Quebec
and the
American
Dream

Quebec and the American Dream

Robert Chodos

Eric Hamovitch

between the lines

© Robert Chodos and Eric Hamovitch, 1991

Published by Between The Lines
           394 Euclid Ave., #203
           Toronto, Ont.
           M6G 2S9
           Canada

Cover design by Counterpunch/Linda Gustafson
Typeset by Techni Process
Printed in Canada

Between The Lines receives financial assistance from the Canada Council and the Ontario Arts Council.

Canadian Cataloguing in Publication Data

Chodos, Robert, 1947 –
     Quebec and the American Dream

Includes bibliographical references and index.
ISBN 0-921284-38-1 (bound)   ISBN 0-921284-39-X (pbk.)

1. Quebec (Province) — Relations — United States.
2. United States — Relations — Quebec (Province).
3. Quebec (Province) — History. I. Hamovitch, Eric.
II. Title.

FC2911.C56 1991   971.4   C91-095460-7
F1052.95.C56 1991

Contents

La Bannière étoilée (The Star-Spangled Banner)

O! Voyez-vous bien, par la lumière luisante,
Qu'on a vue, si fièrement, au jour finissant,
Quelles barres grandes, belles étoiles, dans la nuit périlleuse,
Sur ramparts, en regard, flottaient si galamment.
  Et le feu des fusées, les bombes en air, romprées,
  Donnent preuve, dans la nuit, le drapeau est sauvé!
  O! Dites que cette bannière étoilée encore est ondulant
  Sur le pays de nos libres, et logis des vaillants.

(French words by Clyde LeBlanc, Houma, Louisiana)

for Andrea and Ingrid

1

Introduction:
Quebec in North America

A CLOSE ASSOCIATION between nationalism and anti-Americanism appears to be a fact of modern life, where once the United States—itself born in a revolutionary war against imperial Britain—was an inspiration to emerging nations. Ho Chi Minh, later one of the U.S.A.'s most implacable enemies, used the U.S. Declaration of Independence as a model when (prematurely, as it turned out) he proclaimed the independence of Vietnam in 1945. After the Second World War, however, the view of the U.S.A. as liberator faded quickly and another, darker view took its place. Americans grew accustomed to hearing of Latin American revolutionaries shouting "Yanqui go home", Vietnamese guerrillas engaged in combat with U.S. troops, Iranian students taking U.S. diplomats hostage, and Middle Eastern militiamen hijacking U.S. aircraft. The more recent collapse of the Soviet imperial order makes it plain that nationalist sentiment is something that crosses ideological lines: nobody can feel totally comfortable next to an overweening giant, however benevolent that giant may imagine itself to be. Even in Canada, nationalists have proposed curbs on U.S. investment, demonstrated against U.S. missile tests, and decried the ubiquity of U.S. culture.

But the most intense and potentially destabilizing nationalist movement in the northern part of the North American continent has taken a different direction. Between 1976 and 1985 Quebec was officially committed to a radical reshaping of the province's relationship with the rest of Canada. In a referendum held in May 1980 the Parti Québécois government of Premier René Lévesque asked Quebec voters to approve its sovereignty-association option, though a majority said no. In proposing sovereignty for Quebec, Lévesque had been trying to create a political structure that would express Quebec's national goals and the deep aspirations of many of its citizens; and yet, in the PQ's vision, accession to sovereignty would have little effect on Quebec's relations with the United States. If anything, senior PQ ministers argued, an even closer relationship with the United States could be pursued by a Quebec that was freed of its constitutional ties to Canada.

The PQ was defeated in the 1985 general election and again in 1989, but the trend toward broader links with the U.S.A. continued: the investment-obsessed Liberal government led by Premier Robert Bourassa felt no hesitation at all in encouraging closer economic ties with the great republic to the south, nor did Bourassa's unambiguously pro-business government give off the sort of leftish signals that might irritate the denizens of corporate boardrooms across the border. Under Bourassa the idea of sovereignty-association spent several years in the shadows, although it came to centre stage again after the constitutional squabbles of the late 1980s. If anything, the possibility of a sovereign Quebec was viewed—both north and south of the border—as an even smaller threat to close ties with the U.S. than it had been under Lévesque.

When the enthusiastically pro-U.S. Brian Mulroney led his Conservative Party to a lopsided federal election victory over the more Canadian nationalist and interventionist Liberals in 1984, the stage was set for historic changes in Canada's relationship with the rest of North America. Whereas Lévesque had proposed a sovereign Quebec in economic association with English Canada, Mulroney would soon propose a sovereign Canada in economic association with the United States. Mulroney's version of sovereignty-association was contained in the Canada-U.S. Free Trade Agreement that came into effect on the first day of 1989, only a few weeks after Mulroney was returned to power in a bitterly fought federal election.

Forced to defend the trade deal against unexpectedly vigorous attack from Liberal leader John Turner, Mulroney's Conservatives won outright majorities of seats in only two provinces in the 1988 vote: in the Conservative bastion of Alberta, which was hardly a surprise, but also in the traditional Liberal bastion of Quebec. Polls taken before the election had shown that support for free trade also happened to be strongest in those two provinces. Few Canadians applauded the election results more obviously than the Quebec premier. Robert Bourassa is an economist by training and attaches huge importance to economic growth; what he deems to be good for the Quebec economy has usually taken precedence over other concerns.

QUEBEC IN NORTH AMERICA

Jacques Parizeau is also an economist, and he too applauded the imple-
mentation of the Free Trade Agreement, although for somewhat different
reasons. Parizeau had been finance minister under Lévesque, whom he
succeeded as Parti Québécois leader after a short interregnum. He reasoned
aloud that free trade with the U.S. would weaken the arguments of those
who opposed Quebec independence; no longer could anti-independentist
forces claim that being cast adrift from Canada would leave Quebec on an
economic desert island. Without trade barriers to the south Quebec would
be part of a much bigger market than Canada had ever offered, and so the
Free Trade Agreement that caused such consternation in nationalist circles
in English Canada was viewed as a positive boon by Quebec nationalists.

The divergent views of nationalists across the English-French divide
made it plain that the sympathies and common goals that once served to
suggest a broad mutual understanding had all but evaporated. Many of the
people who helped bring new vigour to the mostly English-speaking Canadian nationalist movement in the late 1960s and 1970s saw Quebec nationalism as a kindred force and even as an inspiration. But English-Canadian
nationalism defined itself largely as resistance to economic and cultural
encroachment by the United States, and when influential sectors of the
Quebec nationalist movement embraced the prospect of closer trade ties
with the U.S., it became plain that the two nationalisms no longer shared a
common ground—if indeed they ever had. By supporting the Conservatives
in the 1988 election Quebec voters were merely acting in what they saw as
their self-interest, but in so doing they left an important sector of opinion in
English Canada feeling betrayed.

Quebec nationalists were joined in supporting the trade deal by a new
and powerful force in Quebec society. Big business, long seen as the unas-
sailable perch of English-speaking interests within the province as well as
outside it, had begun to take on a more French flavour. This was partly
because talented French-speaking managers were finally winning the pro-
motions within English-speaking firms that had been denied to earlier
generations, but more important was the emergence of a dynamic French-
speaking entrepreneurial élite that set about building its own industrial
companies, going after trade and investment opportunities with confidence
and verve. While many of the largest corporate employers in Quebec were
still Anglo-controlled, the economic weight of medium-sized companies
controlled by Francophones rose dramatically through the 1980s. The French-
speaking business élite may have been less inclined than the population as a
whole to favour Quebec independence, but its very existence fed a growing
conviction that Quebec indeed had the ability to go it alone.

The Free Trade Agreement was undoubtedly the most important move toward continental integration in a generation, surpassing in scope the 1965 Auto Pact that allowed automobiles and automobile parts to cross the Canada-U.S. border freely and established minimum production quotas for Canada. The Auto Pact brought in its wake a massive rise in trade in manufactured goods between the two countries and contributed mightily to the prosperity of southern Ontario, where most of Canada's automotive industry is concentrated. But the Ontario government—and a wide swath of public opinion in Ontario—opposed the Free Trade Agreement, partly on the ground that increased north-south flows would weaken the traditional east-west flows that had held Canada together ever since the transcontinental railways were built. Ontario's approach was seen as hypocritical by the governments of most other provinces: Quebec and three of the four provinces to its east (tiny Prince Edward Island being the exception) indicated they would dearly love to see the kind of trade ties with New England that Ontario had long enjoyed with the states across the Great Lakes.

The fact that the debate over the Free Trade Agreement coincided with a particularly intense episode in Canada's never-ending constitutional soap opera brought into relief the different but very real insecurities felt by the country's two biggest and most powerful provinces. Many Ontarians feared that the trade deal would weaken Canada's cultural identity and its political independence. Meanwhile, the Quebec government passed legislation upholding a ban on English commercial signs in defiance of a Supreme Court ruling and continued to insist it would not be part of any Canadian constitution that failed to meet several specific conditions, including recognition of Quebec as a "distinct society".

To an observer from abroad, a more germane question might be whether the rest of Canada could be considered a distinct society. Be that as it may, the "distinct society" clause in the constitutional deal agreed to in 1987 by the prime minister and the ten provincial premiers at Meech Lake just north of Ottawa would lead to years of acrimony and misunderstanding, and in June 1990 the deal finally collapsed after Manitoba and Newfoundland failed to ratify it. Support for Quebec independence, as measured by opinion polls, rose toward new peaks, and many English Canadians began to prepare themselves psychologically for what was starting to look like the impending breakup of the country.

The Meech Lake deal represented an attempt to graft the two-nations concept of Canadian society onto Canada's traditional ten-provinces federalism. Some critics of the deal said that in bowing to provincial demands it went too far in weakening federal authority, and this at a time when the Free Trade Agreement with the U.S. had imposed fresh limits on Ottawa's freedom of action. To proponents of a strong central government it looked like a nightmare come true. And it was Quebec, long a champion of enhanced provincial power and now a keen supporter of closer U.S. links, that was seen to be sawing away at federal authority from both sides.

Important national undertakings, starting with the construction of a coast-to-coast railway network and growing to include such institutions as Canada's elaborate system of equalization payments to assist the poorer provinces, arose from a perceived need to strengthen east-west ties and in turn helped to make sense of these ties: a weaker central authority would erode the ability to build such ties and to resist the ever-present lure of stronger north-south linkages. Constitutional proposals that would lead to a less powerful federal government are not written in a vacuum: they reflect prevailing political pressures. They also accentuate the clash between the divergent nationalisms of Quebec and English Canada, the opposition between which was less evident in an earlier and perhaps more naive period when the apparent strength of Canada's *raison d'être* was greater than it is now.

The pro-U.S. direction of official Quebec nationalism has reflected a deeper pro-Americanism in Quebec society. In 1974 Daniel Latouche, then a McGill University political scientist and later a constitutional adviser to Premier Lévesque, wrote:

> The PQ leadership shares with most Quebec elites a deep admiration for the only North American society that is said to have succeeded in providing itself with an autonomous model of development.... The socio-economic model for the Québécois is not Canada, for it exists only as an act of will, but the United States, which has succeeded in giving form to the North American myth.[1]

In 1977 François-Marie Monnet, former correspondent in Canada for the Paris daily *Le Monde*, marvelled at

> the total absence [in Quebec] of that passionate anti-Americanism that poisons the activities of the international left. The manifest immunity of Quebecers to anti-Americanism is a fact of nature: they belong to one of those rare peoples, if not the only people, which while living in the American orbit feels no inferiority complex toward the Americans.[2]

In 1978 advertising guru Jacques Bouchard, in outlining the stimuli Quebec consumers respond to and the ways they spend their money, debunked the once trendy notion that Québécois were really more European than North American:

> Québécois assume their Americanness and clearly prefer "the American way of life" to the European way. Their daily behaviour proves it beyond a doubt.[3]

And in 1985 the respected political columnist Lysiane Gagnon wrote in the Montreal daily *La Presse* that Quebec

> no matter how French-speaking it is — and maybe precisely for that reason — is the most pro-American province in Canada.

She explained this phenomenon in political, economic, and above all cultural terms:

> Quebecers don't share the feeling of powerlessness and cultural inferiority that feeds anti-Americanism in English Canada. We are much more aware of our difference which, expressed primarily through language, is much more obvious."[4]

Quebec may feel more confident in its cultural identity, but this does not diminish a nagging insecurity. Successive Quebec governments have felt the need to adopt a series of laws and regulations to protect the French language and to restrict, for instance, the use of English on commercial signs. These measures respond to fears that Quebec's dominant language and culture may indeed be less secure than the pro-U.S. bravado of some Québécois has at times suggested. On a continent where Anglophones outnumber Francophones more than forty to one, and in a world where U.S. popular culture seems to transcend all language barriers, the need for vigilance is evident; but have Quebec's language watchdogs chosen the correct targets? French-only signs may please the purists, but such measures can come nowhere close to balancing the lure of U.S. television and U.S. popular music. On the other hand, members of an open society might well feel uneasy about the heavy use of government edicts to curtail foreign cultural influence. Debate on this conundrum has raged for decades, but clear answers have yet to emerge.

Quebec's concerns for its future also have much to do with its precarious demographic situation. In recent decades Quebec's rate of natural population increase has gone from the highest in North America to the lowest. The challenge of getting immigrants to choose to speak French on a continent where English dominates so hugely has been a formidable one; laws requiring children of immigrants to attend French schools have created a new set of problems, with pupils of French mother tongue finding themselves in a minority in some French schools in Montreal.

With its demographic growth sputtering, Quebec has seen a slow decline in its relative weight both within Canada and within North America. But such concerns are far from new. Early in the seventeenth century the majority of the people of European descent in North America north of Mexico were French, although before the end of the century the English would outnumber them. From their bases in the St. Lawrence valley the French controlled trade routes running through the Great Lakes, down the Ohio and Mississippi valleys to the Gulf of Mexico, and westward to the Rockies, while the English remained hemmed in along the Atlantic seaboard; but the authorities in Paris seemed more interested in promoting the fur trade than in populating the vast territories over which enterprising traders from New France were planting the French flag. Not even the St. Lawrence heartland received large numbers of new settlers. Meanwhile a rising flow of British colonists was sent to the shores of North America, enabling England to take good advantage of the territorial gains to be achieved through war, bluster, and diplomacy.

Following the British conquest of New France, the 60,000 remaining French inhabitants embarked on one of the most spectacular demographic adventures in human history. From the late eighteenth century to the middle of the twentieth century, natural reproduction doubled the population, on average, every two decades or so. If all the descendants of these early French Canadians had remained within the borders of present-day Quebec its Francophone population would be between twelve and fifteen million, more than twice what it is today, and Canada might be a majority French-speaking country. But a shortage of suitable farmland, the backwardness of French-Canadian agriculture in the nineteenth century, and the lack of enough industry to absorb surplus labour combined to make emigration inevitable. Some ventured to the U.S. midwest and later others went to the Canadian prairies. Several historians have speculated as to what Canada's linguistic map might look like had greater numbers headed west rather than south; but for the majority of emigrants it was the booming mill economy of New England that beckoned, only a day's train ride from home. Between 1850 and 1930 more than half a million French-speaking Canadians made new homes in the industrial towns of Massachusetts, Rhode Island, New Hampshire,

Vermont, Maine, and Connecticut. Although French is now a dying language in New England, a sixth of the region's inhabitants can claim French-Canadian ancestry.

The memory of those who left is a painful one, and the lost demographic potential they represent can never be recuperated. Natural population growth is now well below replacement level, and tax incentives aimed at encouraging a higher birth rate have achieved little in the absence of adequate child-care facilities for working parents. Immigration has been only a partial answer: laws meant to encourage integration with the French-speaking majority in Quebec have had mixed success against the powerful attractive force of the English-speaking majority in North America.

That immigrants from abroad should be awed by the most influential society on earth ought to come as little surprise to Quebec nationalists. René Lévesque himself developed an abiding admiration for things American while working for the U.S. Office of War Information during the Second World War, and first came to the attention of the Quebec public as an authority on U.S. affairs on television news programs on the CBC's French television network. In his biography *René*, Peter Desbarats recounts Lévesque's reaction to the opening of a radio station in Montreal by Newfoundland entrepreneur Geoff Stirling: "Good God!" Lévesque cried, "We've been colonized by Newfoundland! At least being colonized by the United States is semi-respectable." When Lévesque and the PQ took office in 1976 the tendency of Quebec society toward pro-Americanism was reinforced by the awarding of several top cabinet posts to people holding graduate degrees from U.S. universities.

Clearly nationalists in Quebec are not afraid of the United States, and they have tried, not always with great success, to plead for understanding from Americans and to gain, if not U.S. support, then at least U.S. neutrality. A steady stream of Parti Québécois cabinet ministers, including Lévesque himself, went to speak in New York or Washington. Both sides in the sovereignty debate paraded their views publicly in the U.S.A., though it must be said that opponents of Quebec independence probably got the better of it.

That didn't mean many Americans really cared much about what was going on in Quebec. A survey in *U.S. News and World Report* in July 1978 concluded that "an indifferent U.S. pays little heed to what's going on right next door." The magazine quoted a businessman in Burlington, Vermont, just 150 kilometres from Montreal, as saying, "The separatist issue is like the energy crisis. If it doesn't affect you personally and today, you're not worried." Farther west, even this flicker of interest in the situation faded; as a North Dakotan said, "You would eat a lot of lunches in Bismarck before you'd hear anyone discuss Quebec separatism." Since most Americans take a sustained interest in a foreign country only when that country indulges in some dramatic manifestation of anti-Americanism, Quebec is likely to remain *terra incognita* to them.

Left-wing critics of prevailing trends in Quebec society and of existing strategies for independence have argued that the desire to live in harmony with the United States is incompatible with the goal of maintaining Quebec as a distinct society. Soon after the PQ came to power in 1976 Pierre Vallières, who at one time had been the theoretician of the revolutionary Front de Libération du Québec, wrote:

> The independentist ideology has no future if it does not challenge the very essence of North American society, that is the extension of commodity relationships to all areas of individual and social life, and the domination of these commodity relationships by industrial, financial, military and state monopolies.[5]

A similar position was expressed in 1984 by Gabriel Gagnon, a University of Montreal sociologist and a member of the collective that published the left-wing magazine *Possibles*:

> Despite the mirage of the condominium in Florida or the trip to California, people of all generations continue to hope that a different and autonomous society will be built. Instead of endlessly repeating the vindictive phrases of the first independentists, instead of blindly worshipping the computer as creator and small business as saviour, politicians will have to make a determined effort to adapt their message to this new culture. The emancipation of the men and women of Quebec will be better served by genuine independence, even if we have to wait a longer time for it, than by ersatz independence obtained quickly under the aegis of the American empire.

Such views, however, did not reflect the thinking that prevailed in the mainstream of the independence movement, which became as caught up in the pro-business mood of the 1980s as any of the economic liberalizers who spanned the globe from Valparaiso to Vladivostok. It was the ardent *indépendantiste* Jacques Parizeau, finance minister under René Lévesque, who devised an innovative tax scheme to encourage Quebecers to channel their savings into shares in the multitude of young companies that were being formed by members of Quebec's burgeoning new entrepreneurial élite. The new-found interest of many Québécois in business activity demonstrated not only an obvious desire to enrich themselves financially but also a wish to take fuller control of their personal destinies. This had the incidental effect of making many Québécois think more like Americans, who have not often been known to shy away from business.

Even if it were possible to root out the U.S. presence and build a society entirely free from it in the manner of Cuba, such a course would have the support of only a small minority of Québécois. For the foreseeable future, Quebec will continue to live with the reality, the promise, or the threat of U.S. capital, U.S. material prosperity, U.S. mass culture, U.S. liberal democracy and U.S. homogeneity — in short, of the American Dream. At the same time it will continue to want to maintain itself as an entity apart, whether in or out of Canada, and to see itself as "a people that dwells alone, that has not made itself one with the nations", as the biblical prophet Balaam characterized the ancient Hebrews. Is this duality the eternal lot of the Quebec people? Can Quebec continue indefinitely to avoid choosing one side or the other? Or will Quebec's pursuit of the American Dream eventually mean abandonment of long-held goals?

History offers no simple answers to these questions. The pro-Americanism of contemporary Quebec nationalism has deep historical roots. The French-Canadian rebels of 1837 looked to the American Revolution as a model, and fifty years later Honoré Mercier, perhaps the most strongly nationalist Quebec premier before Lévesque, entertained the idea of the annexation of Canada to the United States. Meanwhile, many hundreds of thousands of Québécois went to live and work in the United States, creating strong human ties between the two societies. Even these Québécois — or Franco-Americans, as they became — did not see their change in residence as meaning they must abandon their language, culture, or other important elements of their way of life, and to the extent that they have disappeared into the U.S. melting pot they have done so slowly, reluctantly, and imperfectly.

In Quebec itself, much of what nationalist thinkers of two generations ago saw as constituting the essence of Quebec's distinctiveness — rural life, large families, Catholic worship and values — was eroded under the inexorable pressures of urbanization, industrialization, and modernization. And, it might be said, Americanization. The Québécois is a stubborn character, capable of preserving an essential part of himself or herself in the most adverse of situations. The American Dream, for its part, is a powerful force, and in its wake proud and ancient cultures have been reduced on the North American continent to struggling remnants.

In these pages we attempt to tell two stories. One is how the French possessed and then lost large parts of the continent and ended by providing the United States with settlers and immigrants from Quebec and its former sister colony Acadia. The other is the story of how the American Dream helped shape Quebec society into what it is today, French-speaking but profoundly North American. These two stories often diverge, but over the centuries they also keep intertwining.

Let us turn now to the sixteenth century and to the triumphs and errors of early European explorers.

2

French Colonization
and American Revolution

1524-1803

THE FRENCH ARE NOT an alien people in North America except in the sense that all peoples of European descent are aliens here. Starting with the earliest era of European penetration they have left their mark on the continent, including that portion of the continent which later became the United States. From Calais in Maine to Boisfort in Washington, from Eau Claire in Wisconsin to D'Iberville in Mississippi—and passing by Coeur d'Alene, Idaho; Pierre, South Dakota; Des Moines, Iowa; St. Louis, Missouri; Terre Haute, Indiana; Detroit, Michigan; New Rochelle, New York; Duquesne, Pennsylvania; Havre de Grace, Maryland; Louisville, Kentucky; Baton Rouge, Louisiana; Beaumont, Texas; and many, many others—U.S. toponymy bears witness to their presence. These place names, and the people of French descent who live in all parts of the continent, are the heirs of one of history's great might-have-beens, the French empire in North America. It is a might-have-been because, while the dreams of the French imperialists were continental in scope, they had to contend with realities that made those dreams impossible to realize.

Like England, France came to North America because what were regarded as the best and richest parts of the New World—the southern parts—were already taken. Chansonnier Robert Charlebois has chided Jacques Cartier in song for sailing to such an inclement destination as Quebec, but by the time Cartier landed on Montreal Island the warm places were already in the hands of the Spaniards and Portuguese. Spain established its rule from Florida to the Andes in the sixteenth century, and found the riches of the New World neither illusory nor long in coming. The Spaniards' most devout hope was to discover gold and silver and to remove large quantities of them to Europe, and this hope was quickly realized. They sent colonists: Spanish America had a European population of 100,000 in 1550, a figure New France had still not attained at the time of the British conquest two centuries later. They encountered highly developed class societies whose lower orders they could put to work for them, while the Native Americans with whom the French and British came in contact were unable to understand even so basic—to Europeans—a concept as land ownership. The relative unattractiveness of North America prevented much from happening there for more than a hundred years after Columbus and Cabot had visited. Only the Newfoundland fishery was of serious and continuing interest to Europeans, and most early voyages to North America were devoted less to exploring the continent than to finding a way around it. Among these were the first expeditions sent by France. According to historian Samuel Eliot Morison:

> In 1500 it was anyone's guess which European power would dominate North America. Eliminating Spain and Portugal, both of whom had little energy left for these supposedly poor and chilly regions of the New World, we have France and England; and anyone estimating their relative power in 1550 would have bet on France.[6]

In 1524 France sent an expedition to North America under the command of the Florentine navigator Giovanni da Verrazzano to look for the Northwest Passage. He sailed from the Carolinas up as far as Newfoundland with frequent stops along the way, including a brief anchorage in the strait between Brooklyn and Staten Island now spanned by the Verrazano Narrows Bridge. All in all he was impressed with what he saw. He thought it would be a good idea to establish French colonies along the coast and bring the benefits of Christianity to the Natives he had met, but the French ruling circles were not interested. A decade later Jacques Cartier of St. Malo found the St. Lawrence River, the great axis of penetration of the North American continent, and established contact with the Huron Indians who were to be the chief allies of the French in their later venture at colonization, much to the Hurons' eventual chagrin. French and Hurons seemed to hit it off, despite occasional acts of treachery on the part of the French. The Huron chief Donnacona regaled the gullible Europeans with tales of the fabulously rich (but unfortunately nonexistent) Kingdom of the Saguenay; Cartier abducted Donnacona so that he could tell his story at the court of King François I, and the chief died in France.

Cartier returned in 1541, under the command of the Sieur de Roberval, to look for the Kingdom of the Saguenay and start a colony on the St. Lawrence. The mission succeeded in neither of its aims. Roberval's party was not ready in time, and Cartier set out without him. The colonists, some of whom had been recruited from French prisons, spent the winter a few miles southwest of Quebec City. The winter was hard, they had scurvy, the Indians turned hostile, they didn't find the Saguenay, and Roberval failed to arrive. In June 1542 they sailed for home, running into Roberval in Newfoundland. Roberval headed for the St. Lawrence to see for himself, but his colony had much the same experience as Cartier's and in 1543 it too broke camp and went home.

The few other sixteenth-century French attempts at North American settlement were similarly short-lived and none of them had the full backing of the French monarchy, which in the latter part of the century was preoccupied with the destructive and seemingly endless Wars of Religion. Many Huguenots—French Calvinists—were traders and shipowners who naturally had a lively interest in American ventures; they also had stronger motives than their Catholic compatriots for wanting to get out of France. Many did so, but their attempts to found new colonies were generally disastrous. At Rio de Janeiro in 1557 the Huguenots were betrayed by the leader of the expedition, who converted to Catholicism, and those who survived his wrath ran afoul of the equally unsympathetic Portuguese. A second group landed in South Carolina in 1562, but fell to quarrelling among themselves and eventually returned to France. In 1564 a third colony was established in northern Florida; it was wiped out by hostile Spaniards on the grounds that the colonists were heretics.

In 1598 the Edict of Nantes established an uneasy peace between Protestants and Catholics, allowing France to get on with the job of national consolidation—and American colonization. The Marquis de la Roche, who had a commission from the king and sixty colonists taken from French jails, planted them on storm-swept Sable Island south of Nova Scotia and shortly returned to France. The few colonists who survived were near starvation when they were rescued five years later. La Roche sold his commission to a Huguenot merchant, Pierre de Chauvin, who established yet another unsuccessful colony at Tadoussac at the mouth of the Saguenay River; the commission eventually passed to another Huguenot, Sieur de Monts, who set out in 1604 with the geographer Samuel de Champlain and a group of colonists. After exploring part of the coast of Nova Scotia and New Brunswick, the group set up a colony on Sainte Croix island in what is now Maine;

those who survived the winter moved to Port Royal on the Bay of Fundy the next spring, and the colonists, more resourceful than their predecessors, for the first time made a success of a French colony in the New World. But in 1607 de Monts' trading monopoly was revoked, and without this economic base the colonists returned home.

In the meantime Champlain had sailed down the coast as far as Cape Cod, checking out reports of the fabulous City of Norumbega and looking for possible sites for colonization. When they resumed their colonizing venture in 1608, however, Champlain and de Monts turned to Quebec on the St. Lawrence. After more than sixty years of failures and false starts, the French had finally found the capital of their future American empire. They might have done better to follow the path of Verrazzano. Morison comments:

> French Canadians exalt Jacques Cartier at the expense of the Italian; but can they deny that the French cause in North America would have prospered more had colonization been directed to Verrazzano's Arcadia (North Carolina), Angoulême (New York), or Refugio (Rhode Island), rather than to Cartier's St. Lawrence?[7]

Even that most strongly nationalist of Quebec historians, Abbé Lionel Groulx, was little inclined to disagree. If Champlain had continued beyond Cape Cod to the mouth of the Hudson, Groulx speculated,

> New France in America would have had a cradle other than Acadia or the St. Lawrence. And Quebec could have been New York. Champlain would continue to regret this failure; he would speak of it later as a great destiny missed.[8]

Groulx wrote of a "secret instinct" guiding the French to the St. Lawrence; others have suggested that its suitability as a base for the fur trade might have been the motive.[9] The French had in fact chosen an excellent spot for commerce and exploration, and with Quebec as their base they would reap vast profits from furs and penetrate west to the Rocky Mountains and southward to the mouth of the Mississippi. The Atlantic littoral, from southern Maine to Georgia, would be settled by the English.

Along with the fishery, the fur trade was the principal form in which North America had yielded up its wealth to Europeans by the time of Champlain. It was to be the chief economic base throughout the 155-year history of New France; but although it provided the driving force for the great French expeditions to the interior of the continent its long-term effects on the growth and development of the colony were at best mixed. With its get-rich-quick possibilities and its exploitation of Indian labour the fur trade met the requirements of the mercantilist theories prevalent in the seventeenth century: that colonies should provide their progenitors with immediate and tangible wealth. New France might not have gold and silver mines, but furs were an acceptable substitute.

In three great thrusts the French penetrated far to the south and west. Champlain explored the lake that bears his name and reached Lake Huron by way of the Ottawa River; he also sent Etienne Brulé into Michigan and Ohio and Jean Nicolet into Wisconsin. The second thrust was set in motion by New France's greatest visionary, Jean Talon, intendant from 1665 to 1672, and was concentrated on the Mississippi River. In the last decades of the seventeenth century Louis Jolliet and Father Jacques Marquette explored the river to within a few miles of its confluence with the Arkansas; Robert Cavalier de La Salle followed the same path and continued on to the Gulf of Mexico; and Pierre Le Moyne d'Iberville founded a new French colony, Louisiana, on the Gulf coast. After their losses in the War of the Spanish Succession were confirmed by the Treaty of Utrecht in 1713, the French undertook their third thrust: Pierre de La Vérendrye pushed westward to present-day Alberta and Montana while other explorers followed the western tributaries of the Mississippi as far as New Mexico and Colorado.

This expansion was fuelled by military considerations, by the hope of converting the Indians to Christianity, and by the Canadians' ripening taste for adventure, as well as by economic motives; but without the prospect of gain from the fur trade it is unlikely that it would have occurred on anything approaching the scale it actually reached. From the time of Champlain the French fur trade was based on exploitation of the Hurons, who were based in what is now southern Ontario. This setup was destroyed by the Iroquois, trading allies of the Dutch at Albany, who in 1650 attacked and devastated the Hurons. The French needed a new labour force and eventually found two: the Ottawas to the north and the Illinois to the south. It was pursuit of these alliances that brought the French to the Great Lakes and the Mississippi as they followed the receding beaver ever deeper into the continent.

Meanwhile they were slow to develop their colonies of Canada on the St. Lawrence, Acadia on the Bay of Fundy, and Louisiana on the Mississippi. In 1627 the Company of One Hundred Associates was given a monopoly of the fur trade in New France, and it promised as part of its charter to bring in about four thousand settlers in the next fifteen years (there were then only seventy-six in the colony). But the promise was never fulfilled, and in 1663 there were still only twenty-five hundred settlers in New France. Acadia had a white population of less than a thousand in 1689. Louisiana had only three hundred in 1712, ten years after the formal establishment of the colony, but a few years later several thousand colonists came out as a by-product of the financial speculation known to history as the Mississippi Bubble. A Scottish financial wizard, John Law, had obtained the confidence of the French regent, the Duc d'Orléans, who was desperately looking for a way to pay off the debts left by the late King Louis XIV. One of his schemes was a joint-stock company that would exploit what was believed to be the vast gold and silver deposits of Louisiana, and shares were sold to an eager French public. In 1720 the inevitable happened: the Mississippi Bubble burst, Law fled to Italy to avoid the wrath of the Paris masses, and emigration to Louisiana halted as abruptly as it had begun. In 1743 Louisiana still had a population of only four thousand whites and two thousand black slaves.

There were a few who tried to put the French colonies in North America on a sounder footing, and foremost among them was Talon, whom Groulx called "the real sculptor of French America". Talon was brimming with ideas for the improvement and expansion of New France. He wanted to acquire, by purchase or conquest, the colony of New York on the Hudson, which Britain had just taken from the Dutch. He tried to link Canada with the ice-free ports in Acadia. He wanted to improve agriculture and set up industries. Under his direction, a tannery, a brewery, small shops for making thread and cloth, and the beginnings of a shipbuilding industry were established. More settlers came to the colony, and more land was cleared. And at the same time Talon dreamed of westward expansion and sent out the explorers who would make it possible.

There were formidable internal obstacles to the success of Talon's policy of developing agriculture and industry. The lure of the west and the promise of a quick fortune were often more powerful attractions than an arduous life in the fields or the manufactories; many contemporary accounts speak of the "indiscipline" of the Canadian *habitant*. But Talon did have one crucial asset: most of his schemes had the full backing of the French government in the person of Louis XIV's powerful minister Jean-Baptiste Colbert. Colbert was a leading exponent of mercantilism, but he interpreted it somewhat more broadly than some of his contemporaries. He agreed that colonies were to be exploited for the benefit of the mother country, but he did not see the development of colonial manufacturing as inconsistent with this: in fact he saw it as beneficial if the colony's dependence on the royal treasury could thereby be reduced. Colbert took an interest in the development of New France and helped promote emigration. Occasionally Talon's enthusiasms were too much for him: when Talon, supporting the demands of the Canadian merchants against the monopoly of traders from the metropolis, referred to New France as "a fair expanse in which can be founded a great kingdom...or at least a very considerable State," Colbert replied that such ideas were dangerous and Talon should confine himself to more immediate concerns. But even with his reservations, Colbert was one of the few boosters New France ever had at the French court. For most royal officials, New France was simply another drain on an already beleaguered royal treasury, and westward expansion a particularly foolish enterprise. The Marquis de Denonville, governor of New France in the 1680s, said that the king of France was not "a great enough lord to develop such a great country". And somewhat later the Comte de Maurepas, minister to Louis XV, argued that New France should avoid expansions that "divide the forces of the colony" and concentrate instead on developing "the inside of the colony". But there was no real policy for developing the inside of the colony either. The growth of shipbuilding was retarded by the reluctance of the French monarchy to buy ships from New France. The opening of the pioneer iron works, the St. Maurice Forges, was held up for twenty years by royal disfavour. Even a hat manufactory at Montreal was suppressed by French fur-trading monopolies.

Ultimately the cause of the weakness of New France lay not in North America but in Europe. On the one hand the France that possessed a North American colony was a France at the height of its glory, France of the *grand siècle*, but on the other it was a France held back by an obsolete social structure and riven by internal contradictions. While in England in the same period the bourgeoisie firmly established its control, in France the bourgeoisie had to share power with a declining feudal nobility and a monarchy that fancied itself absolute. While this alliance functioned reasonably well under creative administrators such as Colbert, French economic policy, and government generally, were more typically characterized by corruption, stagnation, and waste. Louis XIV's ruinous foreign policy virtually bankrupted the state; royal revenues were chronically inadequate even though French peasants were taxed beyond the breaking point.

In 1689 England, under its new Protestant king William of Orange, joined the list of France's enemies in Europe. As a consequence the virtually ceaseless European war spread to North America, and in 1690 Massachusetts mounted a naval expedition against Quebec. The expedition was unsuccessful, and the French survived the first round of the struggle for the control of North America with no loss of territory; in fact, an expedition under Pierre LeMoyne d'Iberville captured the English fur-trading posts on Hudson Bay. The results of the second round were more ominous for the French. By the Treaty of Utrecht in 1713 they were forced to cede the mainland of Acadia, their share of Newfoundland, and the Hudson Bay posts that d'Iberville had won. The French empire in North America had been struck a severe blow.

France was now exhausted from Louis XIV's wars, and New France was given a respite of thirty years. The French used the time to expand the colony militarily, economically, and territorially. With Hudson Bay closed to them, French fur traders opened up the west. The great fortress of Louisbourg was built in Cape Breton, and a chain of forts was established in the Ohio and Illinois valleys. It still seemed possible to maintain a French empire from the St. Lawrence to the Gulf of Mexico and to confine the British to the Atlantic coast; but in 1744 France and England were at war again and in 1745 a force from New England captured Louisbourg. Meanwhile the French had the better of the fighting in Europe and Louisbourg was returned to France. Once again the peace provided only a brief breathing space. Another confrontation in North America, this time a decisive one, was about to begin.

This confrontation began with a series of skirmishes in the year 1755, before war was actually declared in Europe. The results of these preliminary battles were, on the whole, reassuring to the French; especially gratifying was the failure of the British attack on Fort Duquesne, their stronghold at the strategic site of present-day Pittsburgh. The only place they suffered a serious setback was Nova Scotia, the former French province of Acadia: there British regulars and New England volunteers took a French fort, Beauséjour, that stood at the gateway of the disputed territory between Nova Scotia and Quebec, and then, encouraged by this, Governor Charles Lawrence of Nova Scotia used the same troops to deport the entire French population of his domain, thus destroying a way of life that both history and legend have described as idyllic. The most familiar version is that of the poet Longfellow, who wrote that these simple Acadian farmers

> Dwelt in the love of God and man. Alike were they free from
> Fear, that reigns with the tyrant, and envy, the vice of republics.[10]

And other accounts indicate that Longfellow's "Acadie, home of the happy" bore at least some resemblance to the historical Acadia.

But the land in which they tried to build this way of life was a constant battleground of the North American power struggle. Port Royal, their principal settlement, was subject to frequent raids and plundering expeditions and kept changing hands from the French to the British to the Dutch and back again. With the political status of their country more or less permanently uncertain, the Acadians developed a healthy psychological distance from the struggle around them; one of the later French governors of Acadia called them "demi-republicans". As French subjects they still traded with British Massachusetts and as British subjects they still traded with French Louisbourg. British rule was firmly established after 1713, and this only increased their determination to stay out of the great-power conflict. They remained neutral in the war of 1744–48 even though French troops tried to retake Port Royal, and they refused to sign any oath of loyalty to the British crown that required them to take up arms. In the 1720s and 1730s the British had been satisfied with an oath that contained no such requirement, but by 1750 they had come to regard Nova Scotia as strategically important and the so-called French Neutrals as potentially dangerous. Governor Edward Cornwallis explained to the Acadians:

> You deceive yourselves if you think you are at liberty to choose whether you will be the subjects of the King or no.... It is only out of pity to your situation, and to your inexperience in the affairs of government, that we condescend to reason with you; otherwise the question would not be reasoning, but commanding and being obeyed.

With the outbreak of the new war the British, and especially the rigid and insecure Charles Lawrence, were no longer inclined to tolerate this impasse. Heads of families were ordered to appear in churches and were there declared prisoners of the king. They and their families were then taken to the beaches and their villages were burned before their eyes. The sick were allowed to die and were buried in the sand. Those who fled to the woods were pursued and rounded up by force. Finally the ships that had been hastily ordered from a private company arrived and took the French Neutrals to ports unknown. With the war having gone so badly elsewhere in North America, Charles Lawrence reaped what he regarded as well-earned glory for the only British military success of the year.

The events of 1755 were the beginning not only of a new North American war but also of a dizzying series of conquests, revolutions, migrations and diplomatic manoeuvres that would change the face of the continent. Within less than fifty years every part of North America between the Gaspé and the Rocky Mountains would undergo at least one change of sovereignty and some would undergo two or three, and a country that did not yet exist at the beginning of this period would be the continent's dominant power at its end. There had been an arc of French territory stretching from Labrador to the Gulf of Mexico, but after 1803 France was gone from North America and its last hope of a North American empire had vanished. The majority of

French-speaking North Americans now lived under British sovereignty, the rest under the sovereignty of the United States. They derived little benefit from these changes. No less than the other people of the continent, they had been developing an identity distinct from that of their European cousins; unlike the Anglo-Americans, they would have to pursue their national existence under governments that were in no sense their own.

All this took place in the context of the rise of the bourgeoisie and the spread of liberal ideas, developments that had particularly dramatic effects in British North America and in France. French-speaking North America was also profoundly affected by those developments, but they occurred much more slowly there and came largely from the outside, so that their effects were not dominant until much later. In the meantime French-speaking North America came to differ from the English-speaking societies of the continent not only culturally but ideologically. These differences had their roots in early colonial history: they came to full flower only in the late nineteenth century, but it was in the half-century following 1755 that they began to take shape.

QUEBEC AND ITS SISTER COLONIES

Although the British could find few bright spots in the military picture in 1755, their fortunes soon began to improve. In 1758 they took Louisbourg, in 1759 Quebec, in 1760 Montreal. New England rejoiced at the elimination of the French menace to the north. In London there was some sentiment for keeping the West Indian sugar island of Guadeloupe, which British forces had also taken, in preference to Canada, but in the end the forces favouring Canada won out. France for its part was just as happy to have Guadeloupe. After fighting so long for North America France now lost interest in it and considered the defeat something of a blessing in disguise. The French foreign minister said that at last the English were caught, for their American colonies would soon be in revolt. Similar arguments were current in England, where one pamphleteer who favoured the retention of Guadeloupe wrote that:

> The acquisition of Canada might be destructive, because such a country as North America...at such a distance could never remain long subject to Britain.[11]

At the peace France retained as its North American possessions only St. Pierre and Miquelon, two foggy islets that gave it a base for continued participation in the Newfoundland fishery. It ceded Canada and what was then eastern Louisiana to England, and western Louisiana, comprising New Orleans and all the lands west of the Mississippi, to its own aggrieved ally Spain. France had lured Spain into the war and thus was responsible for the Spanish loss of Florida to Britain; Louisiana was turned over as compensation. There would be a brief French return to Louisiana in 1803, but otherwise France's departure from the North American scene would be permanent.

But if France was gone, the French were not. They remained in the struggling towns of Louisiana, in the fur-trading settlements of the Great Lakes and the Ohio and Illinois valleys, and above all in the valley of the St. Lawrence, the heart of the old New France and now of Britain's new Province of Quebec. The province had a white population of between sixty and seventy-five thousand. The fur trade, now in English hands, was still the staple of its economy, but the importance of agriculture was growing. Literacy was not widespread, and the circulation of ideas was limited—in the whole period of the French regime no printing press had ever been allowed in the colony. Nevertheless, the Canadians[12] had often failed to show the proper spirit of submission to their social betters, and resistance to taxes and to seigneurial duties had been common and frequently effective. The social distinction between seigneurs and peasants that was so rigid in France was much less so in the colony; and while the hold of religion on the people seemed secure, Canadian Catholicism seemed to many observers to be more a matter of superficial observance than of inner conviction. In short, Britain took possession of a colony that preserved the forms of feudalism and absolutism but had allowed many of their practices to fall into disuse.

With the example of the Acadians fresh in their minds the conquered Canadians quickly swore unconditional allegiance to King George, but their first opportunity to demonstrate that allegiance showed that it was not very deep. In 1763 the Indian tribes of the interior, led by Chief Pontiac of the Ottawas, rose in resistance to the British occupation of their lands. It was decided that three hundred Canadians should be added to the force sent in to put down the revolt, but although generous inducements were offered to volunteers the British eventually had to resort to not-so-subtle methods, including conscription.

The situation in the province was further complicated by the English merchants who came to Quebec and Montreal on the heels of the victorious British troops. These "old subjects", as they were called (to distinguish them from the "new subjects", the Canadians), are given the villain's role in most accounts of the events of the next two decades; among historians, only A.L. Burt has shown them any sympathy:

There may well have been some rascals among these adventurers on the outskirts of empire, but the majority of the merchants seem to have been of respectable character and of no mean education. For the most part they were young men of spirit and enterprise, men on the make. Those who went to Quebec developed the fisheries of the gulf; those who settled in Montreal greatly expanded the fur trade.

Many of them had lived in the older British colonies to the south and some were American-born. Their background led them to have the same general outlook as their fellow Americans and their self-interest led them to favour a democratic form of government for the new colony—but with Roman Catholics excluded to keep control in their own hands.

For the British, the question of the form Quebec's government should take was a complex one. The disenfranchising of a Catholic majority for the benefit of a small Protestant minority might not seem a credible option in today's terms, but that was precisely what the British were then doing in Ireland. Whatever form the government took, it was certainly reasonable to suppose that an elected assembly would be part of it; all the other settled British colonies in America had assemblies; even Nova Scotia had been given one after the expulsion of the Acadians. The first impulse of the British government was to temporize. The Royal Proclamation of October 7, 1763, said there would be an elected assembly—but not yet. The Proclamation also detached the Great Lakes and Mississippi country from the Province of Quebec and set it off as a closed reserve while the British decided what to do with it. Meanwhile an effort to attract English Protestant settlers was set in motion, and British laws were offered to British subjects settling in Quebec. Like the Acadians before them, the Canadians were given freedom to practise the Catholic religion "as far as the laws of Great Britain permit." (This was said to mean that no "popish hierarchy" could be established in Quebec; but, when it became clear that the clergy would only be satisfied with a bishop, the vicar-general of Quebec City was quietly sent off to Europe to be consecrated as the new bishop of Quebec.) And, although it was hoped that the French could be made to embrace Protestantism, little effort was expended on inducing them to do so.

A more coherent policy took shape in the later 1760s, but by then the context had begun to change. Even at the time of the conquest prophets in both France and England were predicting a revolt in the American colonies, and now a series of British governments set about proving them right. Britain no less than France tried to govern its colonies on the theory that their chief use was to bring wealth to the home country; but implementing this theory in Britain's newly expanded North American empire was not a simple matter. There were new interests to be satisfied, and new needs to be met. The most important of these needs, in the eyes of the British government, was colonial defence, which had become too complex to leave to the colonies themselves; but any new measures taken would cost money, and both mercantilist theory and the state of the British treasury suggested that this money should come from the colonies. The policy worked out by the government of George Grenville, which took office in 1763, involved keeping a standing army in America, enforcing restrictions on colonial trade, and raising a colonial revenue.[13]

Britain's older American colonies were accustomed to only intermittent enforcement of British authority. Under this lax regime they had come to have substantial populations, democratic traditions, and growing manufactures, but this was little understood at Whitehall, where the idea of colonial subordination was firmly held and the contempt of the higher classes of English society for colonials was well developed (Dr. Johnson said he could love all mankind except an American). The gap between the colonial situation as seen from London and the same situation as seen from Boston or Philadelphia would ultimately frustrate the British attempt to make its expanded empire work.

None of Grenville's innovations were popular in America, but least popular of all were the tax measures and especially the notorious Stamp Act by which it was proposed to tax everything from college diplomas to playing cards. The Americans refused to pay the tax, and backed up their protest by refusing to import British goods. In Boston an angry crowd destroyed the new Stamp Office. Colonial assemblies denied the right of Parliament to tax the Americans without their consent. Even in Quebec, a number of the old subjects refused in 1766 to sign a welcoming address for the new governor, Brigadier General Guy Carleton, because it contained a proud reference to Canadian acceptance of the Stamp Act and acknowledged the right of Parliament to legislate for Canada. Parliament finally relented and repealed the Stamp Act, at the same time reaffirming in principle its unlimited authority over America.

In this increasingly heated atmosphere, an idea was germinating in the mind of Guy Carleton. Like all British governors of Quebec until well into the nineteenth century, Carleton was a career soldier. He had little sympathy with the merchants and was not inclined to listen to their arguments. He was also no democrat. As his ideas developed, Carleton poured them out in 1767 and 1768 in a series of letters addressed to Lord Shelburne, who as secretary of state for the southern department had responsibility for the American colonies. Quebec would soon have to be provided with a permanent constitution, and its governor wrote in the first of his letters that this constitution should be based on the principles of

the natural rights of men, the British interests on this continent, and the securing the king's dominions over this province.

He believed that there was in Quebec a potential fighting force of eighteen thousand men, and that all efforts should be made to ensure that in the event of a war this force fought on the side of British power and not against it. His chief worry, at this point, was a possible war with France; the colonial difficulties were only a minor theme. But whoever the enemy turned out to be—and by 1778 Britain was at war with both France and the colonists— successful mobilization of the Canadians was the key to fighting him.

To this end, the new constitution should favour the Canadians and especially the seigneurial and clerical classes who, Carleton believed, would be obeyed by the population as a whole. The seigneurial system and French civil law should be maintained and the Roman Catholic Church should be given back all its privileges. French law had, he said,

established subordination from the first to the lowest...and secured obedience to the supreme seat of government from a very distant province.

There should be no elected assembly, since the better sort of Canadians

fear nothing more than the popular assemblies which, they conceive, tend only to render the people refractory and insolent.

And he added somewhat gratuitously:

It may not be improper here to observe that the British form of government, transplanted into this continent, never will produce the same fruits as at home, chiefly because it is impossible for the dignity of the throne or peerage to be represented in the American forests.

The deepening troubles in America, Carleton believed, were due to an excess of democracy. He thought this mistake could be avoided in Quebec with the help of the clergy and seigneurs, whose hierarchical ideas were compatible with his own, and in 1770 he sailed for England to lobby for his plan.

Carleton's ideas represented everything the Americans opposed, but as yet they were neither aware of his plans nor much interested in Quebec affairs: their attention was focused on much more immediate problems. In 1767, under Charles Townshend, the British again tried to tax the colonies; again there were protests, including a boycott of British goods, and again they were effective: a new prime minister, Lord North, repealed all the duties except the one on tea in 1770, although not before British troops had killed five people in a demonstration in Boston, an event the colonists called "the Boston Massacre". In America it became a matter of pride as well as price to drink smuggled tea. In 1773 the government removed some English duties to relieve the East India Company of some surplus tea and introduce taxed tea into the colonies at a price below that of the smuggled stuff. Enraged Bostonians dumped the tea into Boston harbour, and in the spring of 1774 Parliament revoked the charter of Massachusetts and closed the port of Boston. In June of the same year it passed the Quebec Act, often portrayed as the product of disinterested generosity to the French-Canadian people by the British government. Among those who did not see it that way was the spiritual father of the act, Guy Carleton, nor was its generosity apparent to the parliamentary opposition in London, to Britain's older American colonies, or to the old subjects in Quebec. Already the merchants in Quebec City and Montreal were sending money and grain for the relief of Boston. Soon they would be the leaders of the American Revolution in Quebec.

The colonies whose representatives were now beginning to meet in the Continental Congress in Philadelphia also had good reason to be angry at the Quebec Act, which enshrined many of Carleton's proposals, including establishment of the Roman Catholic Church, French civil law, seigneurial tenure, and rule by a governor and council without an elected assembly. It also returned the whole interior to Quebec, south to the Ohio and west to the Mississippi. Whitehall had been trying to figure out what to do with this territory since 1763, but all of its proposals had aroused intense opposition from one quarter or another. The policy embodied in the Quebec Act was no exception. Albany fur traders saw control of the trade being handed to their rivals in Montreal, and Pennsylvania land speculators saw their schemes being frustrated. The Americans protested as well against the denial of an assembly and of habeas corpus and trial by jury in civil cases and the extension of seigneurial tenure, all signs of the tyranny they abhorred. On the privileges given the church the Congress prevaricated somewhat: in its *Letter to the People of Great Britain* it said

Nor can we suppress our astonishment, that a British Parliament should ever consent to establish in that country a religion that has deluged your island in blood, and dispersed impiety, bigotry, persecution, murder and rebellion through every part of the world.

But in its *Letter to the Inhabitants of the Province of Quebec*, which was translated into French and printed in Philadelphia by the French printer Fleury Mesplet, it asked,

What is offered to you by the late Act of Parliament...? Liberty of conscience in your religion? No. God gave it to you.[14]

The Congress may have been no more disinterested in opposing the Quebec Act than Parliament had been in passing it, and not entirely judicious in its choice of arguments; but American opposition to the act was real, and English merchants who sympathized with the Congress distributed its Quebec *Letter* widely in the province and carried on an intensive propaganda campaign against the Act. Their activities in late 1774 and early 1775 have been described by historian Gustave Lanctôt:

Taking up the ideas of the congressional address, agents spread through the country elementary notions of political theory, and explained the advantages of a form of representative government in which the members, elected by the people, discuss and fix taxes. In short, the campaign constituted a complete social doctrine, illustrated by concrete examples drawn from the local and contemporary scene. To Canadians without experience in public affairs it revealed a whole world of new ideas tending to engender opposition to the Quebec Act and to any attempt to enrol them in the service of England against her rebellious colonies.

In April 1775 British troops met with armed resistance at Lexington and Concord, near Boston. Although the Declaration of Independence was still more than a year away, Britain and the colonies were effectively at war, and the war soon spread beyond Massachusetts. Two ill-defended British forts on Lake Champlain, Ticonderoga and Crown Point, were taken by Benedict Arnold of Connecticut and Ethan Allen and his Green Mountain Boys of what became Vermont, and during the summer of 1775 the Americans prepared an assault on Quebec. A force under Richard Montgomery was to come up via Lake Champlain to St. Jean while another army led by Arnold advanced to Quebec from the east by the Kennebec and Chaudière Rivers.

Carleton meanwhile attempted to organize the defence of the colony. Convinced that the Quebec Act had secured the loyalty of the Canadians, and considering the rebels temporarily deranged and to be pitied rather than punished, he had done little to check the pro-Congress agitation that had been going on in Quebec for the better part of a year. In September 1774 he had sent most of his available troops off to Boston to aid in the counter-revolution there. With no more than seven hundred and fifty British regulars to defend the province, Carleton attempted to raise a Canadian militia. This was an important test of his policy, and the clergy and seigneurs whom he had so carefully cultivated rallied to his side. In May 1775 Bishop Briand said in an episcopal mandate:

> Close your ears...dear Canadians, to the voices of sedition which seek to destroy your happiness by stifling the sense of submission to your lawful superiors graven in your hearts by your education and your religion. Be joyful in the execution of orders from a beneficent government which seeks no other goal than your interests and your happiness.

But it was only with difficulty that Carleton could get Canadians, especially those in the rural areas, to sign up for the militia, and when the expected American invasion actually occurred in September it proved even more difficult to get the militiamen to fight. It now became clear that Canadian support for the Quebec Act was restricted to the privileged classes who derived the most benefit from it. To the ordinary *habitants* the act simply meant the reimposition of tithes and seigneurial dues which had been a major grievance during the French regime. The American propaganda campaign had had its effect. Taxes had been an effective issue, and the pro-Congress publicists had also told the Canadians that the British planned to send them away to fight in foreign wars, a claim that in the light of Carleton's plans was not so far-fetched. When the Americans came, some Canadians actively supported them. A larger number tried to remain neutral, arguing that the fight was between rival groups of Englishmen and didn't concern them. In St. Thomas de Montmagny, when the curé (priest) urged his parishioners to join the militia, they responded: "You are an Englishman, and you want to force us to submit and become English too." Similar incidents occurred in other parishes.

The British had neither the moral force to command the loyalty of the Canadians nor the military strength to inspire them with fear, and the invading Americans scored some notable successes. In September they laid siege to St. Jean; in October nearby Fort Chambly was taken after a two-day siege by a force made up mostly of Canadians; in November St. Jean capitulated, and in quick succession Montreal and Trois-Rivières surrendered peacefully: Carleton had decided to make his stand at Quebec. Meanwhile Arnold and his troops were warmly greeted by the Canadians and joined forces with the American army outside Quebec. Inside the city, Carleton cracked down on dissidents and organized a makeshift garrison. The British force was less than overwhelming, but the army that laid siege to Quebec early in December was even weaker. A surprise attack seemed to be the Americans' only chance of taking the city, and on the night of December 30, in a blizzard, they attacked the Lower Town. They were repulsed, and Montgomery was among the thirty who were killed. Nevertheless the siege, and American rule elsewhere in the province, continued until spring.

Leaders of the American cause emerged from both French and English communities in Canada. James Livingston, a Richelieu valley grain merchant who had been an American sympathizer from the beginning, tried to raise a Canadian regiment. Moses Hazen, who a year earlier had served as a courier for Carleton, now switched sides and tried to raise another, greatly aided by the zeal of two farmers from Ste. Anne de la Pocatière, Germain Dionne and his son-in-law Clément Gosselin, who had come to join the American forces outside Quebec. In Trois-Rivières the American sympathizers were led by two post-Conquest immigrants from France, Christophe Pélissier and Pierre de Sales La Terrière, directors of the St. Maurice Forges.[15]

The American rulers of the captured territory faced much the same problem as had the British. Livingston and Hazen between them were able to recruit only five hundred soldiers: most Canadians were as reluctant to fight for the Congress as for the king. In addition, military rule always has its drawbacks for the ruled and it didn't take long for the Canadians to become acutely aware of them. At first the Americans paid for what they bought with gold and silver. When this ran out they borrowed from sympathetic merchants in Montreal, but soon the only "money" they had was worthless paper. The American commander in Montreal alienated the merchants by cutting off trade with the west for fear that canoes might be used to carry arms to the enemy; he also despised the Canadians and made little attempt to hide it. The army besieging Quebec was being depleted by desertion, the enlistment of those who remained was about to expire, and the reinforcements coming in over Lake Champlain were not sufficient to keep up the fight. Less than awed by British military strength a year earlier, the Canadians were now just as unimpressed by the Americans' ability to hold the colony, and their sympathies began to waver once again.

The Continental Congress tried to save the rapidly deteriorating situation by sending a mission to Montreal in April of 1776. The mission was led by the Americans' most subtle and experienced diplomat, seventy-year-old Benjamin Franklin, and included Charles Carroll of Maryland, the richest man in the colonies and a Catholic, and his cousin Father John Carroll, a Jesuit whose presence, according to one American general, would be worth "battalions" to their cause in Quebec. The French printer Fleury Mesplet was to accompany them and remain in Montreal with his printing press.[16] There was little they could do. The Canadian clergy refused to receive Father Carroll, and the Americans' credit had sunk so low that no one in Montreal would cash Charles Carroll's personal bills. By this time a British force of ten thousand soldiers under Major-General John Burgoyne was on its way to relieve Quebec City. The Americans had already decided to abandon the siege, but the appearance of the first British ships turned their retreat into a rout. There were no major engagements, but rather a series of American flights just ahead of the advancing British.

The Americans failed to take the province of Quebec because too few Canadians rose to join them. According to Marxist historian Stanley Ryerson,

> something was lacking. No general uprising took place on the St. Lawrence. Quebec was far from being at the same advanced stage of social and economic development as the Atlantic colonies: capitalist manufacture scarcely existed there.

Ryerson suggests that the Canadians might have risen in alliance with the Americans on the issue of national independence, but the Declaration of Independence was not issued until July 4, 1776, two days after the last American troops had withdrawn from Quebec.

But the Americans' campaign was only a partial failure. They had successfully exploded Carleton's scheme of using the Canadians to put down the revolt. They had delayed a major British assault from the north until 1777, by which time the rebel colonies were strong enough to deal with it; and they had implanted liberal and republican ideas in Quebec, where they served as a counter-ideal to the dominant conservative tradition and inspired such political leaders as Louis-Joseph Papineau in the 1830s and, much later, René Lévesque in the 1970s.

FRENCH IN CULTURE, BRITISH IN SOVEREIGNTY

What Carleton had begun in the fall of 1776 British general John Burgoyne would try to finish in 1777. He too tried to raise a Canadian militia, and again the results were disappointing. Those who signed up began to desert even in

Montreal, and when Burgoyne's army started to head south the desertions increased precipitously. Burgoyne had other problems as well, and in October, after much delay and disappointment, he surrendered to the Americans at Saratoga. The fate of Burgoyne's expedition was watched with great interest at Versailles. Although the spread of American revolutionary ideas might be dangerous, as Louis XVI would later find out, this was outweighed by his desire to revenge the defeat of 1763 and re-establish the balance of power. French volunteers led by the Marquis de Lafayette were already in America, but Louis was reluctant to offer them official support; Benjamin Franklin was in Paris trying to get the French to change their minds. News of the victory at Saratoga now convinced them that in supporting the Americans they would be backing a winner, and France entered the war on the side of the rebels.

The French alliance reopened the question of Quebec. Among the Canadians the alliance revived hopes that they might be returned to French rule, and the reconquest of Quebec also had popular support in France, but it played no role in the calculations of the French policymakers. Their chief goal was to prevent a rapprochement between Britain and America, and they saw no better way of doing it than by making sure that the new American federation had a British colony on its northern border. In a secret article of its treaty of alliance with the Americans France renounced any intention of regaining Quebec. In theory this left open the possibility of adding it to the American union, but neither party to the treaty wanted to see Quebec in the hands of the other. Nevertheless, the idea of a new invasion of Quebec remained alive throughout the Revolutionary War. Lafayette could always be counted on to support it, and it never failed to have its partisans in Congress. The political situation in Quebec was therefore unsettled throughout the war. Canadians like Clément Gosselin, who had followed the retreating American army south early in the war, now slipped in and out of Quebec as agitators and spies. While Carleton had always been lenient with "His Majesty's deluded subjects" who supported the rebellion, after 1778 a new governor took a harder line and threw some of the more prominent American sympathizers in jail.

In October 1781 a combined American and French force, including Moses Hazen and his Canadians, defeated the British at Yorktown, Virginia, and effectively brought the Revolutionary War to an end. Quebec was still in English hands, and the Americans had made no further attempt to win it in the war: instead they would try to win it at the peace. Benjamin Franklin, the chief American negotiator, demanded the cession of Quebec, New York City, and other places still held by the British. The British, eager but not that eager to conclude a treaty, insisted on retaining Quebec, and dickering began over the boundary. The eventual agreement cut Quebec's old fur-trading hinterland in half by making the Great Lakes the border in the west: the fur-trading posts of Detroit and Michilimackinac and the French settlements in the Illinois and Ohio country became American.

And so the new United States of America came into being without Quebec, which most Canadian historians have regarded as fortunate. If Quebec had become an American state, wrote Gustave Lanctôt, "Canada's French-Catholic personality would gradually have disappeared in the inevitable assimilation of the ethnic group," and most other historians agree; but there is never any certainty about historical speculation, and this hypothesis is no exception. A United States that began existence with Quebec as the fourteenth state would have been a very different United States from the historical one. We can only imagine the additional clauses that would have been needed to satisfy French Canadian delegates to the Federal Convention, but they probably would not have been too far from the religious and cultural guarantees the British gave them in the Quebec Act, and they might not have applied to the Canadians alone. The melting pot became official American ideology only later, and there have always been pockets of resistance to it. While assimilating tendencies were already well under way by the time of the Revolution, there were still Germans in the United States who spoke German and Dutch who spoke Dutch. The Continental Congress issued many of its documents in German as well as English (and occasionally French), and serious consideration was at one time given to making German a second official language of the United States. It is possible— just possible—that the presence of Quebec in the union might have tipped the balance toward a diversity of languages and cultures.

In any case, a group generally retains its identity less as the result of official policy than of social, economic, and geographical factors and its own efforts. Would the Québécois have been any more inclined to give up their French Catholic personality in the United States than they were in Canada? The French-speaking people of Louisiana, without the crucial advantage of being around when the rules of the country were being made, and after being required to share their territory with English-speaking settlers, nevertheless remained French well into the twentieth century; and the French Canadians retained their identity more in spite of official British policy than because of it, especially after explicit pro-assimilation measures were adopted in 1840. So speculation can work both ways. But history does not, and Quebec remained French in culture, British in sovereignty, and outside the United States.

AMERICANS OF FRENCH HERITAGE

By the time of the revolution the American population already had a substantial diversity of background. Probably a third of the two million white inhabitants of the colonies were non-English in origin; some had been absorbed by conquest, others had been attracted by the economic opportunity and religious toleration offered by the colonies in varying degrees. Many of these non-English Americans were of French heritage, and more Franco-Americans would be added to the union through territorial expansion in the first decades of independence. The French group was itself diverse—in religion, in place of settlement, and in circumstances of migration to America—and it had a variety of responses to the influences of Anglo-American society. In the 1780s one French community had already taken its place within the Anglo-American mainstream; and two others that would stay outside the mainstream for generations were in the process of being formed.

The Huguenots, the first French people to arrive in the British American colonies, came as religious and political refugees. They were Protestants, and they had both the means and the motivation to leave France: early in the seventeenth century their intermittent war with the Catholics had ended in a defeat that broke their political power for good. Their first places of refuge were the Protestant countries of Europe, and from there many found their way to America (although they were barred from New France). Guillaume Molines, for instance, along with his wife, children, and servants, arrived in Plymouth on the Mayflower. The defeat of the Huguenots in the 1620s was followed by a period of peace in which the French Protestants continued to play an important role as traders and merchants, but Louis XIV resumed their harassment in the 1660s, finally revoking the Edict of Nantes in 1685. Some two hundred thousand Huguenots left France in the 1680s, and many of them ended up in the British colonies; Huguenot settlements sprang up from Massachusetts to South Carolina.

Their transition to a new life in America was not always smooth. In the 1690s France and Britain were at war, and the Huguenots of Oxford, Massachusetts, on the New England frontier, were attacked so repeatedly by Indians allied to the French that they abandoned the site. A settlement in Rhode Island became embroiled in a land dispute with its English neighbours and was forced to disperse. But, coming as they did largely from the merchant and professional classes, many of the Huguenots prospered, and in the course of the eighteenth century they established themselves as firmly as any group in the colonies. They also lost much of their French character, adopted the English language and were absorbed into the existing Protestant churches (the French Church in Boston opened in the 1680s and closed in 1748, most of its members having gone to other congregations). By the time of the revolution the Americanism of the Huguenots was secure. James Bowdoin (formerly Beaudoin) was one of Massachusetts' leading statesmen; Paul Rivoire, or Revere, warned his compatriots of the coming of the British; and George Washington, who numbered the Huguenot Nicolas Martiau among his ancestors, was at the head of the revolutionary forces.

A very different group of French refugees began to appear in British American ports in late 1755. They were Catholics rather than Protestants; they were farmers instead of merchants; and they were not welcomed by the English-speaking colonists. They had been deported from their Acadian homeland, victims of the war hysteria of 1755 and the narrow and frightened military thinking of Governor Charles Lawrence. The ships onto which they had been herded took them to Boston, Philadelphia, Charleston, and other ports on the Atlantic coast. They arrived accompanied by a letter from Lawrence in which he explained that these French Neutrals were not neutral at all but dangerously sympathetic to the cause of France, and asked his fellow governors to share the burden of caring for them and disposing of them in "such manner as may best answer our Design in preventing their Reunion." To that end, and in violation of a promise made when they were rounded up, families had been split and husbands, wives, and children loaded onto different ships and often taken to different ports. The over-crowded ships were breeding grounds for disease and many Acadians did not survive the voyage.

The recipients of the letter were just as inclined as Lawrence to regard the Acadians as dangerous, but they didn't see why that meant they should have to provide for the outcasts. The governor of Pennsylvania wrote to his colleague in Massachusetts that:

> the people here, as there is no military force of any kind, were very uneasy at the thought of having a number of enemies scattered in the very bowels of the country, who may go off from time to time with intelligence, and join their countrymen now employed against us, or foment some intestine commotion in conjunction with the Irish and German Catholics, in this and the neighbouring Province.

Like some of the other governors, he refused to allow the Acadians to land for a significant time after their arrival, and many who had survived the voyage died waiting in American harbours.

When they did land, many of them were sent to remote parts of the colonies as indentured servants and others became public charges in the cities. Often the Acadians refused to work because they claimed prisoner-of-war status, and often their hosts refused to employ them because they were papists. Disease continued to reduce their numbers, especially in the southern colonies. Those who stayed in the Anglo-American colonies were eventually absorbed into the population; the last mention of the Acadians in the *Assembly Journal* of Pennsylvania is dated January 4, 1766, and concerns a petition from one John Hill of Philadelphia who "has been employed from time to time to provide coffins for the French Neutrals who have died in and about this city" requesting payment from the government for the sixteen coffins he had made since accounts were last settled. Acadians who retained their French names were generally taken for Huguenots, and some even joined the declining Huguenot churches. But there were also many Acadians who left the British colonies within a few years of their arrival and either returned to their homeland or went to England, France, Quebec, Saint Domingue (the present Haiti), and other places where they hoped to find a haven. They endured years of wandering and hardship but they survived as a people; and, frustrating Lawrence's design to "prevent their Reunion", they established two new and enduring Acadias on the North American continent — of which portions of one, and all of the other, eventually became part of the United States.

In England the Acadians fared no better than in the colonies, and after the war ended in 1763 most of them went to France, but even there they continued to be aliens and exiles. They were given a dole that was supposed to tide them over for a few years but was still being paid decades later. There were endless schemes to settle them in various parts of France, but all were badly planned and ended in failure. They were also recruited for the colonizing ventures of the era: Acadians went to Saint Pierre and Miquelon, Saint Domingue, French Guiana, even the Falkland Islands. In the tropical colonies they died of fever, and in Saint Pierre and Miquelon they got caught in the middle of repeated wars with the British. Those who tried to return to Nova Scotia were either apprehended before they got there or shipped out again by Governor Lawrence. Slowly, however, the British began to warm to the idea of exploiting rather than expelling the Acadians: their worth became clear as early as 1759 when the farms of settlers from New England were flooded and only the Acadian prisoners knew how to repair the dikes.

After 1766 British policy toward the Acadians began to soften: peopled as it was largely by New Englanders, Nova Scotia could by no means be counted on to remain loyal to Britain, and it seemed worthwhile to appease the thousand or so Acadians who had remained or returned. Their old lands on the Bay of Fundy were lost to them forever, but they were allowed to settle at the western tip of Nova Scotia and in the St. John valley. In 1768 they were even given a priest. When the American Revolution broke out the dominant sentiment in Nova Scotia was neutrality. There was an attempt by local settlers, including some Acadians, to take Fort Cumberland (once the French Fort Beauséjour) in November 1776, but the British beat it off. The rebels received no aid from the thirteen colonies and did not take up arms again after 1776.

Nova Scotia became a haven for Loyalist refugees, and soon after the war they outnumbered the prewar population. Most of them were granted lands in the St. John valley and in 1784 the new and predominantly Loyalist province of New Brunswick was carved out of the northern half of Nova Scotia. When the Loyalists arrived they showed little regard for the settlers already established there, whether British or Acadian, and once again the Acadians were evicted from their lands. In no position to resist, they decided to establish themselves far enough away to be safe from further encroachment. One group went to the shores of the Baie des Chaleurs and the Gulf of St. Lawrence in northeastern New Brunswick, an area that has remained Acadian ever since. Others went farther up the St. John valley to Madawaska where Maliseet Indians had previously been the only inhabitants. This region was claimed by both Quebec and New Brunswick, and the group that sought land there applied to both provinces. Both governments were favourable and the first settlers, Acadians augmented by a few Canadians, arrived in Madawaska in 1785. They were later joined by others, mostly from Quebec: Madawaska is one of the few areas where Acadians and French Canadians have mixed. Belonging fully neither to Acadia nor to Quebec, they came to consider their territory the homeland of a unique people, *le Madawaska des Madawaskayens*. But, far from being left alone, Madawaska came to be claimed by three jurisdictions: not only was it disputed between New Brunswick and Quebec, but the border between the United States and British North America was undecided for many years; to the dismay of the Madawaskayens, when a border was finally agreed on in 1842 it ran right down the middle of their valley.

A more favoured group of Acadians landed in Louisiana. To be sure, the colony they came to was no paradise and there had been little enthusiasm for it since the Mississippi Bubble. New Orleans was a squalid town of fewer than three thousand people with more than its share of taverns and gambling houses. A start had been made on plantation agriculture based on slave labour, but the vast territory was still sparsely populated. When the Acadians first began to arrive from the English colonies and Saint Domingue in the early 1760s Louisiana was still a French possession, the last of any importance in North America. They were welcomed by the authorities and settled in the Opelousas and Attakapas regions to the west and south of New Orleans. The governor of the colony wrote:

> They are being reborn in Louisiana, and will create wonders there if they are helped a little. Thus, when one would have least expected it, the country will flourish.

Separated from the New Orleans-centred Creoles by geography and social class, the Acadians — over the years it became "Cajuns" — remained a group apart, but they were not immune to the changes that were about to engulf their new home.

France ceded Louisiana to Spain in 1762 by a secret agreement not made known in New Orleans until the spring of 1764. There was immediate consternation among the Creoles, whose trade depended on the colony's remaining in the French system, but their petition asking Louis XV to change his mind had no effect, and in 1768 a popular revolt was led by the Creole officials and merchants of New Orleans. There was also considerable support for it among the Acadians, whose march into New Orleans on October 28, 1768, was one of the revolt's more theatrical events. The rebels were unsuccessful in persuading France to retain the colony, but they did attract the attention of King Carlos III of Spain, who sent Alexander O'Reilly, an Irish soldier of fortune, to New Orleans to deal with the rebels. O'Reilly quickly singled out the leaders of the rebellion, had them tried and executed, and pardoned everybody else. He expelled the English traders and allowed Louisiana to trade only with specified Spanish ports. Then in 1770, after establishing Spanish institutions of government, he returned to Spain. Under O'Reilly's successors both the Creoles and the thousand Acadians who had settled in Louisiana colony became reconciled to Spanish rule, but the general character of the colony remained French. Meanwhile it prospered as it never had under the French, and its population tripled in the first twenty years of Spanish rule. Among the new arrivals were another fifteen hundred Acadians who came from France in 1785. Acadians there had been asking for ten years to emigrate to Louisiana, and the Spanish government was in favour of it: they were to be transported at Spanish expense and given land, seeds, tools, and livestock in Louisiana, but the Revolutionary War had intervened before the scheme could be put into effect. Now the newcomers joined their countrymen who had arrived in the 1760s, and together they laid the basis for the continuing Cajun presence in Louisiana.

NEW LINES ARE DRAWN

North America was still living in the immediate aftermath of one revolution when it encountered the shock waves from another. The effects of the French Revolution of 1789 were not confined to France or even to Europe: democrats and radicals everywhere were inspired by it and reactionaries were moved to denunciations and harsh measures. Its effects were felt in North America both directly and indirectly. The events in France sparked a rebellion in Ireland, where the United Irishmen led by Wolfe Tone fought unsuccessfully for independence from England and a nonsectarian, egalitarian Irish republic; and that in turn helped to reopen what historian Jean-Pierre Wallot has called the "unhealed wound of the American Revolution" in Quebec. In Saint Domingue black slaves, who believed that the ideals of liberty, equality, and fraternity applied to them too, revolted against their French masters and forced the abolition of slavery in 1794—and in the process helped to determine the future of Louisiana.

In the United States, so recently revolutionary itself, political leaders were sharply divided on the merits of the French Revolution. The governing Federalists, strongly influenced by Alexander Hamilton, the self-acknowledged champion of the "rich and well-born", were opposed to the revolution in Europe on grounds of both philosophy and self-interest, while the emerging Republican opposition led by Thomas Jefferson was strongly sympathetic to it. In 1793 the American position was further complicated by the outbreak of war between France, to which the United States was still bound by the alliance of 1778, and Britain, with which the merchants who made up Hamilton's constituency had a lucrative commerce.

Through the early years of the war the United States maintained an uneasy neutrality. Popular sympathy in the early 1790s was heavily on the side of the French. Citizen Edmond Charles Genêt, called by historian Samuel Eliot Morison "the quaintest of many curious diplomats sent by European governments to the United States", was given a tumultuous welcome in city after city as he proceeded to Philadelphia, then the capital. The mission of Citizen Genêt was not altogether straightforward: in addition to organizing support for the French Revolution in the United States, he was to attempt to detach Canada from Britain and Louisiana from Spain.

The Canada toward which Citizen Genêt's activities were directed was in a period of transition, newly divided by the Constitutional Act of 1791 into two provinces: Lower Canada was primarily French—the old settlements in the St. Lawrence Valley; Upper Canada was English-speaking—the new Loyalist settlements in the west. In the summer of 1793 Citizen Genêt and a young French Canadian, Henri Mezières, met in Philadelphia and drafted a pamphlet calling on Mezières' countrymen to rebel: "This land is yours. It must be independent.... The hour is propitious, and Insurrection is for you the most sacred of duties." The pamphlet charged that Britain had granted only "a shadow of a constitution"—and would not have done even that but for the fear that Canada would follow the example of the United States and France in "founding a government on the inalienable rights of man"—and it proposed the abolition of seigneurial duties, tithes, and other unloved accoutrements of the regime. The pamphlet was widely circulated in Lower Canada and contributed to the general unrest in the province. A new Militia Act in 1794 and measures to impose the corvée (forced seigneurial labour) in 1796 both provoked riots and demonstrations, and when the British took repressive action it led only to further agitation.

There was no official U.S. support for any of this activity. Even the sympathetic Jefferson was soon alienated by Genêt's intrigues; the U.S. government demanded his recall, and Paris complied. At the same time Jay's Treaty papered over the outstanding differences between the United States and Britain, leaving the Federalists free to manoeuvre toward war with France, and between 1798 and 1800 the Americans and the French were engaged in an inconclusive naval conflict. In the same years repressive legislation in the United States was directed against supporters of the French Revolution and the United Irishmen.

But although the U.S. government was increasingly on the side of France's enemies, individuals in the United States continued to engage in pro-French activity, some of it directed at Canada. In early 1797 a U.S. ship with a cargo of French arms was sequestered by the British on suspicion that the arms were to be used in an attempt to drive the British out of the Canadas. The owner of the cargo maintained that they were for the Vermont militia, and after a lengthy court battle he recovered them; but David McLane, an Irishman involved in the agitation in Lower Canada, was accused of conspiring to overthrow the British regime with the help of men and arms from Vermont, convicted of high treason, and hanged, dismembered, and disembowelled in the public square in Quebec City. The popular agitation died down, but the British authorities in the Canadas continued to watch the U.S. border closely, and in 1801 they arrested the leaders of the Montreal Civil Society, a secret organization of Americans in Montreal inspired by French revolutionary principles and the United Irishmen and allegedly involved in a new conspiracy against British rule. No French Canadians were involved. The people seem by this time to have lost their taste for U.S.-based liberation movements; the clergy and the élite were, as always, vocal in their loyalty to the Crown; and the calling up of the militia to deal with the apprehended insurrection received a somewhat less tepid response than usual.

If the threat to British rule in Canada during the French Revolution was never serious, the threat to Spanish rule in Louisiana most certainly was. With the end of the Revolutionary War settlers from the United States began to push westward, heralding the end of the sleepy isolation of Louisiana. By the 1790s U.S. settlement stretched to the Mississippi; this was the most convenient trade route for the new states of Kentucky and Tennessee, and they insisted that the United States obtain navigation rights on the river. Spanish officials, for their part, conspired to detach the western territories from the older states of the union. With Spain and the United States looking covetously across the Mississippi at each other's territory, French interest in the area also began to revive. Not only strategic and commercial arguments but revolutionary principles as well argued for its recovery: it had been a crime for the *ancien régime* to sell a people to a foreign power against their will. The revolution also heightened the desire of the Louisiana Creoles to return to French rule. The first attempt to recover Louisiana was set in motion by Citizen Genêt, who enlisted the aid of a number of Americans in a proposed expedition against the colony but was unable to get American financing for the scheme. Genêt was eventually repudiated by the French government and the expedition was never mounted. Nevertheless, France still hoped to get Louisiana back. Diplomatic overtures for the retrocession of the colony continued throughout the 1790s, and in 1800 Napoléon Bonaparte finally obtained it.

While the United States could easily tolerate a decaying imperial power like Spain on its western border, the presence of France, with its formidable military strength, was another matter. Thomas Jefferson, elected president in 1800, wrote:

> There is on the globe one spot, the possessor of which is our natural and habitual enemy.... It is New Orleans.... The day that France takes possession of New Orleans...seals the union of two countries who in conjunction can maintain exclusive possession of the ocean. From that moment we must marry ourselves to the British fleet and nation.[17]

For Jefferson, who in the 1790s had tried to steer U.S. policy toward France and away from Britain, that was quite a statement.

Bonaparte had had visions of a new French empire in the New World, centred in Louisiana and Saint Domingue; but by 1800 Saint Domingue, under the black revolutionary leader Toussaint L'Ouverture, had only loose ties to France, and by late 1803 the blacks had repelled a French army sent to retake the colony and restore slavery and had instead driven out the French and established the independent republic of Haiti. With Spain refusing to part with the Floridas, which Bonaparte also wanted, the United States being unfriendly, and Saint Domingue refusing to submit, there no longer seemed to be much point in re-establishing French sovereignty over Louisiana. The colony might do him just as much good in the hands of the United States, which it could help build into a serious rival to his real enemy Britain. When Jefferson's emissary James Monroe arrived in Paris in April 1803 he found the French surprisingly ready to sell Louisiana. There only remained a little haggling over the purchase price.

With the incorporation of Louisiana into the United States, the present political borders of North America were well on their way to taking shape. The United States now stretched from the Atlantic to the Rocky Mountains, and Spanish apprehensions about its designs on Mexican territory to the south and west would later prove justified. North of the United States was a loose collection of British colonies that lagged behind the republic in both political and economic development.

The cultural borders of the continent, however, were far from firmly established. There were pockets of French-speaking people in both the United States and British North America, and they formed the majority in one of the British colonies, Lower Canada. Neither the British nor the Americans yet had a firm policy for dealing with cultures other than their own. The British had from the time of the Conquest entertained vague hopes of Anglicizing the French Canadians, but under the pressure of political realities had in practice done little to interfere with their language and culture. When the Lower Canada Assembly met for the first time in 1792 there was a long discussion of whether French should be an admissible language of debate. While English remained the sole official language, the French-Canadian majority was able to win *de facto* recognition of French as a language of the Assembly's proceedings. In the United States, a resolution in the House of Representatives in 1795 proposing that federal laws be printed in German as well as English was defeated only by a vote of forty-two to forty-one. The ideology of cultural uniformity that was to characterize the United States in later years had not yet taken full hold.

Although the Louisiana Purchase incorporated into the republic some forty thousand people who were French in language and culture, there seemed to be more concern about the political than about the cultural orientation of these new citizens. During the debates on the Louisiana treaty doubts about the propriety of encompassing an alien people were addressed by Rep. Samuel L. Mitchill: they will not remain alien, he said in effect; they will be educated, and we will keep them in tutelage until they are.

> It is intended, first, to extend to this newly acquired people the blessings of law and social order.... In this way they are to be trained up in a knowledge of our own laws and institutions. They are thus to serve an apprenticeship to liberty; they are to be taught the lessons of freedom; and by degrees they are to be raised to the enjoyment and practice of independence.... The act we are about to perform will not confer on them this elevated character. They will thereby gain no admission into this House, nor into the other House of Congress. There will be no alien influence thereby introduced into our councils. By degrees, however, they will pass on from the childhood of republicanism, through the improving period of youth, and arrive at the mature experience of manhood.[18]

But at no point in the debate was the question raised of what language the Louisianians would speak, or what values they would hold in the private sphere. Americanism, at this point, was a purely political idea.

The events of the eighteenth century had left French-speaking North Americans without a political entity of their own, but the cultural implications of this circumstance were only beginning to manifest themselves. The seeds of the vast economic and social changes of the nineteenth century had already been planted. As a result of those changes cultural borders would come to correspond to political ones even less than they had in 1803, but nowhere in North America would there be an easy acceptance of the existence of different cultural communities within the same political entity. Americans would develop their dream, with its implications of cultural homogeneity, while French-speaking North Americans would develop their counter-ideal of *survivance*. Where these two came in contact, as they would both in the United States and in French Canada over the next century and a half, conflict would be frequent, emotion would be intense, and compromises would be made whose full implications often would not be understood until much later.

3

Democracy at Issue, Farms in Crisis, and an Industrial U.S.A.

1803–1850

As THE UNITED STATES grew physically and economically it gained in self-confidence as well; in fact self-confidence was one of the most striking characteristics of the early republic. It was based on a faith in progress, economic opportunity, the apparently endless availability of arable land in the west, democracy (variously defined), and the fundamental belief that in America a new and different kind of society could avoid the mistakes of the Old World. By the time of the American Revolution that idea had already gained wide currency. Michel-Guillaume Jean de Crèvecoeur, a Frenchman who lived in New France before the conquest and later settled in Orange County, New York, anticipated Emma Lazarus's inscription for the Statue of Liberty a century later when he wrote in the name of his adopted country:

> Welcome to my shores, distressed European; bless the hour in which thou didst see my verdant fields, my fair navigable rivers, and my green mountains! —If thou wilt work, I have bread for thee; if thou wilt be honest, sober, and industrious, I have greater rewards to confer on thee—ease and independence.

Although the more conservative Founding Fathers of the United States believed that power should be largely confined to an élite, the forces favouring greater popular sovereignty won important gains with the election of presidents Thomas Jefferson in 1800 and Andrew Jackson in 1828. Democracy, a term of opprobrium in the first years after the Revolution, was being used by its supporters with pride in the Jackson era. One could be for democracy or against it, but few seemed to doubt that it prevailed in the United States. Count Alexis de Tocqueville, who visited the United States during Jackson's first term, considered democracy to be fundamental to the U.S. experiment, for better or for worse, and he took note of what he regarded as its inherent dangers, especially its tendency to lead to conformity.

An earlier visitor, Irish poet Tom Moore, also recognized the power of U.S. ideals, although he criticized the reality those ideals had produced:

> No longer here shall justice bound her view,
> Or wrong the many, while she rights the few;
> But take her range through all the social frame.
> . . . .
> Oh golden dream!

As Moore saw it, the United States failed to realize its golden dream, but the dream was still a potent force. Most Americans who expressed themselves publicly on the matter believed implicitly in the dream, and did not share the doubts entertained by Tocqueville and Moore. They saw it as their duty not only to give life to the dream themselves but also to bring it to the less fortunate peoples who surrounded them, even at the risk of confrontation with other powers. Commercial considerations and British acts of aggression on the high seas initially impelled the United States to take a warlike stance toward Britain in the early years of the nineteenth century, but by 1810 they had other reasons to take up arms. The war hawks, led by the young Congressman Henry Clay of Kentucky, saw the possibility of acquiring new territory by force. Clay's fellow Kentuckian Richard M. Johnson proclaimed that:

> The waters of the St. Lawrence and the Mississippi interlock in a number of places, and the great Disposer of Human Events intended those two rivers should belong to the same people.

The U.S. attempt to conquer Canada in 1812–14 ended in failure, but the United States dismembered northern Mexico in the 1830s and 1840s, after declaring itself the protector of the whole western hemisphere under the Monroe Doctrine in 1823. The Mexican adventure provided the republic with the future states of Texas, New Mexico, Arizona, Utah, Nevada and California, and with a popular phrase to describe its relation to the North

American continent: New York newspaper and magazine editor John L. Sullivan wrote of

> our manifest destiny to overspread the continent allotted by Providence for the free development of our yearly multiplying millions.

Progressive and intelligent Americans like William Cullen Bryant, Ralph Waldo Emerson, and Walt Whitman agreed. For Whitman, expansion was justified because it would result in "the increase of human happiness and liberty."

Thomas Jefferson advocated the simple life and an agricultural vocation for the American people, and these ideas continued to have at least some influence through most of the nineteenth century. To imitate the manners of aristocratic Europe was to be subject to ridicule in democratic America: in the presidential campaign of 1840 the Whigs portrayed Democratic incumbent Martin Van Buren as an effete drinker of European wine while their candidate, William Henry Harrison, was satisfied with hard cider. Harrison was elected.

In a country whose territory was vast and increasing the land maintained a powerful hold on the public imagination, but by mid-century it had to share that hold with the nation's growing industrial prowess. At the World Exhibition in London in 1862 the United States was represented by an impressive display of machines, including devices for making shoes, binding books, and manufacturing paper bags, as well as advanced farm machinery. The London *Standard* commented:

> It is one of the cardinal points of an American's system to do nothing with his hands that he can do by a machine.[19]

There were other developments, varied and sometimes contradictory, but nevertheless all suggestive of the direction in which the United States was moving. There was a growing public school system, based on the principle that education should be available to everyone. There were a number of idealistic communities set up, most based on the ideas of Robert Owen of Scotland and Charles Fourier of France. There was a proliferation of new religions, including Unitarianism, Universalism, Seventh-Day Adventism, Christian Science, and Mormonism. There was a widespread belief that worldly success was not incompatible with godliness, and that God in fact bestowed riches as a means of doing God's works.

There was an interminable debate over whether American literature could be truly distinct from European literature, until Walt Whitman issued a convincing declaration of literary independence with *Leaves of Grass*:

> The United States must found their own imaginative literature & poetry, & ... nothing merely copied from & following out the feudal world will do.

He infused his verses with vigour, self-confidence and faith in the future, as in "Roaming in Thought (After Reading Hegel)":

> Roaming in thought over the Universe, I saw the little that is Good steadily
>   hastening towards immortality,
> And the vast all that is call'd Evil I saw hastening to merge itself and become
>   lost and dead.

In short, a distinctive American culture was developing, arising out of the culture of the colonial era but strongly affected by the political ideas of republicanism and democracy. The relation of non–Anglo-Saxons to that culture was just beginning to be a subject for serious thought. The American Dream did not *a priori* exclude anybody, or at least not anybody who was white; but the republic was home to increasing numbers of people who were born to other values, customs, and ways of life. When they came they accepted the economic ground rules of the United States (that was, after all, why most of them came) and they by and large accepted its political ideals; but did they accept the cultural corollaries?

After the War of 1812 a number of immigrant groups petitioned Congress for special credit terms so that they might set up colonies in areas of the west previously uninhabited by people of European descent. Such colonization, reasoned the Irish Emigrant Society of New York, was the best form of immigration, because it would allow

> those whose birth place is in common, who have the same feelings and habits—the same connections and attachments...[to] join together, assist and support each other... [and to] form a community into which they all can enter, where they will find persons and usages to which they are familiar, and which create a resemblance to their own country...[and thus] raise up a young and happy Erin, in the midst of abundance and freedom.

In anticipation of objections that

the foreign nationality, which such a mode of settlement is calculated to cherish, may be at variance with the attachment they ought to form to their adopted country

the society argued that

the operation of colonization is to destroy the foreign character of that nationality... early affections and partialities would be gradually withdrawn from the foreign country, and transferred to the colony— they would become blended with his devotion and gratitude to the government, the laws and institutions under which it had been raised and flourished. In his domestic and interior relations, he might have some Irish feelings and propensities; but in the performance of his duties as a citizen, he would be exclusively and ardently American.[20]

With clarity and prescience, as well as a certain amount of cheek, the Irish Emigrant Society was asking the United States to embark on a policy of cultural pluralism, of permitting a variety of cultures to flourish under a single political umbrella. Congress said no. There would be no special encouragement for immigrant groups to settle, as groups, in the United States. "Probably no decision in the history of American immigration policy," wrote historian Marcus Lee Hansen more than a century later, when the consequences of Congress's action had had full opportunity to manifest themselves, "possesses more profound significance."

Nevertheless, despite that historic decision, the United States already contained islands of unassimilated minority cultures. It would soon acquire others. There were the French-speaking people of Louisiana, whose language rights were recognized for the first time in the state constitution of 1845. As a result of the Mexican War the United States absorbed a long-established Spanish-speaking society in the Southwest. Germans preserved their language and old-country ways in Pennsylvania, and as their numbers increased they would do so in the Midwest as well. Some of them dreamed of establishing a German-speaking state; when the American union broke up (as they expected it to do) this state would become an independent Teutonic commonwealth. That did not happen, but a "German belt" nevertheless developed that stretched from Pennsylvania to Texas.

The possibility of a conflict of values was increased by the large number of the new Americans who were Roman Catholics, and thus brought with them beliefs that many Protestant Americans regarded as alien. Continuing efforts were made to reconcile the doctrines of Catholicism with those of Americanism; perhaps the most tireless advocate of such reconciliation was a former Universalist minister and secular preacher named Orestes A. Brownson, who converted to Catholicism in 1844. Brownson wrote in 1850:

> How is it possible to regard Catholicity as likely to impede modern civilization, since modern civilization is undeniably the product of the Catholic religion?

Positions stiffened on both sides. In the 1850s the anti-Catholic American Party, the "Know-Nothings", gained a considerable if short-lived following, and in 1864 Pope Pius IX issued his *Syllabus of the Principal Errors of Our Times*, errors that included freedom of religion, separation of church and state, public education, and, in general, the idea that "the Roman Pontiff can and ought to reconcile itself and come to terms with progress, with liberalism, and with modern civilization." The *Syllabus* was addressed primarily to Europe, but it was bound to have profound consequences in the U.S.A. as well. Anti-Catholic forces eagerly seized on it, and Orestes Brownson now denounced the values of progress and modernity he had previously stood for.

The controversies over cultural relations and reconciliation of values reached their height in the late nineteenth and early twentieth centuries. The masses of French Canadians who crossed the border to New England in these years stepped into the middle of these controversies, were deeply affected by them, and developed positions on them that reflected their own history and intellectual environment as well as their new situation in the United States.

THE RISE AND FALL OF RADICAL NATIONALISM

In French-speaking Lower Canada the liberal and democratic ideas that had come in at the time of the American Revolution in the 1770s and the French Revolution in the 1790s continued to have their effect through much of the nineteenth century, allied in the thinking of the popular leaders of the era with the sense of collective identity that was just beginning to develop into French-Canadian nationalism. This association was quickly noted by the English-speaking and anti-democratic rulers of the colony. The first opposition newspaper, *Le Canadien*, wrote early in the century that "in the ministerial dictionary, a bad fellow, anti-ministerialist, democrat, *sans culotte*, and damned Canadian, mean the same thing."

This conflict of ideas was part of an increasingly bitter constitutional struggle between the popularly elected legislative assembly with its limited powers and the appointed officials who were responsible not to the assembly but to London, and it took place in the context of economic changes from which the mass of French Canadians derived little advantage and not infrequently suffered real distress. Anglophone merchants, in alliance with British officials, dominated the colony, and they not only spoke a different language and professed different ideas from those of the French-Canadian doctors, lawyers, and notaries who controlled the assembly, but had different economic interests as well.

Furs no longer played an important role in the economy of Lower Canada after the Montreal-based North West Company lost its long battle with the Hudson's Bay Company for control of the western fur trade. Their place was taken by timber, which had a growing market in Britain; with the help of imperial preferences Canadian timber was able to fill a large part of that market. The Montreal merchants, who invested heavily in the timber trade, thus had a direct economic stake in the British connection. There was also a British market for agricultural products, although a much less stable one, but for many reasons French-Canadian agriculture had entered into an apparently irreversible decline and the farmers of the St. Lawrence valley were in no position to take advantage of occasional high prices in Britain.

When the leaders of the assembly began talking about independence in the 1830s there was therefore no conflict between their ideas and the economic interests of the farmers who supported them. Like the Americans of the 1760s and 1770s, these leaders came to the idea of independence only reluctantly: until late in their long struggle with the Anglophone merchants and British officials, they saw themselves as defenders rather than opponents of British constitutional theory and practice. In the early days *Le Canadien*, whose nationalist slogan was "our language, our institutions, and our laws", portrayed the French Canadians as the natural allies of the British Crown against the Americanizing influence of the merchants: the French Canadians were loyal and peaceful children of the soil; the Americans were a commercial people and hence linked to the merchants who were trying to "Yankify" the province by bringing settlers from New England into the Eastern Townships. When American troops invaded Lower Canada in 1812 they found much less support among the population than had existed in 1775. French Canadians proved much readier than usual to serve in the militia, despite some resistance in Montreal: one of the most important British victories of the war, at Châteauguay, was won by a largely French-Canadian unit under a French-Canadian commander, Colonel Charles-Michel de Salaberry.

The French Canadians' attachment to British institutions waned as the defects of the colonial constitution, the high-handedness of the British governors, and the not-so-benign neglect of London led to increasing frustration. Sir James Craig, governor from 1807 to 1811, dissolved a newly elected assembly when it refused to bow to his wishes, and later suppressed *Le Canadien* and jailed its editors. In 1822 a bill was introduced in the British House of Commons that, if passed, would have reunited Upper and Lower Canada and phased out French as a language of debate in the assembly of the combined province within fifteen years. News of this bill aroused intense opposition in Lower Canada, and a delegation was sent to London to make those feelings known; the bill was eventually dropped. In 1827 another authoritarian governor, Lord Dalhousie, after a long battle with the assembly over the control of provincial finances, prorogued the assembly rather than accept its choice for speaker, Louis-Joseph Papineau. The dispute was resolved only when a committee of the British House of Commons intervened in favour of the assembly.

Papineau, who had first been elected speaker in 1815, was the most important French-Canadian political leader of the day. Although he worked within the British constitutional system for more than twenty years, he became increasingly sympathetic to the republican ideas of revolutionary America and France. In his last public speech Papineau said:

> The good teachings of modern times, I have found condensed, explained, and given over to the love of peoples...in a few lines of the Declaration of Independence of 1776 and of the Declaration of Rights of Man and the Citizen of 1789.

In the 1830s, under Papineau's leadership, the French Canadians went some distance toward replaying the events that had first been staged by the people of Massachusetts sixty years earlier. The victory of the assembly in its struggle with Lord Dalhousie and his recall in 1828 ushered in a brief period of co-operation. Two events in 1832, however, brought an end to the truce and led to an even wider divergence between the assembly and the administration. One of these was a cholera epidemic, which was blamed on the British policy of sending the "redundant population" of the British Isles to Quebec as immigrants, with little attention to health and sanitary conditions aboard ship or how the immigrants would be cared for when they reached their destination. The other event occurred during a hotly contested election in Montreal: when partisan crowds battled with sticks and stones in

Place d'Armes, British troops fired into the supporters of the radical candidate, killing three. This became known as "the Montreal Massacre", in analogy with the Boston Massacre of 1770.

The Massachusetts assembly had voted in 1768 to stand fast in its opposition to the hated Townshend Acts by a margin of ninety-two to seventeen, and so the number ninety-two had become a symbol of colonial resistance: Paul Revere made a silver punch bowl dedicated to the "Immortal 92". Now, in 1834, Papineau and his supporters framed their grievances and demands in ninety-two resolutions enumerating the ills the existing system had given rise to and setting forth the main political demands of Papineau's party, which had adopted the name "Patriotes", again evoking American antecedents.

The key demands were for a more powerful assembly and an elective legislative council, and the resolutions raised the possibility of independence if these demands were not met:

> This House would esteem itself wanting in candour to the people of England, if it hesitated to call their attention to the fact that in less than twenty years the population of the United States of America will be as great or greater than that of Great Britain, and that of British America will be as great or greater than that of the former English colonies was when the latter deemed that the time had come to decide that the inappreciable advantage of governing themselves instead of being governed, ought to engage them to repudiate a system of colonial government which was, generally speaking, much better than that of British America now is. [Resolution 50]

The ninety-two resolutions were passed by the assembly, and the Patriotes went into the 1834 election with the resolutions as their platform. Despite their position as representatives of French-Canadian nationalism the Patriotes in this crucial election based their appeal almost entirely on an ideological rather than an ethnic foundation, and they succeeded in winning significant support among English-speaking as well as French-speaking voters. Their most enthusiastic English-speaking supporters were the Irish, who saw analogies to the situation in their home country; Papineau's Irish lieutenant Edmund O'Callaghan was an ally of Daniel O'Connell, the leader of the Catholic Emancipation movement in Ireland and an influential supporter of the French-Canadian cause in the British House of Commons.

Patriote candidates won seventy-seven of the eighty-eight seats in the assembly, but the seriousness with which the demands embodied in the ninety-two resolutions were being put forward made little impression in London. A royal commission sent out to examine the situation recommended against an elective legislative council and a government responsible to the assembly, and ten resolutions in the House of Commons repeated the commission's recommendations and went on to authorize the governor of the province to spend public money without the consent of the assembly. In Lower Canada these provocative British resolutions were met with even more determined resistance. The intensifying political conflict coincided with an economic crisis, the result of bad harvests combined with fallout from financial panics in Britain and the United States, and French-Canadian discontent reached the point of open revolt. Defiance first took the form of a boycott of British goods—another leaf from Boston's book—and Patriotes pointedly attired themselves in *étoffe du pays*, Canadian homespun. Those who favoured more direct resistance also followed a Massachusetts model in calling themselves the Fils de la Liberté, after the American Revolution's Sons of Liberty.

Early in November 1837 the Fils de la Liberté clashed with Anglophone conservative paramilitary groups in the streets of Montreal; then there was a skirmish between British troops and Patriotes on the road between Chambly and Longueuil, southeast of the city; six days later, at St. Denis on the nearby Richelieu River, a battle with British troops ended in a Patriote victory. It was their last. The armed phase of the rebellion never spread beyond the Richelieu Valley and the Deux Montagnes district northwest of Montreal, and it was put down within three weeks. The rebel leaders fled to the United States—including Papineau, who had never supported the resort to arms. The rebels had hoped for U.S. support, but President Van Buren quickly issued a proclamation of neutrality. Still, one group of Patriotes kept up the fight: but their first attempt at an invasion from U.S. soil ended when they were disarmed by the U.S. Army; the second was easily dispersed by volunteers and British regulars and twelve of its leaders were hanged for treason.

Although the British authorities had the military situation well in hand, they now recognized that something was amiss. One of the most consequential governors ever sent out by Britain to Canada arrived in 1837, completed his brief tour of duty, and returned home. Lord Durham's mission was to see what could be done about the discontent that had caused the Lower Canadian rebellion and the simultaneous uprising in English-speaking Upper Canada, and his recommendations were forceful and unambiguous. First, responsible government, demanded explicitly by the rebels in Upper Canada and implicitly by those in Lower Canada, should be granted. Second, since Durham interpreted the Lower Canadian conflict as "a struggle, not of principles, but of races," steps should be taken to break down the "unreasoning tenacity of an uneducated and unprogressive people" — the French Canadians. He wrote in his report:

> There can hardly be conceived a nationality more destitute of all that can invigorate and elevate a people, than that which is exhibited by the descendants of the French in Lower Canada, owing to their retaining their peculiar language and manners. They are a people with no history and no literature.

Durham's second recommendation was followed by the British government, but his call for responsible government was not. Upper and Lower Canada were united to create an English majority, with English as the only official language of the new province. The legislative assembly was to play the same subordinate role in United Canada as it had in the old divided colonies. The program of 1822, which had aroused such fierce opposition in Lower Canada, was now implemented. This created a dilemma for French-Canadian liberal nationalists. They had become accustomed to working within the parliamentary system, but the new assembly with its English-Canadian majority would not be the rallying-point for national sentiment that the Lower Canada assembly had been. Nevertheless a moderate group led by Louis-Hippolyte Lafontaine resolved to accomplish what it could within the Union, and in alliance with Upper Canadian reformers it succeeded in winning some important changes. Responsible government was granted in 1848, French was made an official language in the same year, and there came to be an understanding that significant decisions required a "double majority" — a majority of the delegates from each half of the colony.

For the radical democrats who kept alive the tradition of 1837 these reforms were incomplete and unsatisfactory. The radicals were in touch with the currents of progressive thinking that swept through Europe at the time and culminated in the revolutions of 1848, currents that closely linked liberalism and nationalism and were inspiring other "peoples without history" in southern and eastern Europe to take their place as nations in the modern world. Papineau, who returned from exile in 1845, was among the most prominent of the radicals, but they also attracted considerable support from younger French Canadians. They founded a fraternal society, the Institut Canadien, in 1844, and with it Montreal's first public library; a youth newspaper, *L'Avenir* (The Future), in 1847; and later a political party, the Parti Rouge. Politically, they stood for abolition of the Union, nothing less, and for elective legislative and executive councils, expansion of education, modernization of agriculture, and other progressive reforms.

When annexation to the United States was advanced as a solution to Lower Canada's problems by a group of English Montreal merchants in 1849, many French-Canadian radicals, including Papineau, had their own reasons for supporting the proposal. The merchants had been hurt by the British adoption of free trade and the consequent loss of their protected markets for grain and timber, and their arguments were entirely economic:

> The proposed union would render Canada a field for American capital, into which it would enter as freely for the prosecution of public works and private enterprise as into any of the present States. It would equalize the value of real estate upon both sides of the boundary, thereby probably doubling at once the entire present value of property in Canada.... It would also introduce manufactures into Canada as rapidly as they have been introduced into the northern states; and to Lower Canada, especially, where water privileges and labour are abundant and cheap, it would attract manufacturing capital, enhancing the value of property and agricultural produce, and giving remunerative employment to what is at present a comparatively non-producing population.[21]

The merchants' vision of Quebec has survived into our time. A radical supporter of annexation, writing in L'Avenir on July 4, 1849, saw distinctly different benefits arising from it:

> Masters of the election of our own officials, we shall have a legislature and an executive truly French-Canadian in personnel; our laws will be in reality official laws, and our language an official language; we shall no longer be forced, as today, to submit our laws to the stroke of a pen of an English Queen, or to sacrifice our language to the necessity of being understood by our public officials. Furthermore, our general interests will be represented in the House of Representatives and the Senate of the United States by a sufficient number of members to make them known and respected.

While the merchants were content with the limited form of free trade with the United States adopted in 1854, annexation continued to be a popular radical cause. In 1864, when the confederation of the British North American provinces was beginning to be seriously discussed, one member of the Institut Canadien, Gonzalve Doutre, supported the idea only because he saw confederation as leading to a larger North American union.

But in the 1860s the radicals were inexorably losing their battle with the conservative forces in Lower Canada, a battle that pitted them against the most powerful institution in French Canadian society, the hierarchy of the Roman Catholic Church. Conflict between the radicals and the clergy was not new. Papineau and the Patriotes were mildly anticlerical, and an attempt by the Patriote-dominated assembly to legislate the democratization of parish structures had aroused clerical opposition. Bishop J.J. Lartigue of Montreal condemned the 1837 insurrection, ordering priests to refuse absolution to those who preached resistance to "the government under which we have the happiness to live," and denounced the "pernicious doctrines" of democracy and the concept of the "sovereign people"; indeed the church's opposition to the insurrection was a major factor in its disastrous outcome.

Under Lartigue's successor, Monsignor Ignace Bourget, the church took the offensive. The ideological foundation of its campaign was ultramontanism, whose main tenets were submission to papal authority and the supremacy of the church over the state. Ultramontanism had first arisen in the seventeenth century as a response to the pretensions of the king of France to some say in the running of the French church, and was thus in its origins antinationalist. In French Canada, however, the ultramontanes embraced nationalism, although it was a very different sort of nationalism from that of Papineau and the Rouges. While Rouge nationalism was progressive, outward-looking, and oriented toward the recognition of political rights, ultramontane nationalism was reactionary, mystical, inward-looking, and based on the French Canadians' "providential mission" to establish a "profoundly Christian people" on the land given them by God.[22] The ultramontanes frowned on contact between ordinary Catholics and their Protestant neighbours: one of Bishop Bourget's complaints against his favourite target, the Institut Canadien, was that it admitted Protestants to membership. On the other hand, they favoured collaboration with the British secular rulers of French Canada, to whom they owed the privileged position of their church; they supported the Union and campaigned for its successor, Confederation, in both cases winning out over the opposing Rouges.

Confederation gave the new Province of Quebec its own legislature with considerable authority over cultural matters, and thus gave the clergy its best chance yet to put its doctrine of church supremacy into practice. It carved out a position for itself as cultural guardian of French Canada which was not seriously challenged until the 1960s, and successive provincial governments acquiesced in the doctrine that education should be left to the church. Politicians of all stripes had to reckon with its power: ultramontane support was equally important to George-Étienne Cartier in promoting

Confederation in the 1860s and to Honoré Mercier in defending provincial autonomy in the 1880s. Even the Liberal Party, heir to the Rouge tradition, was largely forced to abandon that tradition in order to gain respectability in Quebec, and Wilfrid Laurier, in his youth a member of the Institut Canadien, adopted a conciliatory attitude toward the church well before becoming Liberal leader in 1887. Nevertheless, it was 1897 before a Quebec Catholic could vote Liberal without being guilty of a mortal sin.

When Pope Pius IX declared war on the modern world with his *Syllabus of Errors* in 1864 he found no more enthusiastic supporter than Bishop Bourget. Backed by the authority of the pope (who in 1870 persuaded the First Vatican Council to declare him infallible), the bishop carried on his battle against the Institut Canadien, which he accused of encouraging the circulation of Indexed books and being generally wrongheaded as well as of harbouring Protestants. The battle reached a climax with the unseemly Guibord affair, in which the bishop refused to allow a deceased member of the Institut, Joseph Guibord, to be buried in consecrated ground. Spurred on by her husband's friends at the Institut, Guibord's widow took the bishop to court and ultimately won a favourable judgement from the British Privy Council in 1875, six years after Guibord's death and two years after her own. A mob still prevented Guibord's burial. He was finally laid to rest under the protection of British troops, but the bishop had the last word by deconsecrating his grave. By this time, the Institut was a spent force, and it folded soon afterward.

At the same time that Americans were increasingly inclined to identify the ideology on which their country was founded with a single culture, French Canadians were identifying their culture with a single ideology. This was the position when the period of most intimate contact between the two groups began.

A CAPITAL PLACE FOR MILLS

The militant Protestantism of New England was a significant and continuing influence in the events that led to the political and cultural configurations of 1803. Refugees from religious intolerance in Britain, the founders of New England tended to be equally intolerant, and the Catholic Acadians and Canadians who lived on New England's northern border were natural targets for their hostility. New Englanders were early advocates both of a harsh policy toward the Acadians and of vigorous action to bring about the conquest of Canada.

New England was more culturally homogeneous than the mid-Atlantic colonies, and it was largely rural despite its scattering of coastal towns based on overseas trade; but by the beginning of the nineteenth century changes were already under way that would transform New England into the first great U.S. industrial region, into a point of attraction for newcomers, notably from Ireland and Quebec, and eventually into one of the most heavily Catholic areas of the United States. The main driving force of these changes was the textile industry. The first cloth manufactory in America had been established at Rowley, Massachusetts, in 1643. In the next century English inventions mechanized the making of textiles and heralded the dawn of a new era of industrial capitalism, and when these inventions came to America they came first to New England.

In 1789 a young Englishman named Samuel Slater secretly left home, bound for New York to make his fortune. Slater had worked for a partner of Sir Richard Arkwright, inventor of the most advanced and successful cotton-spinning machine of the era, and he was well aware of the stringent regulations the British had enacted to prevent knowledge of the new machines reaching foreign competitors—hence the secrecy of his departure. Soon after his arrival an opportunity presented itself: a Pawtucket, Rhode Island merchant named Moses Brown had purchased textile manufacturing machinery but was unable to get it to work. Slater looked at the machines, told Brown that "these will not do", and agreed to build wholly new machines after the Arkwright patents in return for a fifty per cent interest in the business. By late 1790 the first yarn was being spun in the Pawtucket mill, and Slater's yarn was soon being sold in Salem, Hartford, and Philadelphia as well as at the mill. Not surprisingly, this first success begat others: Slater himself started a second mill in 1799 just across the state line in Rehoboth, Massachusetts, and former employees established other mills elsewhere in Massachusetts and Rhode Island.

The mills established by Slater and his imitators at the end of the eighteenth century were spinning mills only: the yarn they produced was still woven by hand. An enterprising group of Boston capitalists eventually changed that. In 1811 Francis Cabot Lowell visited mills in Scotland and England and memorized the construction of the British power looms; and by 1814 he and his mechanic had succeeded in building a practical loom. Lowell and other members of the Boston mercantile élite incorporated the Boston Manufacturing Company, bought water-power rights on the Charles River at Waltham, Massachusetts, and built a mill there. It was the first fully mechanized textile mill in North America, and its potential markets soon outran its limited capacity. The Boston Associates set about looking for places with more plentiful water power—a prerequisite in the days before steam—and in 1821 they found one in bucolic East Chelmsford, on the Merrimack River northwest of Boston. The Boston Associates' agent, one Kirk Boott, is said to have bilked the farmers of a fair price for their lands and water rights by saying he intended to raise wool and fruit, and a satirical song about the transaction became popular in the area:

> There came a young man from the old countree,
> The Merrimack River he happened to see.
> "What a capital place for mills!" quoth he,
>   Ri-toot, ri-toot, ri-toot.
>
> ....
>
> And these same farmers so cute
> They gave all their lands and their timbers to Boott,
>   Ri-toot, ri-toot, ri-toot.[23]

By late 1823 the new factory town of Lowell had been built on the banks of the Merrimack, and in the ensuing decades other towns would grow up on the same model: Fall River, Massachusetts; Manchester, New Hampshire; Woonsocket, Rhode Island; Lewiston, Maine, and many more. By 1860 cotton textile manufacturing was the leading industry in the country in terms of value-added, and seventy-five per cent of its capital was invested in New England mills. Related industries such as men's clothing and textile machinery were also assuming substantial significance, as were woollen textiles.

To achieve all this the industry needed a labour force, and in obtaining one it wrought profound economic and social changes. Slater, following English practice, had employed whole families in the mills, but Lowell and his associates took a new approach: they recruited the daughters of the Yankee farmers who still made up the bulk of the region's population. To induce New England women to leave the farm for the unknown life of a factory town, the Boston Associates had to make that life respectable, and this they did through a paternalistic system that in its time was the wonder of the industrial world. The mill girls were accommodated in boarding houses, company-owned and strictly chaperoned, for $1.25 a week, leaving them take-home pay of a dollar (for seventy-two hours and more of work). In Lowell, where the mill-girl system achieved its fullest flowering, care was taken to provide not only for the worker's morals but also for her intellect. She could borrow books from the Lowell Circulating Library and attend lectures at the Lyceum, and the *Lowell Offering*, a journal devoted entirely to stories, poems and essays by the mill girls, appeared regularly between 1840 and 1845.[24]

If Lowell had ever lived up to its self-image as one big happy family, it clearly no longer did so in the late 1840s. Cotton profits were declining, and mill-owners everywhere responded by putting ever greater pressure on the workforce. Wages were reduced, the machines were speeded up, and the Yankee mill girls simply left. By 1860 they had all but disappeared. Their place was taken by the immigrants from Ireland who made up a growing proportion of New England's population, and the presence of these strangers may have strengthened the bad reputation that mill work was acquiring in rural New England. The Irish had been coming to the region since the early part of the century. They dug canals, built roads, laid foundations, worked as farm hands, and in the 1850s mill work in the region was largely an Irish occupation; but after the Civil War, as the textile and other industries grew, yet further sources of labour were needed. One enterprising shoe manufacturer brought in Chinese from California, but they proved unsuited to eastern factory conditions; others encouraged immigration from England, but the class-conscious English workers had a distressing tendency to organize labour unions. The mill-owners wanted a labour force that had no such deficiencies, and they found it in Quebec.

THE CRISIS OF RURAL QUEBEC

One point of agreement between Patriote and ultramontane nationalism was the belief that French Canada was and should remain a fundamentally agricultural society. The Patriotes' organ *La Minerve* said in 1828 that:

> Agriculture is the architecture of social life; it is the mother of all occupations. It is toward this kindly mother that all eyes must turn, it is to her that we look for succor, we must all have a special veneration for her.

The ultramontanes agreed, and also attached to agriculture a moral significance: Christian values and the family were thought to flourish best in a rural setting, and French Canadians who abandoned the countryside were considered traitors and lost souls. But the high regard in which agriculture was held could not mask its progressive deterioration and its chronic inadequacy as an economic base for French Canada's increasing population. The French-Canadian farmer remained attached to the cultivation of wheat, although after 1830 wheat production was in most years unable to meet domestic needs, let alone provide a surplus for export to Britain. Other grains were slow to win acceptance because they were considered inferior to wheat and did not have the same export potential. Increasing quantities of potatoes were grown but they were seriously affected by the potato blight of the 1840s. Meat produced on French Canadian farms was generally of poor quality and local demand could be better met by meat imported from the United States.

The French-Canadian agricultural crisis was a product of many factors. As in neighbouring New England, the soil had deteriorated significantly — from an initial mediocrity — in the hands of the French-Canadian farmer, whose reluctance to adopt improvements in agricultural methods was often noted by early nineteenth-century observers. Ploughing was haphazard, the seed planted was poor, the use of easily available manure as fertilizer was not widely practised, cattle were scrawny and ill-tended. Then a series of natural catastrophes precipitated a crisis. The wheat crop was badly damaged by the Hessian fly between 1805 and 1816 and virtually wiped out by the wheat midge in the 1830s. The 1837 rebellion occurred when the ravages of the wheat midge were at their worst, and one contemporary observer wrote:

> I verily believe that the almost total destruction of the wheat crops by the wheat fly... was in one respect an incidental cause of that rebellion.[25]

There was wide consensus on the need for better agricultural techniques: it was something of a motherhood issue in the politics of the time. The land question, however, was more complex and more politically charged. The constitution of 1791 had established two coexisting land tenure systems, the seigneurial system in the St. Lawrence valley area traditionally inhabited by French Canadians and the English freehold system in other parts of the province. It was thought that freehold tenure would attract English-speaking settlers, and to a limited extent it did. It also ensured the existence of geographically separate English- and French-speaking areas: English-speaking Protestant farmers, many of them from the United States, were reluctant to establish themselves in the French Catholic environment of the seigneuries, while French Canadians were slow to leave the seigneuries for the English Protestant Eastern Townships. The seigneurial system thus came to be seen as important to French Canadian survival. While *habitants* often protested against the rents and other burdens the system involved, French Canadians in the early nineteenth century rarely attacked the system itself. Papineau, himself a seigneur, was an ardent defender of the system, and only the most radical of the Patriotes were in favour of abolishing it, although that position became more popular in French-Canadian liberal circles after the 1837 rebellion.

Throughout the early nineteenth century both land tenure systems worked to the disadvantage of French-Canadian farmers. The French-Canadian population in 1844 was five times that of 1784, but the land occupied by French Canadians had increased by only an estimated 275 per cent. Under French inheritance law, retained under the British, a man's farm was inherited in equal shares by all his sons; one son usually bought out the others, who would then find farms in the ungranted portions of the same seigneury or a neighbouring one. This system worked so long as the land was available and seigneurs were willing to make new grants. In the nineteenth century land was increasingly scarce, and the seigneurs—more and more of whom were English—were increasingly reluctant to grant the land that was still available. They were tending to see themselves less as feudal holders-in-trust than as capitalist investors: if a seigneur could make more money by exploiting the ungranted portion of his seigneury as timberlands or through pure speculation than by making new grants to farmers, then that is what he would do. He would also squeeze as much rent out of his *censitaires* (seigneurial tenants) as he could, and sometimes the rent demanded for new lands was more than farmers were willing to pay. But it was even more difficult for land-hungry *habitants* to obtain farms in freehold-tenure areas. Land in freehold required an immediate cash outlay that was beyond the means of most *habitants*.

The land policies of the regime, which combined favouritism with incompetence, contributed to the difficulty. One governor of Lower Canada granted huge tracts of land to himself and other government officials; the one-seventh of the land in the freehold regions that was reserved for the support of the Protestant clergy was a further complication; and in 1834 the British government turned over 850,000 acres to the British American Land Company with the ostensible purpose of encouraging settlement, but one of the effects was to keep land prices high.

With seigneurial land difficult to obtain and freehold land out of the reach of most *habitants*, repeated subdivision of farms was inevitable, and it often went beyond the point at which the farms ceased to be economic. By the middle of the nineteenth century the average farm size in Lower Canada was only twenty-eight hectares, and in many parts of the province the typical holding was much smaller than this. In Montmorency county, below Quebec City, about forty per cent of the holdings were less than three and a half hectares. Many *habitants* were only able to obtain *emplacements*, plots of ground large enough for little more than a house and a small vegetable garden; their occupants formed, in effect, a landless rural proletariat who worked as day labourers on surrounding farms, in nearby villages, or in the lumber industry to support their families—when work could be found.

For French Canada to solve its deep-seated agricultural problems far-reaching changes were needed in agricultural patterns and techniques, new lands needed to be opened up, and the economy needed to be diversified. All of these things happened, but none of them happened quickly enough to prevent thousands of French Canadians from resorting to a fourth and more drastic solution: emigration.

In the latter part of the nineteenth century grain gave way to livestock as the staple of French-Canadian agriculture. French-Canadian farmers also showed increasing openness to new ideas and techniques, and agricultural schools were started in L'Assomption, St. Hyacinthe, and other Quebec towns. But modernization often meant mechanization: the same amount of land could now be cultivated by fewer people. The Richelieu valley, one of the areas of the province where agriculture was most advanced, was also among the areas that contributed most heavily to the textile towns of New England.

The colonization of new lands within Quebec was vigorously promoted by the church and the provincial government, and the campaign had some results: new lands were settled in already inhabited territories such as the Ottawa valley and the Gaspé, and entirely new areas were opened up, notably the Saguenay–Lac St. Jean and the Laurentian Mountains northwest of Montreal. The Eastern Townships, still essentially an English enclave at midcentury, slowly lost that character: Shefford and Wolfe counties had French majorities by 1861, Drummond by 1871, Richmond and Sherbrooke by 1881. In all, the area of land under cultivation more than doubled between 1851 and 1901.

Exploitation of Quebec's vast forest resources continued to be the most important nonagricultural economic activity. Controlled by the English Montreal merchants and their London allies and oriented toward export markets, the timber trade was also the first Quebec industry to attract the attention of U.S. capital: New England entrepreneurs got their hands on large tracts of Quebec forest as early as the 1830s, and others, such as E.B. Eddy of Vermont who began making matches in the Ottawa valley in 1851, followed in succeeding decades. French-Canadian enthusiasm for the industry was generally muted, for reasons that ranged from its domination by the English to its effect on the morals of the province's youth: the lumberjack in the nineteenth century had a reputation similar to that of the *coureur de bois* in the seventeenth. One Father Bourassa lamented in 1851 that the money earned in the lumber industry "by the flower of our people at the price of a thousand sacrifices" was "consumed in the fire of the most deplorable passions." A few days in the taverns of Bytown or Quebec City could account for a whole year's earnings. The industry was also under constant attack for competing with agriculture for land and manpower—although by providing employment in previously unexploited regions like the St. Maurice valley and the Saguenay it made possible their initial development and facilitated agricultural colonization. Another cause for unease was the lumber industry's vulnerability to external market conditions; this was especially clear in the 1840s when Britain's adoption of free trade caused a crisis in the industry.

Lumbering was nevertheless an important source of employment for French Canadians and gave rise to the beginnings of manufacturing industries: Quebec City was already a shipbuilding centre in the 1820s, and 1,065 sawmills in Lower Canada employed 3,634 hands in 1851. The increasing number of sawmills reflected the growing importance of the U.S. market for sawn lumber, which picked up the slack caused by the disappearance of the British market for squared timber. In the last half of the century the pulp and paper industry made its appearance, and grew from a gross product of $500,000 in 1871 to $5 million in 1901. This was a period of growth for other industries as well: the manufacture of food products, leather goods, and clothing, all already established by 1850, underwent significant growth, while new industries such as textiles, tobacco products, transportation equipment, and iron and steel became important for the first time. Nevertheless industrialization in the sense that it was understood in the English Midlands and the northeastern United States was still in its infancy in Quebec at the end of the nineteenth century.

A lumber entrepreneur wrote in 1855:

The *habitant* has no other love than that which he bestows on his small farm. He prefers the spot where he was born to all other places in the world, even if his life is sometimes very hard.... He asks nothing else but to live and die where his ancestors lived and died.[26]

In the last two-thirds of the nineteenth century many *habitants* continued to cultivate the land worked by their ancestors, while others remained in the country but worked in the forests or in small rural factories. But in the same period thousands of others left: for new agricultural lands in Quebec, for the cities—the population of Montreal grew from 57,715 in 1851 to 267,730 in 1901—and for other parts of North America. The U.S. economy continued to develop much faster than Quebec's, and by the end of the nineteenth century perhaps half a million French Canadians had gone to try their luck in the States.

THE FIRST EMIGRANTS

The emigration of French Canadians to the United States took place in a restless era: fifty million people left Europe in the nineteenth century, about three-quarters of them destined for North America, the rest for Latin America, Australia, New Zealand, and South Africa; and within North America itself, millions uprooted themselves and pushed the frontier of white settlement steadily westward. Historian Marcus Lee Hansen emphasizes the continental nature of this movement:

> The North American of the nineteenth century had a restless spirit and a wandering foot.... He passed from the jurisdiction of the United States to that of the British Crown; and often he, his son or his grandson went back to the land of their fathers. The international boundary proved the least troublesome of the barriers created by Nature or by man that fell athwart his path.

Americans from New England and New York State pioneered in Upper Canada, Upper Canadians helped settle the U.S. midwest, and when the Canadian prairies were opened up large numbers of midwestern Americans poured in and took up homesteads.

The part French Canadians played in this movement was conditioned by their culture and history. Americans entering Canada or English Canadians entering the United States generally blended fairly easily into their new homes; French Canadians in the United States, on the other hand, were unquestionably "immigrants", an epithet that came into common usage in the nineteenth century and said as much about the economic, social, and cultural status of the people it described as about their having moved from one place to another. Franco-Americans, as they came to be called, did not always willingly accept that status. They belonged to a people that had been in the New World for two centuries; as the heirs of Champlain, Marquette, La Salle, and d'Iberville, they have often maintained that their language and culture were at least as entitled as any other to a place on this continent. In 1886 a French newspaper in Fall River, Massachusetts, editorialized:

> The French Canadians were Americanized long before the Yankees. Of all the races of the Old World, ours is the only one which has perfectly adapted itself to North America, and if the Yankees are unable to get used to our manners and habits it is because they have not become sufficiently Americanized themselves and they are still imbued with the prejudices which they have brought from the British Isles.[27]

Nearly a century later one of the delegates at a gathering of French-speaking North Americans in Quebec City objected when Quebec Premier René Lévesque referred to Franco-Americans (U.S. citizens of French descent) as immigrants. She sharply told the premier:

> Not all Franco-Americans are immigrants. I'm from the Great Lakes and we were there with the Indians when the first English settlers arrived.

For those who went to New England, the proximity of their old homes also had an effect: the dream of making some money and then going home was more realizable for them than for Europeans. Most French Canadians who went to New England saw it as a temporary move; many thousands of them actually did go home and thousands more planned to do so as soon as they had saved just a little more money. Others settled permanently in the United States but made annual visits to relatives in Quebec and read the Quebec newspapers that circulated in New England, so that communication with the homeland was never cut off. Still, what is most striking in the experience of French Canadians in the United States is not the differences from the experience of European immigrants but the similarities.

In the early years of the nineteenth century there were three areas in the United States with significant French-speaking populations. While Louisiana was the most important of these congregations, it developed in almost complete isolation from the French-speaking society on the St. Lawrence until well into the twentieth century. The other two areas were the border region — the northern parts of New York State, where the French-Canadian veterans of the American Revolution had settled, and Vermont — and the still largely unpopulated land south of the western Great Lakes; both of these populations were regularly replenished by new arrivals from Lower Canada.[28]

The movement across the border to Vermont and New York State was in the nature of a steady trickle. Permanent settlers were outnumbered by casual labourers, working for a season on a farm, in the forests, on construction sites, or in the marble quarries of Vermont, but gradually small communities began to form, and in 1815 several children of French-Canadian parents were baptized in Burlington, Vermont, by a French priest from Boston. Some of the areas of southern New England that later became major Franco-American centres also received their first French-Canadian settlers in these years. According to local tradition the first French-Canadian settler in Woonsocket, Rhode Island, François Proulx, arrived in town in 1815, and there were undoubtedly French Canadians there in the 1820s. In 1832 Abraham Marois, a carpenter from St-Ours, Quebec, was living in Worcester,

Massachusetts, when he heard there was a French-speaking person in Southbridge, thirty kilometres to the southwest, so he decided to move there; he arrived after a two-day journey by ox-cart and settled next to his French friend.

The U.S. midwest, once part of the great arc that was the French empire in North America, continued to attract adventurous French Canadians, although the French settlements there were about to be swamped by the influx of Yankees from the east. The Detroit *Gazette*, founded in 1817, carried a column in French, and on one occasion "Vieux Philippe" warned his readers:

> French people of Michigan, you must begin immediately to give your children an education. In a short time, there will be as many Yankees in this territory as French people, and if your children are not educated, all the jobs will be given to Yankees.

The people of nearby French Town, anticipating a presidential visit, changed the name of their community to Monroe; President Monroe never came but the name stuck. The French-speaking people of Monroe regarded the Yankees as mercenary and domineering, but that didn't prevent the more enterprising among them from making money by selling land to the newcomers. Illinois also had a French-speaking population that predated English settlement, and when it was admitted as a state in 1818, the first lieutenant-governor was Pierre Menard, a native of St. Antoine sur Richelieu, Quebec, who had lived in the region as a fur trader, entrepreneur, judge, and politician for fifty years. French Canadians who set out for the forests of Michigan or the farmlands of Illinois were thus going to an area that could offer not only economic opportunity but the nucleus of a French community as well, and in the early nineteenth century the states and territories on the Great Lakes were the area most eagerly sought by emigrants from Quebec.

This first haphazard phase of the French-Canadian migration to the United States lasted roughly until the rebellion of 1837. The migration would later become a mass movement; but first, in the wake of the rebellion, two atypical Franco-American communities were created, one of them short-lived, the other remarkably durable.

REFUGEES AND VALLEY FOLK

It is common in immigrant communities for groups whose migration stemmed from idealistic rather than economic motives to be held in special esteem: hence the importance in U.S. history of the Pilgrim Fathers, or the status among German-Americans of the "Forty-eighters"—the political exiles who fled Germany after the failure of the 1848 revolution. Among Franco-Americans, a similar position is accorded the refugees of 1837. For most of the refugees exile in the United States was an unhappy experience, and Quebec writer Antoine Gérin-Lajoie's mournful song "Un canadien errant", expressing a refugee's deep longing for his homeland, probably reflected the sentiments of many.

President Van Buren's neutrality proclamation of January 1838 forced the Patriotes to recognize that the United States had no intention of allowing them to jeopardize its currently good relations with Britain. This was a severe blow to the exiles. So was the discovery that their U.S. sympathizers were, in the words of historian Robert Rumilly, "neither as numerous nor as generous as they had hoped." Most of the refugees had come without money; some had left families behind. Many, especially the professionals who were the leaders of the movement, could not find work. Médard Hébert and Pierre-Paul Desmarais, two notaries who succeeded in opening a grocery store in Plattsburgh, New York, were among the lucky ones.

The refugees lived in an atmosphere of fear and suspicion, and friends and relatives in Canada were afraid of compromising themselves by writing to them. Divisions and recriminations erupted within the exile community itself, especially over the abortive attempts to mount a second rebellion in 1838, attempts that increased the size of the community but also intensified its fears. Some of the refugees went as far as Wisconsin, Missouri, and Louisiana, but the largest concentration was in the border areas of Vermont and New York State, and it was in Burlington, Vermont, that Ludger Duvernay, who in Montreal had been the editor of the Patriote paper *La Minerve*, now started an exile newspaper. The first issue of *Le Patriote Canadien* appeared on August 7, 1839, and listed a network of twenty-five correspondents stretching from nearby Montpelier to New Orleans. Throughout its brief life *Le Patriote Canadien* was plagued by the fears and pressures endemic in the exile community. The paper was banned in Canada, and few exiles in the U.S. could afford a subscription. Tory newspapers in Canada reprinted the names of its correspondents as a sort of hit list. When it published a poem by George-Étienne Cartier, who had fled to the U.S.A. after the rebellion but had since returned to Montreal (eventually to become a Father of Confederation), Cartier felt he had been put in danger and wrote a reproachful letter to Duvernay. In late 1839 William Lyon Mackenzie, the Upper Canadian rebel leader who was attempting to publish a paper in Rochester, New York, was arrested for violation of U.S. neutrality, and Duvernay expected a similar fate. He escaped it but, devoid of funds, *Le Patriote Canadien* ceased publication of its own accord on February 5, 1840.

The hope of another rebellion that had inspired the exiles slowly faded. Some of them became part of the growing Franco-American communities of Vermont and New York State, but when amnesty was declared in 1842 the majority, including Duvernay, went back.

Another group whose lives were directly affected by British-American relations and whose interests were, if anything, given even less consideration than those of the rebels were the Acadian and French-Canadian settlers of the upper St. John valley, the *Madawaskayens*. As one chronicler of the Madawaska dispute has put it, the controversy showed "how pine trees were more important than people in playing international chess."

The Madawaska dispute had its origins in a maddeningly vague clause in the 1783 Treaty of Versailles, the agreement that ended the American Revolutionary War. The second article of the treaty purported to establish the boundary between what were then northern Massachusetts and western Nova Scotia, but it was written with little knowledge of the geography of the area and left a legacy of confusion that lasted sixty years. The border was supposed to follow the Sainte Croix River, at the mouth of which Champlain and de Monts had established their historic settlement in 1603. Unfortunately nobody was quite sure just which river was the Sainte Croix until 1794, when the ruins of a settlement were found on an island in the Schoudic River. The Schoudic was duly renamed the Sainte Croix and recognized as the border. From the source of the Sainte Croix the border was to follow a line due north to the "Highlands which divide those Rivers that empty themselves into the River St. Lawrence from those which fall into the Atlantic Ocean." The task of agreeing on which highlands were meant made identifying the Sainte Croix look easy by comparison. The Americans favoured a ridge north of the St. John River and within a few kilometres of the St. Lawrence, deep in what is now Quebec, and they had a strong case since the St. John flows into the Bay of Fundy, an arm of the Atlantic. The British, reasoning that the Bay of Fundy is not "the Atlantic Ocean," argued for a different set of highlands considerably father south. In between lay thousands of square kilometres of valuable timberland, and the Madawaska settlement.

For thirty years after its founding in 1785 this settlement managed to live untouched by the international boundary dispute. If the *Madawaskayens* were affected by any jurisdictional disagreement it was the one between New Brunswick and Lower Canada, each of which regarded Madawaska as part of its territory: in 1792 a magistrate appointed by New Brunswick arrested a militia lieutenant appointed by Lower Canada for enforcing a Lower Canadian judgement against a Madawaska settler. As time went on New Brunswick took *de facto* charge of governing the area, although the dispute remained unsettled. More serious problems for the *Madawaskayens* were the yearly floods that forced them to move their farms up from the banks of the St. John and the September frosts that sometimes ruined their wheat crops. One such frost in 1796 was followed by a winter of real famine, brightened only by the heroism of Marguerite-Blanche Thibodeau, the legendary *tante du Madawaska* who trudged from farm to farm on snowshoes bringing help to stricken settlers.

Meanwhile the settlement of the Sainte Croix dispute put the fate of the *Madawaskayens* on the international agenda. A satisfied British official who had been involved in the Sainte Croix negotiations wrote:

> As it is, we lose not a single British settlement. A few miserable Frenchmen at Madawaska on the route to Canada fall within the Territory.

The "miserable Frenchmen" remained oblivious. Farming was their main activity. Education was haphazard and literacy rare. Contracts were verbal and going back on one's word earned severe reproof from the community. Disputes were referred to a court consisting of the curé and assessors appointed by each of the parties. Rivalries grew up between settlers on the north side of the St. John and those on the south, and between those farther up the river and those farther down, but the peace of the community was rarely disturbed. Madawaska seemed unaffected by its location on the main communication route between Quebec and Halifax. Even the War of 1812 caused hardly more than a ripple. (The Treaty of Ghent that ended the war left the boundary as confused as before.)

By the 1820s the settlement had even begun to enjoy a modest prosperity. By that time, however, history had also begun to catch up with the *Madawaskayens*. The most important change that had taken place was the growth of the lumber industry, which quickened the interest of distant entrepreneurs, both British and U.S., in the disputed territory. In 1817 the first U.S. settlers arrived in Madawaska. Three years later the state of Maine was carved out of the northern part of Massachusetts, and much of the impetus for U.S. expansion into the region was to come from the aggressive government of the new state. The *Madawaskayens* on the whole favoured New Brunswick jurisdiction, which at least had the virtue of familiarity, but their interests lay less in any particular side than in an early settlement of the dispute so that they could get legal title to their lands; some of the first settlers had received New Brunswick titles in the 1790s, but because of the interprovincial and international disagreements no land titles had been granted since then.

From 1825, when land agents for the states of Maine and Massachusetts arrived in Madawaska to grant U.S. titles to settlers in the valley, to 1839, when Maine touched off the "Aroostook Bloodless War"[29] by sending a force into the area to suppress the activities of trespassing lumbermen, the location of the border was the subject of active and often hot contention. Each side periodically resolved to exercise jurisdiction in Madawaska, which led to a cycle of side A conducting a census, holding an election, or performing some other act of sovereignty; side B protesting loudly and perhaps arresting side A's officials; one side or both moving troops closer to the area; Washington and London intervening to cool the situation down; both sides agreeing to work through diplomatic channels — and then one side or the other committing yet another act of provocation soon afterward. Usually it was Maine that made the first move in these little dramas, but Sir John Harvey, lieutenant-governor of New Brunswick in the late 1830s, was capable of acting as impetuously as any Maine governor.

With the conclusion of the "Aroostook Bloodless War" both Washington and London decided that the dispute had gone on long enough. Both were concerned about its interference with lumber operations; and, for the British, the still unsettled conditions in Upper and Lower Canada and the presence of Canadian rebel leaders as exiles in the United States were an additional impetus to settlement of a dispute that threatened to disrupt good relations with the Americans. Whitehall sent Lord Ashburton, a member of the financial house of Baring which had extensive investments in North America, to Washington in 1842 to negotiate with U.S. secretary of state Daniel Webster, and they agreed on the St. John River as a compromise border. In Maine there was a widespread feeling that the state had been sold out by Webster, and in London there was talk of the "Ashburton Capitulation", but the compromise was reluctantly accepted.

As for the *Madawaskayens*, Webster denied that there was any cruelty in dividing them between two countries, maintaining that the international line need not disrupt social and family relations. Through the long years of isolation and dispute their principal loyalty had been to Madawaska itself rather than to any larger entity, and there was no indication that a border run through their settlement by faraway officials would make them change. Still, the *Madawaskayens* on the south bank were now U.S. citizens, and the state of Maine sent an agent, James Madigan, to instruct them in the duties inherent in their new role. Madigan, an Irish Catholic proficient in French, opened a school for children and held classes in U.S. civics for adults, in addition to acting as postmaster, tax collector, and magistrate for the area. Meanwhile the *Madawaskayens* on the south bank received U.S. titles for their lands, and in 1846 they elected their first state representative: the historian of Madawaska, Father Thomas Albert, relates that this legislator, Joseph Cyr, was easily distinguishable by his suit of *étoffe du pays* from his more soberly dressed colleagues.

In 1851 Madawaska was divided again when Canada and New Brunswick (which would not become part of Canada until 1867) finally settled their boundary dispute and some of the northern parts of the territory were awarded to Canada. There was also a movement for ecclesiastical division of the territory, instigated by the inhabitants of Carmel, a religious settlement of uncertain origin on the south bank, and perhaps motivated as much by the old *rivalité du bord* (rivalry of the riverbanks) as by the political separation. The ecclesiastical dispute took almost as long to resolve as the political one, and separation was finally achieved in 1870 after appeals to Rome by both sides. But the essential unity of Madawaska was in many ways preserved, and one of the unifying factors was what Father Albert called "*l'engouement des États*", the infatuation with the United States that swept the north bank as well as the south; for this infatuation was no respecter of boundaries, and after 1840 it was felt with increasing strength throughout French-speaking North America.

4

Textile Towns, Cultural Struggles, and an Industrial Quebec

1850-1929

THE MASS MIGRATION of French Canadians to the United States that began in the 1840s lasted almost a century. There are no completely reliable figures for the total number of people who crossed the border from Quebec and Acadia between 1840 and 1930, but informed estimates run from the neighbourhood of half a million up to almost a million.[30] The significance of the migration for French-Canadian society is suggested by comparing this with the French-speaking population of Canada reported by the 1851 census: 669,528. At the time, and often since, many French Canadians who stayed behind regarded emigration as a rejection or even betrayal of the distinctive values, traditions, and institutions of French Canada. In the eyes of those who left it was no such thing, although it was unquestionably a rejection of the attempt by some of the leaders of French Canada to develop those values, traditions, and institutions in isolation from the rest of North America.

At first the stream of migrants was divided, with one branch leading to New England and New York State and the other to Michigan and Illinois. The Quebec clergy tended to regard the first branch as the more dangerous, because in the northeastern U.S.A. the migrants would be going to an existing urban, English-speaking, and Protestant society that would surely swallow them up, rather than to a largely unpopulated agricultural area where they might have some chance of retaining their French and Catholic character. Attempts to divert the flow of migrants were unsuccessful, but it turned out that they were also unnecessary: it was in New England that French Canadians came closest to reproducing both the religious and the national life they had known in Quebec.

One of the most influential advocates of the western migration was a priest named Charles Chiniquy, "Quebec's apostle of temperance". Brandishing a golden crucifix and aided by his legendary eloquence and a talent for exaggeration and self-promotion, Chiniquy toured the province drawing large crowds and exacting from thousands of Québécois a pledge of total abstinence from strong drink. Chiniquy's crusade had the support of Bishop Bourget of Montreal, but relations between the two soured: when Bishop Van De Velde of Chicago came to Montreal in 1851 to find French-speaking priests for his diocese all three parties were gratified when Chiniquy went as curé to Ste. Anne de Kankakee in the heart of the growing French-Canadian area of Illinois.

Chiniquy always denied being an advocate of emigration; he said it was simply inevitable, an "immense fact that reveals to us the infinite mercy of God," and if French Canadians had to leave Quebec it was best that they come to Illinois, a land sanctified by their forebears. Nevertheless both spiritual and temporal leaders in Quebec reacted bitterly to the enthusiastic reports about Illinois that Chiniquy sent to Canadian newspapers, and he was accused of being "antipatriotic". Meanwhile he had become embroiled in a dispute with Van De Velde's successor, Bishop O'Regan, over the ownership of both the French-Canadian church in Chicago and his own church in Ste. Anne—a foretaste of later conflicts between Franco-Americans and the Irish hierarchy in the church. In 1856 O'Regan first suspended and then excommunicated Chiniquy, and when Chiniquy went on as if nothing had happened he was excommunicated again, this time publicly. The deposed priest first formed his own Christian Catholic Church and then in 1859 embraced Presbyterianism, taking many of his parishioners in Ste. Anne with him through these changes. He spent the rest of his long life preaching widely in Canada, the United States, and Europe, undertaking a mission to convert French Canadians, and proving to his own satisfaction—if to no one else's—that the assassination of Abraham Lincoln (who as an Illinois lawyer had once represented Chiniquy in a civil suit) was a Jesuit plot.

The Chiniquy episode gave the U.S. midwest a bad odour in respectable circles in French Canada, but in any case the structure of French-Canadian society simply did not accommodate the kind of pioneering that was necessary there. According to U.S. historian Marcus Lee Hansen,

> The young British Canadian had only one obligation and that was to relieve his parents of the burden of his support. The young Frenchman, however, felt obliged to contribute to the cash income that was increasingly necessary to the

economy of the household. What he desired was a job with wages, good hard cash delivered into his hand on Saturday night. When the opportunity for such payment arose within what to his sturdy legs was walking distance, the attraction of the West dimmed.

With the completion of railway connections between Lower Canada and New England in the 1850s the pull of the factory towns became even stronger. French Canadians continued to cross the border during the American Civil War, and both those already in the United States and newcomers from Quebec enlisted in the Union army, although the traditional estimate of forty thousand is surely an exaggeration. Americans could avoid the draft by procuring a substitute, and many French Canadians served in place of the sons of Yankee farmers. The war also caused a labour shortage in the textile mills, and this brought more French Canadians across the border.

After the Civil War the textile towns grew rapidly and needed ever greater numbers of workers; mill owners sent recruiting agents to the Quebec countryside and French Canadians came to the mills in the tens of thousands. The last third of the nineteenth century was the era of the French Canadians in the textile mills of New England. In 1900 one-third of the work force in the New England textile industry was French Canadian, and in some areas and some branches of the industry the concentration was much higher: nearly seventy per cent in the cotton mills of Maine, sixty per cent in those of New Hampshire. But mill workers were let go as easily as they were taken on, and French Canadians who answered the call of the recruiting agent might soon find themselves without a job. They went to another town, or back to Quebec, or perhaps out west for a while, and they might move several times before they finally settled down.

Those who ended up in New England were no longer scattered migrants but part of a recognizable group, and the humble "Little Canadas" where they congregated in the mill towns—similar in some respects to the Chinatowns and Little Italys that sprang up in some other U.S. cities—formed an archipelago of French-speaking islands in the Anglo-American sea. They began to be communities, with community institutions dedicated both to adaptation and to cultural preservation. They celebrated St. Jean Baptiste Day and the Fourth of July with equal gusto; naturalization clubs and St. Jean Baptiste Societies existed side by side. Félix Gatineau's history of the Franco-Americans of Southbridge, Massachusetts, contains an 1896 photograph of the author standing in front of a white horse and dressed as Paul Revere in honour of Patriots' Day. Three years later this same Félix Gatineau was instrumental in the founding of the Union St. Jean Baptiste d'Amérique, which was to become the largest Franco-American mutual benefit society.

Among the institutions founded by the Franco-Americans of the late nineteenth century the most important were the national parish, the parochial school, the mutual benefit society, and the newspaper. All four carved out limited spheres for themselves, reflecting the hesitancy of a people that had never had full control of its national life. Primacy in economic affairs was conceded to Yankee capitalists, a concession in which Franco-American workers generally acquiesced and one that was greatly valued by their bosses. Politics also had a fairly low priority: although community leaders took a stand when Franco-American cultural survival was directly affected and urged Franco-Americans to become citizens and to vote, they did not organize a political force that could operate with continuing effect within the U.S. system. When Franco-American community leaders did intervene in economic and political matters it was often to exercise a conservative influence. During the Fall River textile strike of 1878 Father Pierre Jean-Baptiste Bédard, a fierce French-Canadian patriot and orator whose influence spread far beyond his own Notre Dame de Lourdes parish, took the position that, while workers had the right to strike, other workers had an equal right to act as strikebreakers—an attitude that did not endear him to the Yankee, British, and Irish strikers.

It was in the religious, linguistic, and cultural areas that Franco-American community institutions believed their efforts could be most fruitful, and within these areas they were in fact successful for a long time. The network of institutions established toward the end of the nineteenth century remained largely intact until after the Second World War, and portions of it survive even into the 1990s. Its principal aim and most important achievement was *survivance*, cultural and religious survival, a goal it shared with the leading institutions of French Canada itself.

The "national parish" was the device that allowed Franco-Americans to preserve the style of Catholicism they had known in Quebec, which differed not only in language (except for the language of the Mass, which was Latin in both countries) but in other essential respects from the form practised in the United States. The first French-Canadian national parish in New England was established in 1851 in Burlington, Vermont, with the support of a French-Canadian priest who acted as vicar-general of the Diocese of Boston, and in 1869 Monsignor Louis-Joseph de Goësbriand, a native of Brittany who became the first bishop of Burlington, launched an appeal for separate parishes and French-speaking priests to serve the French-Canadian flock. With the increasing number of immigrants to New England national parishes were being founded all over the region, and many Quebec priests responded to Monsignor de Goësbriand's appeal. Later, however, the national parishes were to run into opposition from the Irish-dominated U.S.

hierarchy, which preferred ethnically mixed territorial parishes and, in response to nativist accusations that the church was a foreign institution, demanded a high degree of cultural conformity from Catholics.

A crucial adjunct of the national parish was the parochial school, which educated Franco-Americans in the French language as well as the Catholic religion and was often staffed by teaching orders from Quebec. At first English was taught as a foreign language in these schools; later, in response to state requirements, half the school day was devoted to secular subjects taught in English while in the other half such subjects as religion and French-Canadian history were taught in French. For many years a large majority of Franco-American children in major centres went to parochial schools (in Woonsocket, Rhode Island, it was three-quarters in 1926). In 1904, the Franco-American educational system in New England was further enriched when priests from France established the Collège de l'Assomption in Worcester, a French-language institution comparable to the classical colleges in Quebec.

The two large mutual benefit societies, the Union St. Jean Baptiste and the Association Canado-Américaine, grew out of small local organizations that in addition to social and cultural activities provided burial expenses and perhaps sickness and accident benefits to their members in return for a small monthly payment. This activity bore a suggestive resemblance to insurance, and when the local clubs federated into region-wide societies at the turn of the century (after a number of previous attempts) these bodies were able to establish themselves as full-fledged insurance companies. The insurance business has given the societies an ongoing financial base for the cultural activities they have never entirely abandoned despite the attenuation of the cultural distinctness of their members: each of the societies maintains a library, publishes a magazine, and has been responsible for the publication and distribution of books. The Association Canado-Américaine, for a long time the smaller of the two, has traditionally been the more uncompromising on cultural issues and has also expanded into Quebec with an office in Trois-Rivières; the Union St. Jean Baptiste, which has tended to take a more conciliatory approach, has restricted its activities to the United States.[31]

Franco-American newspapers had numerous obstacles to overcome. Their constituency was not a highly literate one, and they had to compete both with local English-language newspapers and with French-language papers from Quebec, but despite these difficulties the Franco-Americans of New England produced a vigorous press. Many of the early newspapers had a short lifespan, but when one shut down it was rarely long before another arose to take its place. Some eventually won a stable following, and a few — among them *Le Messager* of Lewiston, *L'Étoile* of Lowell, *L'Indépendant* of Fall River, *L'Avenir National* of Manchester, and *Le Courrier* of Lawrence — survived into the post – Second World War era. At their height these were far more than ethnic newsletters: they were full-fledged newspapers that nevertheless reflected the particular interests of the Franco-American community. In the 1870s Ferdinand Gagnon, editor of *Le Travailleur* of Worcester, was the principal voice of the Franco-Americans, and for a long time journalists were reckoned among the leaders of the community.

Franco-Americans who established these and other institutions saw them as compensation for the absence of the majority status, control of the church hierarchy, and dominant position in the state apparatus that French Canadians had known in Quebec. The cultural conditions of Quebec could not be reproduced in New England; but even if they failed in their ultimate aim, they laid the institutional foundation for an active cultural life that lasted several generations, and they helped to give the textile towns of New England a French character that they have not completely lost even today, when many of the physical neighbourhoods have been demolished. In Lowell, for instance, only a plaque remains where the heart of Little Canada once lay. But some of the Little Canadas survive at least partly intact, recognizable by their characteristic three-decker multifamily housing and the French names on many of the businesses. Government statistics and official reports have documented the squalid conditions that often existed in the Little Canadas of New England, but statistics do not show the very real sense of community that prevailed, with all that this implied in terms of emotional sustenance and psychological security, or the nostalgia that some older people still feel for those crowded, noisy, unsanitary neighbourhoods.

In recent times many New England mill towns have had a down-at-the-heels look. Starting in the late 1970s several of the more fortunate ones — Lowell is a noteworthy example — underwent something of a renaissance as businesses ranging from high-tech research and manufacturing to factory outlet shops for clothing or furniture took over and refurbished some of the old mills, giving them a new lease on life. But a number of less privileged communities are almost ghost towns, with Main Streets full of boarded-up stores and river or canal banks lined with abandoned mills. (Even Lowell headed for a slump in 1989 following massive layoffs by Wang Laboratories, the biggest local employer.) Although close in distance, the mill towns have tended to be far removed in mood from the metropolitan New England of Boston, the Yankee New England of Bennington, the intellectual New England of Cambridge, the exclusive New England of Newport, or the tourist New England of Sturbridge. Only the most vivid imaginations have ever been able to find them picturesque. A 1972 travel guide described Fall River as "very dreary", Worcester as "very unattractive", and Manchester as "a cultural and intellectual wasteland" and, along with nearby Concord, proof that "New Hampshire wasn't cut out to have cities."[32]

In strictly esthetic terms it is difficult to argue with these judgements, but to dismiss the mill towns to which French Canadians came and on which they made their mark is to deny as important a part of New England's past as the landing at Plymouth Rock or the Battle of Bunker Hill. A hundred years ago the mill towns were no more pleasing esthetically than they are today, but they were vibrant, optimistic, growing, and much more interested in their future than in their past. They saw themselves as well on the way to becoming great cities, a status they never quite attained, although within the textile industry they did win international pre-eminence. Fall River, which of all the towns enjoyed the most spectacular and unruly growth, eventually came to produce more cotton textiles than any other place in the world. Between 1865 and 1880, the period of its most precipitous expansion, the number of spindles in operation in Fall River quintupled and its population nearly tripled, almost entirely through immigration. In 1883 Fall River produced three-fifths of the print cloth manufactured in the entire United States. Its growth was marked by speculation, stock manipulation, and almost continuous labour strife.

A number of towns—Worcester, Manchester, Lewiston—at different times claimed the status of capital of the Franco-American archipelago, but it was in Woonsocket, a town in northeastern Rhode Island that became one of America's most important producers of woollen and worsted textiles, that Franco-Americans came closest to building a lasting, integral French-speaking society in the United States. In the 1920s immigrants to Woonsocket from Italy and eastern Europe learned French as well as English, and one English-speaking visitor who spent an hour at Woonsocket city hall in 1924 heard not a word of English spoken except to him. What made Woonsocket unusual was that French was the language used not only at home and on the street but also, to a large extent, in the factory. This was due to the efforts of Aram-J. Pothier, a native of Yamachiche, Quebec, who became mayor of Woonsocket and eight times governor of Rhode Island. Pothier had developed extensive business contacts with French and Belgian woollen manufacturers and he induced them to bring their technically advanced system to Woonsocket, the prospect of a French-speaking labour force being one of the attractions.

Eventually not even Woonsocket could fully withstand the forces of cultural homogenization, but in the late nineteenth and early twentieth centuries that was still far from clear. Franco-Americans who had left the land for the factory, shifted their political allegiance, and even, perhaps without being fully aware of it, made some cultural accommodation, were inclined to feel that they had undergone enough changes; when further accommodations were required of them they would balk, and sometimes even resist.

LOST SOULS OR ADVANCE GUARD?

Emigration to the United States began to have an impact on French Canadian thought as early as the 1840s. The Legislative Assembly was sufficiently concerned about it in 1849 to set up a committee to study it: the committee took note of Father Chiniquy's estimate of seventy thousand French Canadians who had left the province in the previous five years but rejected it in favour of a more modest estimate of twenty thousand. All the familiar ills of French-Canadian agriculture were recounted to the committee to explain the migration, but in addition to the exodus from the farms, a commercial depression in the province was causing a substantial southward emigration from the cities. As time went on and the number of emigrants increased the response in French Canada became both more intense and more complex. The emigration was an occasion for French Canada to look at itself critically as a society and to attempt to devise a program for keeping French Canadians in Quebec; but it also raised the question of the responsibility of Quebec's leaders toward French Canadians who lived outside their territorial jurisdiction, and in a limited way it revived the old vision of a French-speaking entity with Quebec as its centre but all of North America as its field of activity.

The primary alternative to emigration that French-Canadian society attempted to offer was the colonization of its own lightly populated areas. The clergy, which at least in the early years of the emigration regarded those who left as lost souls, took the lead in the colonization movement. Colonization societies were set up under church patronage, and priests were sent to areas where colonization was just beginning. There was no more tireless promoter of the movement than the curé of St. Jérôme, Antoine Labelle, who did much to bring colonists to the Laurentian region. When a department of colonization was set up by the provincial government of Premier Honoré Mercier in the 1880s, Curé Labelle was appointed its deputy minister.

While the colonization movement had impressive results in opening up new areas of the province, the number of people for whom it actually provided new farms was modest. Both lay and clerical leaders were forced to

re-examine their attitude toward more profound economic change in the
province, for despite the ultramontane bias in favour of agriculture it was
increasingly clear that unless French Canadians had the option of becoming
industrial workers in Quebec many of them would become industrial workers in the United States. Bishop Laflèche of Trois-Rivières, a leader of the
ultramontane school, might believe in theory that of all forms of work
agriculture was "the one most favourable to the development of [a person's]
physical, moral and intellectual faculties, and above all the one that puts him
most directly in touch with God"; but when it came to the development of
his own diocese, rich as it was in minerals, forests, and hydroelectric power,
the bishop believed that it was the intention of Providence that industry
should predominate, and he wrote to Labelle suggesting that the curé's
efforts to promote agricultural colonization might better be pursued elsewhere in the province. Curé Labelle's plans did not exclude industry either,
however devout his belief in colonization. He told a meeting in Montreal in
1872:

> Emigration is devouring us. Our resources are lying inert in the bowels of the
> earth. Our wood is rotting on the soil. Are we going to perish in the midst of
> abundance? No, gentlemen — we need industry to develop our country.

In the period of growth that began just before the turn of the century the
local curé in town after town, far from opposing industrial development,
worked hand in hand with the outside (often U.S.) industrialist to ensure
that it was accomplished without undue social disruption. The government
of Quebec followed the lead of the church. According to Jean Hamelin and
Yves Roby, the leading authorities on the economic history of late nineteenth-
century Quebec:

> It does not seem exaggerated to state that emigration to the United States was a
> problem that traumatized the collective conscience of French Canada and that
> the totality of government policies was a response to this problem.

The government built roads and disseminated information to encourage
colonization (although it adopted a laissez-faire policy toward the large
landowners and speculators who were a major obstacle to the development
of new lands), but it also provided generous terms to foreign investors to
facilitate industrialization.

The government also undertook a repatriation program in the 1870s, in
an effort to entice French Canadians in the United States back to Quebec.

The repatriation movement had several circumstances in its favour, the most important of which was that the depression of that decade had left many textile workers in New England wandering from city to city in search of jobs. That New England French Canadians had not lost their attachment to Quebec was amply demonstrated on the occasion of the 1874 St. Jean Baptiste Day celebration in Montreal, organized by the St. Jean Baptiste Society as a homecoming, a meeting of French Canadians on both sides of the border. Franco-American communities vied with one another to see which could send the largest delegation, and U.S. railways offered special rates and promised French-speaking conductors. In all, some eighteen thousand people from the United States made the trip, and the event was judged a great success. Its immediate effect, however, was not at all what the organizers intended. The Franco-Americans were out to impress their cousins in Quebec with both their economic advancement and their continuing Frenchness, and so they did: the celebration was followed by a large wave of emigration.

The next year the Quebec legislature voted a subsidy of $60,000 to encourage immigration, part of which was to be used to repatriate French Canadians from the United States, and appointed Ferdinand Gagnon of Worcester its agent of repatriation. Land was made available at advantageous prices, and a colony of returning emigrants was established at La Patrie in the Eastern Townships; Gagnon demonstrated his commitment to the movement by repatriating his own father to La Patrie. The Canadian government also got into the act and tried to persuade French Canadians in the United States to move to Manitoba, but there was no mass response to either initiative. Gagnon estimated in 1881 that the Quebec government had repatriated about six hundred families, and that of those only three hundred had stayed. The number repatriated under the federal program was even smaller. Whatever momentum the movement had was lost with the return of prosperity at the end of the 1870s, and even Gagnon eventually lost interest. By 1880 it was clear that the French Canadian community in the United States was a permanent one. A substantial number of French Canadians had become naturalized U.S. citizens, with the encouragement of community leaders like Gagnon; there were Franco-American selectmen in many towns and, in Connecticut, a member of the state legislature.

If the Franco-Americans had started to take an interest in the political life of the United States, they had by no means stopped being an important part of the political life of French Canada. The death sentence handed out to Louis Riel in Regina in 1885 aroused resentment among the Franco-Americans of New England as well as the French Canadians of Quebec; indeed the

Franco-Americans felt a particular identification with the Métis leader, who had spent some of the darkest days of his exile in their communities, received the protection of their leaders, and become a U.S. citizen after settling in Montana. In Fall River, where the Riel affair became entwined with a local conflict between Franco-American parishioners and the Irish church hierarchy, feelings were particularly intense. The naturalization club, the most active political organization in the Franco-American community, sent resolutions of protest to the government and opposition in Ottawa, and the editor of the local French newspaper, Rémi Tremblay, wrote strongly worded articles deploring the sentence. Gabriel Dumont, Riel's lieutenant, came to New England and spoke to large audiences in Franco-American centres.

Some of the more visionary leaders of French Canada like Bishop Laf`eche of Trois-Rivières envisioned a French-Canadian state incorporating Quebec and New England. Even for many whose visions were more firmly rooted in reality the Franco-Americans remained an integral part of the French-Canadian community, with as large a stake as anyone else in French Canada's collective destiny. Both religious and temporal leaders in Quebec saw their area of responsibility as extending beyond the boundaries of the province. The church had at one stage been reluctant to provide for the spiritual welfare of French Canadians in the United States for fear of making it easier for people to emigrate, but it was shaken by the Chiniquy episode and the dark picture of religious need painted by Bishop de Goësbriand of Burlington. Bishop Bourget of Montreal responded to de Goësbriand's appeal by sending missionaries to the United States, and a new willingness on the part of priests in Quebec to go to the United States made possible the proliferation of Franco-American parishes.

Quebec politicians also regarded the Franco-Americans as part of their constituency. This idea was perhaps most fully developed in the mind of Honoré Mercier, who saw the government of Quebec not merely as a provincial government but as the national government of French Canadians. In keeping with this conception, Franco-American affairs were part of his concern as premier of Quebec, and he stepped into the middle of a bitter controversy within the Catholic Church over cultural policy in the United States.

In 1891 a memorial was presented to Pope Leo XIII demanding that Catholic immigrants in the United States whose native language was not English be served by bishops, priests, churches, and schools of their own language. The guiding spirit behind this Lucerne Memorial was Peter Paul Cahensly, a member of the German Reichstag and general secretary of the St. Raphael's Society, an organization promoting the welfare of German emigrants, and among its signatories were the German and Austrian representatives at the Vatican and Premier Honoré Mercier of Quebec. The alliance, at first glance a strange one, arose out of the common struggle of German-Americans and Franco-Americans against the assimilationist policies of the Irish-dominated U.S. church hierarchy, to whom "Cahenslyism" became a catchword for foreign influence and cultural pluralism in the church. Mercier was in Europe when the Lucerne Memorial was being drawn up, and representatives of Cahensly approached him in Paris. Later, in Rome, Mercier had an audience with Pope Leo and repeated the demands of the memorial. The Irish-American bishops eventually prevailed, however, and Cahenslyism was rejected by the Vatican.

Mercier was dismissed as premier by the lieutenant-governor in 1891, but he retained a large following both in Quebec and in the United States. In 1893, in a speech before six thousand people in Montreal's Sohmer Park, he advocated the full independence of Canada from Britain, suggesting two subsequent possibilities: the independence of Quebec, or the annexation of Canada to the United States. Annexation was a live issue, and had support both among Anglo-Americans imbued with the spirit of manifest destiny and among Franco-Americans for whom it would mean a political reunification with their fellows in Quebec. Mercier was invited to take his campaign for Canadian independence to the United States, and, accompanied by great fanfare, he toured the Franco-American centres of New England, comparing Canada unfavourably with the United States, ascribing Canada's continuing economic difficulties to the British yoke, calling for an independent Canadian republic, and suggesting that Canada could then join the United States if its people so desired. His highly sympathetic biographer, Robert Rumilly, has expressed the suspicion that Mercier's campaign may have been financed by rich annexationists in New York. In Canada, political opponents accused him of "talking treason with his American friends" and denigrating his race and country. The climax of his tour was an appearance at a national convention of Franco-Americans in Chicago as a registered delegate appointed by the St. Jean Baptiste Society of Boston. His very presence as a delegate was hotly contested, and he thought it wise to speak on the uncontroversial topic of the need to maintain the French language, although he closed by expressing his hope of seeing an independent Canada. Like his involvement in the Cahensly movement, Mercier's campaign for Canadian independence and possible American annexation bore no immediate fruit; but the alliance of Quebec nationalism with pro-Americanism that he inherited from the Patriotes and helped keep alive would prove durable. Whether or not the isolation of Quebec from the rest of North America was desirable, emigration had made it impossible: it was only the nature of Quebec's links to the United States that was subject to variation, not their existence.

In fact for many French Canadians the border to the south was a political and economic demarcation but hardly a barrier: they moved back and forth across it as their interests dictated and found no paradox in being both French Canadian and American. Nevertheless there was a tension—although not necessarily a contradiction—between those two elements. Perhaps no one synthesized them so well as the composer Calixa Lavallée: he was *notre musicien national* to both French Canadians and Franco-Americans; a French Canadian who spent the greater—and by far the most successful—part of his adult life in the United States; tireless advocate in the U.S.A. and official ambassador in Europe for "American" music (which included his own); and composer of two patriotic songs, the Franco-American *Restons français*—and *O Canada*, commissioned for the 1880 St. Jean Baptiste Day celebration in Quebec City, premiered by massed bands from Quebec and Massachusetts, and eventually the national anthem for all of Canada.

Calixa Lavallée was born in 1842 at Verchères, near Montreal. His father worked for an organ-maker and on the side tuned and repaired musical instruments of all sorts, repaired firearms, did other copper and iron work, and taught music. Little Calixa showed promise as a pianist, and at twelve he was taken to Montreal for formal study and placed in the care of Léon Derome, a wealthy butcher who became his lifelong patron; but the courses were not much to his liking, and in 1857, barely fifteen, he ran off to New Orleans. By the time he was twenty he had toured South America as accompanist to a Spanish violinist, served in the Union army as a musician, and been wounded at Antietam.

He returned to Montreal in 1863 and tried to establish himself as a music teacher and concert pianist, but seventeen of the twenty concerts he gave there were benefits: he could not make a living, and in 1865 he went back to the United States. He turned his hand to any musical task that offered, including playing the cornet in blackface: he went to San Diego, then to New Orleans where he taught music, then to Lowell in the growing Franco-American archipelago. By 1870 he was musical director of the Grand Opera House in New York. He wrote the music for a comic opera, *Loulou*, but just before its opening night Jim Fisk, owner of the opera house and the most flamboyant of the nineteenth-century robber barons, was killed in a quarrel over a woman. The opera house closed and Lavallée returned to Montreal and to Léon Derome, who sent him to study in Paris for two years.

In 1875 Lavallée began his most serious attempt to put music on a solid footing in Quebec. He opened a studio in Montreal with soprano Rosita del Vecchio and Belgian violinist Frantz Jéhin-Prume; Guillaume Couture, music critic for *La Minerve*, wrote that their first public concert "ushers in a new musical era." Lavallée was also choirmaster of St. Jacques church, and used his choir to stage Gounod's lyric drama *Jeanne d'Arc* with del Vecchio in the title role. It was the most ambitious musical project ever undertaken with local talent in Montreal, and it was a great success. The English-language Montreal Conservatory had just opened, and Lavallée hoped (in vain) that the interest generated by *Jeanne d'Arc* might persuade the Quebec government to fund a French-language conservatory. In 1878 he had a success in Quebec City with his *Cantata*, and another in 1880 with his setting of the poem *O Canada, terre de nos aïeux*; but 1880 was his last year in Canada. He was increasingly discouraged in Quebec, and after one last hectic concert tour with Jéhin-Prume and del Vecchio he decided not to return. Quebec's brief musical awakening was over.

Lavallée had little difficulty in resuming the U.S. musical career he had left behind eight years earlier. He was briefly reduced to playing the piano on the Boston-New York steamboats, but before long he had a studio in Boston and was professor of composition at the Carlyle Petersilea Academy of Music and choirmaster of Boston's cathedral church—and he also wrote the martial rallying song *Restons Français* for the Ligue des Patriotes of Fall River.

Although still far behind Europe, music in the United States was growing in both popularity and sophistication, and Boston was one of its leading centres. Lavallée became a tireless worker on behalf of U.S. music. At the 1884 convention of the Music Teachers' National Association he staged a landmark concert of unpublished works by U.S. composers, and he was the U.S. delegate to the 1887 World Congress of Music, where he captivated London society with his performance of his own newly composed *American March* and the Lord Mayor gave a dinner in his honour. In his speech to the congress he reviewed the difficulties that had stood in the way of the development of American music; but, he said,

it had now acquired enough momentum to assure it of a bright future. Immense possibilities are before us. We were present at the dawn of a day whose glorious noon cannot be imagined.[33]

Like many of his compatriots, Lavallée found greater scope for his energy and talents in the United States than in Quebec, but he never stopped being thoroughly French Canadian. One writer on the Franco-Americans has called him "a man of multiple but not of divided loyalties." If he had lived a few decades later it is doubtful whether even Lavallée could have achieved such a balance, for developments were already under way that would make what was difficult in the nineteenth century all but impossible in the twentieth.

A HORDE OF INDUSTRIAL INVADERS

In the textile towns the Franco-Americans gradually grew accustomed to an existence circumscribed by the discipline of mill life. Probably the most authoritative account of the lives mill operatives led in the 1870s and 1880s is contained in the annual reports of the Massachusetts Bureau of Statistics of Labor, a state agency whose conception of its function went far beyond the dry collections of figures suggested by its name. Under the direction of Col. Carroll D. Wright the bureau published detailed, opinionated, and often controversial studies of the major social problems of its time. The influence of its reports spread far beyond the boundaries of the state, and in London they were read with interest by a diligent researcher named Karl Marx.[34]

It is not surprising then that the bureau's 1881 report caused widespread dismay among the leaders of the Franco-American community. The occasion for its displeasure was the report's discussion of the advisability of restricting women and children to an average of ten hours of work a day. Only three objections to the ten-hour system were given: first, that small mills would be damaged by a ten-hour law, and so it proposed exempting them; second, that operatives would spend their extra hour of freedom in drinking, smoking, and loafing, but "the well-behaved ought not to be punished...for the sake of putting a restraint upon the ill-behaved." The report went on:

> The third objection to the ten-hour law is the presence of the Canadian French. Wherever they appear, there their presence is urged as a reason why the hours of labour should not be reduced to ten. The reasons for this urgency are not far to find.
>
> With some exceptions the Canadian French are the Chinese of the Eastern States. They care nothing for our institutions, civil, political, or educational. They do not come to make a home among us, to dwell with us as citizens, and so become a part of us; but their purpose is merely to sojourn a few years as aliens, touching us only at a single point, that of work, and, when they have gathered out of us what will satisfy their ends, to get them away to whence they came, and bestow it there. They are a horde of industrial invaders, not a

stream of stable settlers. Voting, with all that implies, they care nothing about. Rarely does one of them become naturalized. They will not send their children to school if they can help it, but endeavour to crowd them into the mills at the earliest possible age. To do this they deceive about the age of their children with brazen effrontery.

The bureau then accused the French Canadians of living "in the most beggarly way" so that they could take as much money as possible out of the country; attributed to them only "one good trait", that of being "indefatigable workers, and docile"; and characterized "drinking and smoking and lounging" as the sum of their amusements. The report concluded:

> Now, it is not strange that so sordid and low a people should awaken corresponding feelings in the managers, and that these should feel that, the longer the hours for such people, the better, and that to work them to the uttermost is about the only good use they can be put to.[35]

But once again it argued that "society should be shaped to the better portion of the people" and not to "these lowest ones."

In town after town across Massachusetts Franco-American organizations passed resolutions taking strong exception to the bureau's remarks. They insisted on being allowed to correct the impressions left by the report, and at a hearing in the State House in Boston they were allowed to have their say. In sometimes halting English, buttressed by statistics they had collected and testimony from prominent citizens in the towns where they lived, they effectively countered the picture presented in the ten-hour study and succeeded in impressing even the strong-minded Col. Wright.

According to their statistics, which covered thirty-two towns in six states, French-Canadian children made up twenty-four per cent of the school population of these towns, although French Canadians were only twenty-one per cent of the total population. Many of these children attended the forty parochial schools that had been established. Among the 88,653 French Canadians in the towns surveyed there were 4,480 naturalized U.S. citizens and 2,516 who owned real estate. Ferdinand Gagnon, a leading voice for the Franco-Americans, recounted the failure of the repatriation movement and effectively demonstrated that most of the French Canadians in the United States intended to stay. Charles Q. Tirrell, a state senator from Marlborough, reported that while French Canadians made up roughly a fifth of the population of that town, only forty-three of the 383 criminal cases brought before the Marlborough trial justice in the previous year involved French

Canadians. Of $3,580.42 paid out by the town for the assistance of the poor, $496.81, or fourteen per cent, was to French Canadians. In Fall River, according to Constable Edward J. L'Herault, 562 of 12,651 people brought before the courts between 1875 and 1880, or fewer than one-twentieth, were of Canadian birth, although about a sixth of the population of the town was French Canadian. Community leaders characterized the Franco-Americans as law-abiding citizens, so law-abiding that they did not like to get involved in strikes, but were inclined to "accept the wages fixed by the liberality, or sometimes the cupidity and avarice, of the manufacturers." While they favoured a ten-hour law, they did not favour the agitation that was necessary to effect the passage of the law, and had incurred the enmity of labour reformers. As for their living "in the most beggarly way", Father Millette of Nashua, N.H., told the bureau that "one of the great reproaches we make is, that they spend too much, they live too high, and they dress too fine. That is the great evil that we put on them."[36]

In justifying his previous report Col. Wright took refuge in some rather unconvincing excuses. The bureau's description of French Canadians had not been meant to apply to those in Massachusetts, where a ten-hour law already existed. While the description might not be true for the generality of French Canadians, it was undoubtedly true for some—as it was true for some English, Irish, and Americans. And anyway, the bureau was only reporting what it had heard from the people it had interviewed, who had no reason to be malicious. But Wright conceded the main points that the Franco-Americans had made. French Canadians were going to school "to an extent not realized a very short time ago"; they had become permanent settlers, and they were making rapid progress toward naturalization. He concluded with what he considered a high compliment:

> With such aspirations and purposes as were manifested at the hearing, complete assimilation with the American people is but a question of time.

The next annual report of Wright's bureau contained the transcript of the Franco-Americans' hearing, and also another document of equal interest, a section entitled "Fall River, Lowell and Lawrence". The growth of Fall River had been accompanied by continuing labour discontent, strikes, and violence, while the towns of Lowell and Lawrence had been almost entirely free of these phenomena. The Bureau wondered what caused this difference, and in looking for an explanation probed into almost all aspects of the material life of operatives in the three towns. All three towns were heavily dependent on the textile industry, which in each case accounted for about eighty per cent of the capital invested in all industries. Wages did not vary greatly among the three towns, being perhaps a little higher in Fall River, where a weaver handling eight looms or a spinner could earn as much as nine dollars a week. In one Lowell corporation wages ranged between $3.60 and $6.30 a week, while in Lawrence an operative estimated them as between $5.40 and $6.90, but in neither town did the bureau find any "absolute dissatisfaction" about wages. In all three towns, operatives were likely to have their wages "trusteed" or garnisheed by grocers or other merchants, a frequent source of complaint.

The bureau's agents found unhygienic conditions in many Fall River tenements. In those owned by the Richard Borden Manufacturing Company,

> The drinking water is in the yard, supplied by one pump, to which the inmates of these sixteen blocks have to come for water. In the yard of these houses, which is a large open space, are 36 closets for the use of 96 families. The place was dirty, and so were the people.

In the King Philip Mills tenements,

> The arrangement of the rooms was very poor for ventilation, and the sleeping-rooms in the attic were close and stuffy, and the height not over eight feet. The privies were in the centre of the large court-yard, and the stench from them was quite strong, and in warm weather must be much stronger.

In a privately owned tenement at No. 19 Almond Street,

> The condition of these tenements was most wretched, filth and decay abounding in all quarters.

But such conditions were by no means unique to Fall River, and the bureau was no kinder to the "Little Canada" section of Lowell:

> The general appearance of "Little Canada" was very demoralizing, the people being crowded into the smallest possible space, and the local board of health powerless to prevent the over-crowding, except in a case of an epidemic.

Fall River operatives complained about the system of blacklisting, by which an operative fired by one mill for being a troublemaker could find a job nowhere else in the city. The blacklist was applied with particular force against members of the Spinners' Union, the operatives testified. There was no blacklist in Lowell or Lawrence, but in firing employees mill owners could withhold the "discharge paper" they were required to present when seeking employment in another mill. This amounted to the same thing as a blacklist, but since there were no unions in Lowell and Lawrence the owners there did not have much occasion to resort to it.

Drunkenness was frequently mentioned as a cause of the troubles in Fall River, and one former operative said that "the great curse of this city is the liquor traffic," but judging by the numbers of arrests, most of which were for drunkenness and misdeeds related to it, this does not seem to have been a greater problem in Fall River than in Lowell and Lawrence. In Fall River in 1880 there were thirty-seven arrests per thousand population, while in Lowell the figure was forty-six and in Lawrence fifty-nine. One interesting aspect of the police statistics is that they corroborate the evidence presented by the Franco-Americans, for French Canadians were only a small proportion of those arrested between 1874 and 1881 (five per cent in Fall River, four per cent in Lowell, three per cent in Lawrence, in all cases well below their proportion of the total population). In Lowell, almost three-quarters of those arrested were Irish. The Irish and the English each tended to blame the other for the unsettled atmosphere in Fall River, and neither side much liked the French Canadians, who were willing to work for wages that the others considered too low.

The real difference between Fall River and the other towns seemed to be in what one Fall River operative called the "unreasonable spirit of competition that destroys all of the feelings of humanity among the overseers and agents, as well as among the operatives." This competition was not at the level of the mill owners, for there was a high degree of interlocking ownership and control of the mills and a strong consciousness of common interest among the rich mill-owning families. The Board of Trade, the organization of the manufacturers, was widely believed by the operatives to set production standards for the mills, although the owners denied this. It was at the lower levels that competition was bitter. Said one operative:

> The Board of Trade drives the agent, the agent drives the superintendent, he drives the overseer, and the overseer drives the operative. They drive us, and we drive each other.

Because of Fall River's rapid growth and the rickety financial structure of its mills there was none of the paternalism of Lowell or Lawrence. The owners demanded immediate returns, and production was increased at the expense of quality. Extra minutes were added to operatives' working day, extra yards were added to the "cut" they were expected to produce. Cheap cotton was used, producing yarn that broke easily and making the weaver's task more difficult. An English operative testified:

> The trouble is caused by the mixture of the English and American systems, not the best but the worst of each. High speed, English; and poor cotton, American.

The operatives were shown no respect by either the manufacturers or the overseers, and one of them said that:

> There is no feeling, no humanity, no Christianity manifested, and it seems to be growing worse instead of better. Until the operatives are recognized as somebodies by the manufacturers, they will always cause them trouble.

What comes through most clearly in the bureau's reports is how little was asked by the mill workers in general, and the Franco-Americans in particular. Fairness in applying the rules the manufacturers themselves had laid down, a pace of work that did not leave the operatives completely exhausted at the end of the day, and some common courtesy were enough to buy social peace. In the case of the Franco-Americans, their acceptance of the conditions of the mills was evidence less that they possessed some innate "docility" than that they did not see changing their economic status as being within their power. In areas where they felt their efforts could have some effect, the "truculent Canadians", as one of their most powerful adversaries called them, were bonny fighters indeed.

MATERIAL FOR THE MELTING POT

In October 1908 a play that was to enjoy a long run and wide popularity opened at the Columbia Theatre in Washington. It was called *The Melting-Pot*, and it was in the long literary tradition, dating back to Thomas More's *Utopia*, of seeing the New World as a place where the mistakes and failures of Europe could be avoided. The hero of the play, David Quixano, is a young Jewish musician in New York, a Russian immigrant who fled the Kishinev pogrom and is wildly enamoured of his new country. He is writing an American symphony to express his feelings about the United States. By chance he meets Vera Revendal, also from Russia but gentile, who works with immigrants at a settlement house. They fall in love, but when he meets Vera's father David recognizes him as the Russian army officer who stood by while his mother and sister were massacred in Kishinev, and the romance founders on this ancestral enmity. In the end, David's American symphony is played and is a success, he and Vera get back together, and he speaks rapturously of America as they look out into the sunset and the orchestra and chorus break into *My Country, 'Tis of Thee*. The title of the play quickly gained currency as a metaphor for the U.S. process of assimilation, and it has remained in the language. This is not without its ironies. The author of *The Melting-Pot* was Israel Zangwill, a British Jew who never lived in the United States, and many of those who picked up Zangwill's phrase missed one of his central points—that the culture into which the immigrants were to be melted was not the original Anglo-American culture but an alloy of the best that all the nationalities coming to the U.S.A. had to offer.

The America in which *The Melting-Pot* was performed—amid much controversy—was a country far more aware of cultural questions, particularly those posed by large-scale immigration, than it had been a few generations earlier, and there were numerous theories about the way the U.S.A. had dealt and should deal with these issues. While assimilation was by far the most influential of these theories, two others, nativism and cultural pluralism, either de-emphasized assimilation or rejected it entirely. The divisions among these three were by no means absolute: some of the harsher assimilation theories were barely distinguishable from nativism, and assimilation in its more generous forms contained some of the elements of cultural pluralism. It is nevertheless possible to see the three as separate precepts: that immigrants should be assimilated, that they should be kept out, or that they should retain their own cultures. To understand what happened to the Franco-Americans in the twentieth century, it is useful to look at where these ideas came from and what influence they had.

The importance of cultural pluralism in the U.S.A. has often been underestimated because the most active and committed cultural pluralists have generally been immigrants themselves. Their ideas have usually been expressed within their own communities, often in languages other than English, and whenever they have reached the larger "American" public the most common responses have been incomprehension and hostility; but, despite the limited nature of their circulation, cultural pluralist ideas have been significant in determining the shape of U.S. society.

French Canadians, as we have seen, came to the United States with a firm belief in the value of their language and religion and considerable determination to retain them. A Franco-American correspondent for the Montreal intellectual monthly *L'Action Française* tried to define "our national status" in 1921:

> We must be, first of all and simply, American citizens. For that there is no need to abandon our Catholic faith and our language and to lose our ethnic qualities.

After elaborating on the duties of a U.S. citizen, he came back to this point: "We are American citizens of Catholic faith and French language." He was taking for granted a cultural pluralist vision of U.S. society in his belief that "an American citizen of Catholic faith and French language" was something it was possible to be. It was a belief that not all Americans shared.

The Franco-Americans were far from alone in their ideas. The Spanish-speaking people of the Southwest, absorbed into the United States as a result of the Mexican War, showed little sign of adopting the language, culture, or values of the *gringos* who moved into the area in increasing numbers. New Mexico entered the union in 1912 as an officially bilingual state, having had a Spanish-speaking majority until the beginning of the twentieth century. It has been estimated that in 1910 German was the mother tongue of roughly nine million Americans, many of them U.S.-born of U.S.-born parents. Cincinnati had begun to establish a bilingual English and German public school system in the 1830s, and this system still existed in the early twentieth century and had served as a model for similar networks in several other cities. German-language newspapers in the United States had reached a combined circulation of roughly eight hundred thousand. The Creoles and Cajuns of Louisiana remained largely French-speaking, and substantial numbers of Poles, Czechs and other groups remained faithful to their native tongues.[37]

It was an American Jewish philosopher, trained at Harvard, who became the principal voice in the society at large for cultural pluralism not only as a description of reality but as a U.S. ideal as well. Horace Kallen argued that cultural pluralism was implicit in the freedoms guaranteed by the Declaration of Independence and the Constitution. " 'Equal' in the Declaration of Independence," he wrote, "is an affirmation of the right to be different." But Kallen's was a lonely voice, and even as he began a half-century of writing on the subject with a 1915 article called "Democracy *versus* the Melting Pot", a brutal and concerted assault on cultural pluralism was being prepared by powerful elements in the English-speaking mainstream.

A world of difference separated one extreme of the assimilation movement, the settlement-house workers who believed that the immigrants could make an important contribution to the life of the United States, from the other extreme, the high-pressure Americanizers; but both believed that people who came to the United States could and should undergo a cultural transformation that would produce, in the end, a homogeneous, culturally uniform society. The perceptive British observer G.K. Chesterton suggested that Americanization was what was unique about America. English or Spanish or Italian was something you were born. American was something you could become.

All this, of course, still left open two crucial questions: how this process was supposed to take place, and what its end product should be. Much of the rhetoric of assimilation made it sound like the melting pot in the Zangwillian sense — different elements fusing to create something new — but in practice assimilation usually meant something closer to what the Franco-Americans called pan-Saxonization and some sociologists have called Anglo-conformity. According to this model, the United States is fundamentally an English country, peopled by the English "race", speaking the English language, based on English traditions and values; the essential pattern of U.S. life was established at the time of the Revolution and before; and the proper role of an immigrant is to conform to this pattern. While this view ignores both the presence of substantial numbers of non–Anglo-Saxon Americans even in colonial times and the vast changes wrought by nineteenth-century immigration, it describes a process that many immigrants did in fact undergo.

As for the "how" of assimilation, it was assumed in the late nineteenth century that it would be a voluntary and fairly gradual process. Immigrants themselves, or their children, would perceive the superiority of the American way of life and would join the mainstream in the natural course of events. Spanish, German or French-Canadian cultural islands were seen as temporary phenomena that would disappear as their inhabitants adjusted fully to their new surroundings (even if the inhabitants themselves saw things very differently). As long as economic progress continued and social ferment was kept within tolerable bounds this optimistic, relatively open view of assimilation prevailed. There were occasional events, like the Haymarket affair of 1886 and the assassination of President McKinley by Leon Czolgosz in 1901, that cast non–Anglo-Saxon Americans in an unfavourable light and brought on a wave of hysteria aimed at "foreign influence", but these were exceptions rather than part of a consistent pattern.

Confidence in the easy operation of the melting pot had already begun to wane when it was further shaken by reverberations from the war that broke out in Europe in 1914. Americans were shocked at the "discovery" of millions of unassimilated "foreigners" in their midst, many of them Germans, potential agents of the Kaiser. In a book published in 1916 Frank Julian Warne wrote:

> It has consciously become all of a sudden of the very greatest importance to us as a nation that the immigrants whom we have welcomed into our society... should be an integral part of that society and not foreign to it. We have found that our forces for assimilating this foreign element have not been working.

At a time when a high priority was placed on national cohesion, when patriotic zeal was directed toward achieving "preparedness", and when political candidates vied with one another in the ferocity of their denunciations of "hyphenated Americanism", the assimilating forces had to be *made* to work. It was time to turn up the heat on the melting pot. The result was an intense campaign for "Americanization", and the slogan was "one hundred per cent American". Although many immigrants voluntarily joined in U.S. preparation for and participation in the war, manifestations of their loyalty were never quite enough to satisfy the hundred-per-centers. Among the chief apostles of Americanization was automobile magnate Henry Ford, who set up his own English School and compelled his foreign employees to attend it. John Higham, the chronicler and interpreter of U.S. nativist movements, has described a pantomime that was enacted at this school:

> In this performance a great melting pot (labelled as such) occupied the middle of the stage. A long column of immigrant students descended into the pot from backstage, clad in outlandish garb and flaunting signs proclaiming their fatherlands. Simultaneously from either side of the pot another stream of men emerged, each prosperously dressed in identical suits of clothes and each carrying a little American flag.

While German-Americans were the chief targets of wartime xenophobia in the United States and provided the principal rationale for the Americanization campaign, its effects spilled over onto other foreign-language groups as well. Repressive measures were directed at all non–English-speaking Americans. The governor of Iowa banned all languages except English in schools, churches, and public places and on the telephone. In fifteen states, instruction in languages other than English in public and private primary schools was made illegal. Oregon decreed that all primary-school children had to go to public schools, and ordered foreign-language newspapers to display prominently a literal English translation of their entire contents.

Although the Americanization campaign did have some lasting results in creating institutions to facilitate assimilation, its immediate effects were inevitably disappointing to its proponents. When it turned out that millions of hyphenated Americans remained hyphenated despite the best efforts of the hundred-per-centers, and when the emotional energy unleashed by the war and the Big Red Scare that followed it in 1919 and 1920 was dissipated, the crusade was abandoned as quickly as it had been put together. With the decline of Americanization, the field was left open to outright nativism.

Suspicion and fear of foreign influence and foreign ideas were longstanding components of U.S. nationalism. John Higham traces three continuing threads in nativism, and two of them, anti-Catholicism and antiradicalism, had to do with keeping the U.S.A. safe from ideologies and conspiracies imported from abroad. Both made their first appearance early in American history—anti-Catholicism at the time of the first English settlements and antiradicalism during the conservative reaction to the French Revolution in the 1790s—and both had periodic revivals thereafter. Anti-Catholicism fuelled the Know Nothings in the 1850s and the American Protective Association in the 1880s and 1890s, and outbreaks of antiradicalism occurred in the hysteria following the 1886 riot in Chicago's Haymarket Square when police attacked a march in which foreign-born anarchists were prominent, and again in the Big Red Scare of 1919–20. While both these elements were present in the nativist surge of the 1920s, its dominant theme was a third and much newer antiforeign theory based on notions of racial purity.

Racial theories of history enjoyed a considerable vogue in the early twentieth century, particularly among the upper classes. Their basic assumption was that heredity was the principal determining factor of history, and that superior moral and intellectual qualities were more likely to be found in some races than in others. The race with the largest helping of these qualities was the "true whites", the blond, blue-eyed Nordics who predominated in northern Europe. This noble race was in danger of extinction because it had allowed itself to be diluted by the blood of the inferior races of Europe—the round-headed Alpines, the swarthy Mediterraneans, and the Jews. In allowing large-scale immigration, especially from southern and eastern Europe, the United States ran the risk of losing the racial advantage that made it great; one of the chief proposals of the racists, therefore, was that immigration should be severely restricted. Such proposals had been made in the past, but they had never been able to prevail against two powerful counterarguments. First, there were the U.S. tradition of regarding the United States as a haven for the poor and oppressed, the commitment to equality in the Declaration of Independence, and the humanitarian sentiments inscribed on the base of the Statue of Liberty. Second, and more important, there was the indisputable fact that immigration had been an economic boon for the country, providing pioneers for the frontier and abundant low-cost labour for the mines, mills, and factories. Madison Grant, a New York patrician whose *The Passing of the Great Race* was the most popular of the racist tracts, reluctantly acknowledged the force of the economic argument:

> During the last century the New England manufacturer imported the Irish and French Canadians and the resultant fall in the New England birth rate at once became ominous. The refusal of the native American to work with his hands when he can hire or import serfs to do manual labor for him is the prelude to his extinction and the immigrant laborers are now breeding out their masters and killing by filth and by crowding as effectively as by the sword.
>
> Thus the American sold his birthright in a continent to solve a labour problem.

But after the First World War even the economic argument was not enough to prevent restriction. The resumption of immigration in 1919 and 1920 after its wartime interruption coincided with a postwar depression, and this helped create the climate that frightened Congress into legislating the first general restrictions on immigration. A temporary restriction, providing for country-by-country quotas, was enacted in 1921 in the face of big-business opposition; but increasing mechanization had reduced the need for large numbers of immigrant labourers, and business came to accept the new regime. With that stumbling-block out of the way, Congress made a quota system permanent in 1924.

Of all the immigrant groups affected by the Americanization and nativist movements, probably none got off as lightly as the Franco-Americans. The Protestant upper class of New England had not taken well to the changes that the nineteenth century had brought to the region and had fallen into a mood of pessimism and self-pity, fuelled by the gloomy theories of the racist historians and anthropologists, but the heaviest blows against non – Anglo-Saxon Americans were struck elsewhere in the country. Even Henry Cabot Lodge, a bearer of Yankee traditions, an early convert to racism, and for years a leader in Congress of the movement to restrict immigration, nevertheless had kind words for Franco-Americans whom he regarded as not really immigrants at all, since:

> They have been, in the broad sense, Americans for generations, and their coming to the United States is merely a movement of Americans across an imaginary line, from one part of America to another.[38]

French Canadians escaped even the restrictions on immigration, since neither the 1921 law nor its successor in 1924 applied to the western hemisphere.

They were not, of course, completely immune. A number of New England legislatures considered measures to restrict foreign-language teaching in parochial schools, but only Rhode Island did so. In 1923 Republican Assemblyman Frederick Peck introduced a bill that required parochial schools to teach all the subjects covered by the public schools in English (other subjects could be taught in French). The Peck bill passed despite determined Franco-American opposition, but was overturned two years later and a milder regulation substituted. But while Franco-Americans were spared the worst prejudices and the most drastic effects of specific measures, they could not escape the change in climate. It was palpably more difficult to be a "hyphenated American" or an "American citizen of Catholic faith and French language" in the 1920s than it had been before the First World War. Many non–Anglo-Saxon Americans responded to the new climate by proclaiming their ethnic identity even more loudly than before and becoming more intensely involved with the problems and prospects of their own groups. Similar forces to those that led Jews to Zionism and black Americans to Marcus Garvey's Universal Negro Improvement Association led Franco-Americans to a transnational ethnic movement of their own.

THE WARS OF RELIGION

From the point of view of the hierarchy of the Catholic Church in the United States the arrival of the French Canadians, with their strong predilection for retaining the language and customs they had brought with them from Quebec, occurred at a very inopportune time. Since the early days of the republic the church had been performing an often difficult balancing act, reconciling the demands of being Catholic with those of being American; and it had to accomplish this reconciliation not only in its own eyes but also to the satisfaction of suspicious Protestants in the United States and skeptical Catholics in Europe.

Looking at such matters in the light of late-twentieth-century perceptions and prejudices, with the role of religion fading in the daily lives of many North Americans and the influence of religion decidedly secondary in matters of public policy, it may seem hard to imagine what all the fuss was about. Three or four generations ago, however, when the Roman Catholic Church in the United States was coming to grips in fiercely divisive fashion with questions of language and national identity, the dispute between the church and some of its most loyal followers seemed crucial to a great many individuals. In the Franco-American community, with its twin allegiance to Catholicism and the French language, it came to be perceived as a matter of life and death to important institutions. The consequences of some of the conflicts in this long-running dispute were to hasten the erosion of the French language and of the cultural identity of which it was an integral part.

The problem had already been perceived in 1835 by John England, the first Roman Catholic bishop of Charleston, South Carolina. At that time the church in the United States was dominated by priests from France who had fled the anticlericalism of the French Revolution, and Bishop England wrote:

> One of the strongest topics of prejudice against our religion is that it is a foreign religion, and it is not American, that it is the religion of strangers, of aliens.... The French clergy are generally good men and love religion, but they make the Catholic religion thus appear to be exotic, and cannot understand why it should be made to appear assimilated to American principles.

A number of developments later in the nineteenth century accentuated the difficulties addressed by Bishop England. Although the French clergy faded from the scene and the Irish took over the most important positions in the U.S. hierarchy, they were now called upon to preside over a flock that included an increasing number of "foreigners" speaking strange tongues — first Germans, then French Canadians, and later Poles, Italians, and other southern and eastern Europeans. In addition, the rise of the Know Nothings and other nativist movements in the decades before the Civil War left a deep impression on their chief targets, the Irish, who drew the lesson that the church had to be made as American as possible to avoid a repetition of such outbursts. A further complication was the conservative direction in which the church was steered by Pope Pius IX during his long reign. Liberal prelates had to fight their battles for a palatable American Catholicism on two fronts, in the United States and in Rome.

Toward the end of the century the Americanizing movement in the church was under the direction of two of its greatest leaders, the archbishop of Baltimore, Cardinal James Gibbons, and Archbishop John Ireland of St. Paul. In manner and method the slight, gentle, diplomatic Gibbons and the imposing and sometimes impulsive Ireland were opposites, but they shared similar ideas and were lifelong allies. On social questions Gibbons and Ireland were, in Catholic terms, progressives—Ireland to the point where he became known in Europe as "the socialist bishop" even though he was a firm believer in private property. In 1891, well ahead of his time, Ireland came out against all forms of racial segregation. Gibbons, a southerner by upbringing, disagreed with him on that, but on the question of the Knights of Labor they were in full agreement. At the urging of Archbishop Elzéar Taschereau of Quebec (who in the context of the church in French Canada at the time was considered a clerical liberal) the Holy Office in Rome condemned the Knights in 1884 as a secret society forbidden to Catholics. Gibbons and Ireland fought the ban, and while in Rome in 1887 to be invested as a cardinal Gibbons successfully pleaded with the Holy Office to reverse its condemnation. Neither prelate missed an opportunity to praise U.S. institutions. Ireland proclaimed that:

> My Catholic heart and my American heart are one.... I do not think that anyone is fit to enter the kingdom of heaven who is not capable of taking care of, as far as the opportunity affords, this magnificent kingdom given to us here, the republic of America.

Gibbons took the uncharacteristically bold step of defending—in Rome itself—the separation of church and state, which was foreign to European Catholic thinking, and attributing the growth of the church in America "to the civil liberty we enjoy in our enlightened republic." The Americanism of the leading U.S. Catholics went so far that some European clerics thought they detected heresy in it, and in 1899 Pope Leo XIII condemned opinions which "some comprise under the name of Americanism." But the pope confined his condemnation to purely theological issues, and Gibbons and Ireland were able to deny that "Americanism", in this sense, existed in the United States.

The need to reconcile Catholicism with Americanism also underlay the attitude of Gibbons and Ireland on cultural questions. They were aware of the need to serve non-Anglophone Catholics in the United States, and that this often meant providing them with priests who spoke their native languages; but if the Catholic Church was to be American it had in their eyes to be English-speaking and to play an active role in assimilating immigrants to the American way of life. It was the latter consideration that prevailed, to such an extent that the Catholic Church has been called the second most important assimilating force in the United States, exceeded only by the public school system.

But this policy of public conformity did not triumph without serious opposition. The Germans, in numerical terms second only to the Irish among U.S. Catholics, insisted on having German priests and German bishops in proportion to their numbers; Polish disagreements with the hierarchy led to the establishment of an independent Polish National Catholic Church; and as soon as they were numerous enough to make their presence felt the Franco-Americans were also fighting for the preservation of their cultural traditions within the church. Their sense of the relationship between culture and religion was very different from that of Gibbons and Ireland. To the Franco-Americans being French and being Catholic were inseparable; they saw the French language as the guardian of their Catholic faith. This identification was expressed by Jules-Paul Tardivel, the Kentucky-born editor of the Montreal newspaper *La Vérité*, advocate of ultramontanism and Quebec independence and enemy of liberalism, freemasonry, and the "Americanism" of the Irish-American bishops. "For our compatriots," wrote Tardivel in 1885, "language is intimately tied to Faith. If they lose one, they run the risk of losing the other." A generation later, in 1918, Henri Bourassa told a Montreal audience:

> The French language in America is completely devoted to the Catholic Apostolate, to Catholic teaching, to Catholic exegesis.... In contrast, the English language is a language of error, of heresy, of revolt, of division, of dogmatic and moral anarchy.

From the point of view of the Franco-Americans the assimilationist policies of the Irish bishops were very far from essential to the growth of the church in the United States: they were ruinous. Maintaining the French language was especially important in the United States, where French Canadians were surrounded by error and heresy on all sides. To bring up one's children in English was to expose them to temptations that might tear them away from Catholicism; ultimately, it was to risk their marrying outside the faith. In 1909, the *Guide Français de Fall River* warned in an article entitled "Le Mariage entre étrangers: un crime contre dieu et une abomination nationale" (Intermarriage: a crime against God and a national abomination) that:

> Knowledge of the English language is useful and even necessary in commerce, industry and politics, but it is very dangerous and even deplorable in the too familiar relations it engenders between our young people and strangers to our manners, ways and customs. Out of these unfortunate relations, first of

friendship and then of love, have come marriages that are often contracted frivolously, not to say in defiance of the sacred principles that make up the honour of our race and the glory of our religion.

Parish by parish, diocese by diocese, the struggle went on, from the first major engagement in the 1880s to the final spectacular defeat of the militant Franco-Americans in the 1920s. The specific issues they contested varied from place to place, but underlying all the battles was the question of language and its relationship to religion.

Notre Dame de Lourdes parish in Fall River was for ten years the preserve of the energetic and uncompromising Father Pierre Jean-Baptiste Bédard, who gained a large following among Franco-Americans but made enemies of many of his Irish coreligionists, including his superior, Bishop Thomas Hendricken of Providence. When Bédard died of apoplexy in 1884 Hendricken had his revenge by appointing an Irish priest, Rev. Samuel McGee, as his successor. The dissatisfied Franco-American parishioners sent a delegation to Providence, but Bishop Hendricken only asked, "Why do you want a French priest? Within ten years, everyone in your parish will be speaking English." Seeing that they would get nowhere with the bishop, they began to make life uncomfortable for the unfortunate Father McGee: coughing epidemics broke out when he tried to read the announcements during Mass, and some of the more hotheaded parishioners issued threats against him. In early 1885, McGee was removed but his replacement was another Irish priest, and the Franco-Americans began boycotting Mass. Hendricken placed the parish under interdict, effectively closing the church.

Neither side was willing to budge. The Franco-Americans took their case to Rome. The church remained closed until September, and when it reopened with yet another Irish priest in charge attendance was sparse. The Sacred Congregation of the Propaganda in Rome reaffirmed the right of the bishop to name whoever he liked as pastor but suggested that in the interests of peace and for the good of souls it might be best to appoint a French-Canadian pastor to Notre Dame de Lourdes. Father J.-M. Laflamme was brought in from Quebec—as curate under an Irish pastor. The Franco-Americans, anticipating victory, interpreted this as a face-saving device on the part of the bishop, and they were proved right in March 1886 when Laflamme was confirmed as pastor.[39]

The struggle left its mark on the Franco-Americans of Fall River. Along with the intense interest aroused by the fate of Louis Riel, it brought French-Canadian nationalist feeling to a high point and led to the creation of new newspapers and organizations, and to a rallying song, *Restons Français,* written by two of the era's more interesting figures: the words were by Rémi Tremblay, a Civil War veteran who had come to Fall River from Ottawa to edit the newly founded newspaper *L'Indépendant*, and the music by Calixa Lavallée.

Not all the Franco-Americans' battles ended as happily as the Fall River conflict. In Danielson, Connecticut, they fought endlessly and unsuccessfully to have a French-Canadian pastor appointed to their mixed but French-majority parish; a pastor from France, appointed by the bishop of Hartford as a compromise, failed to satisfy them. In North Brookfield, Massachusetts, Franco-Americans were refused a separate parish by the bishop of Springfield, and attended unauthorized services conducted by a French-Canadian priest under pain of excommunication. An important advance was made in 1907 when Georges-Albert Guertin became bishop of Manchester, New Hampshire—the first Franco-American bishop. In neighbouring Maine, as in New Hampshire, Franco-Americans made up the majority of Catholics, but an Irish bishop, Monsignor Louis Walsh, was appointed to the diocese of Portland in 1906. Relations between the previous bishop and Maine's Franco-Americans had been touchy, and as Walsh was not only Irish but a militant assimilationist as well they soon moved toward open confrontation.

The issue on which the Franco-Americans challenged Walsh was control of church property and finances. In Quebec parish property was administered by a *fabrique*, a board of lay trustees who made financial decisions in collaboration with the curé, but the diocese of Portland used the Corporation Sole system, by which all church property was under the authority of the bishop. The Franco-Americans appealed to the Maine legislature in 1911 to order adoption of the trustee system, on the American principle of "no taxation without representation"; after that failed, they appealed to Rome. Bishop Walsh resorted to the harsh ecclesiastical penalty of interdict; when one active opponent of the Corporation Sole system died he was refused a funeral Mass by the bishop. The issue of church property in Maine came before the annual meeting of American archbishops in Washington, the St. Jean Baptiste Society in Montreal, and the Sacred Congregation of the Council in Rome, which pronounced itself against the Corporation Sole system but in favour of a compromise that permitted the appearance of decentralization but left most of the power still in the hands of the bishop. Some Franco-Americans saw this as a significant concession, but the more militant considered it another defeat and were determined to avenge it.

The assimilationist design of Gibbons, Ireland, and their supporters was never fully realized: important elements of ethnic diversity remain in the Catholic Church in the United States even now. But while part of their struggle had been won, Franco-American leaders just before the First World War were more conscious of what had been lost. The French language was being eroded, and the areas of life that were being lived within the Franco-American community were becoming fewer. There were two responses to this, a moderate one that emphasized adaptation to changing times and a militant one that advocated resistance to all outside influences. The divergence between these two tendencies in the Franco-American leadership was becoming sharper as events within the church led toward a final epic encounter.

DAIGNAULT'S LAST STAND

The byzantine atmosphere of conspiracy and counterconspiracy that pervaded the Franco-American archipelago in the latter half of the 1920s had as much to do with a breakdown of trust as with any concrete issues. The embattled factions saw each other as on the one hand bad Catholics, rebels disrespectful of the authority of the church, and potential schismatics, and on the other as bad Franco-Americans, lacking a sense of patriotic duty, instruments of the assimilationist designs of the Irish bishops. Their common enemy was the threat of Americanization, but they had very different ideas about how to meet that threat and very different visions of the Franco-American community.

The radical faction took its name from its newspaper, *La Sentinelle*. The Sentinellistes held the traditional view that French Canadians in Quebec, those in other provinces, and Franco-Americans were all part of one community, engaged in a single struggle for *survivance*. Their opponents were inclined to see excessive attachment to Quebec among Franco-Americans as coming dangerously close to validating the nativist accusation that they were "fifty-fifty Americans". Both nevertheless sought support from Quebec, and it was a well timed series of articles in a Montreal newspaper that delivered the *coup de grâce* to the Sentinellistes.

The Sentinelle movement followed some forty years of resistance to assimilationist tendencies within the Roman Catholic Church in the United States, but it surpassed all previous resistance efforts in its emotional intensity, its geographic extent, the degree to which it affected the entire institutional life of the Franco-American archipelago, and its international repercussions. It was also unique in being largely an internal struggle within the Franco-American community itself. The Sentinellistes were scarcely less heated in their denunciations of the Franco-American, Bishop Georges-Albert Guertin of Manchester (one of them referred to him as "O'Guertin"),

than in their attacks on the Irishman, Bishop William Hickey of Prov
And opposition to the Sentinellistes was led as much by Elie Vézina,
secretary-general of the Union St. Jean Baptiste d'Amérique, and Albert
Foisy, editor of *La Tribune* of Woonsocket, as by Bishop Hickey. Their
struggle left a legacy of bitterness of which echoes could still be heard two
generations later.

The epicentre of the struggle was the quintessential Franco-American
city of Woonsocket, Rhode Island, *la ville la plus française d'Amérique*.
Woonsocket was the birthplace and home of the leader of the Sentinelle
movement, Elphège Daignault, lawyer, politician and, after 1922, president
of the Association Canado-Américaine (whose chapters were sometimes
referred to collectively as *les Canados*). It was in Woonsocket that Daignault
and his chief collaborators published their militant weekly newspaper *La
Sentinelle*. It was also in Woonsocket that Elie Vézina directed anti-Sentinelliste
strategy from the head office of the Union St. Jean Baptiste, and it was
Woonsocket's French-language daily, *La Tribune*, that became the most
important anti-Sentinelliste organ.

The issue that brought the divisions in the community into the open was
the old and still unresolved one of the control of church finances. Bishop
Hickey was funding his diocesan projects by assigning each parish a quota
which, if not filled from contributions, had to be made up out of general
parish funds. There was increasing emphasis within the church on the
importance of Catholic—but not necessarily French—high schools; Hickey
continued to indulge his taste for building new institutions, implementing
the diocesan centralization that he believed was necessary to avoid state
control. Rhode Island Franco-Americans, in whose eyes institutions that
were under the control of the Irish bishops were little better than state
institutions, grew increasingly resentful. But it was not simply a question of
resistance by Franco-Americans to the use of their money for "Irish" institutions. A new commercial high school in Woonsocket was the pet project of
Monsignor Charles Dauray, a venerable Franco-American priest whose
more than eighty years did not prevent him from participating vigorously in
the anti-Sentinelliste cause. To Monsignor Dauray and his allies, the new
school was a necessary addition to Franco-American institutional life, but
for the Sentinellistes it was potentially another tool for assimilation. It was to
be under diocesan control, which meant out of the hands of the Franco-
Americans; it was to be bilingual, which meant that in practice the main
language of instruction would be English; and it meant the closing of a
Franco-American boarding school in nearby Central Falls, which helped to
turn Central Falls into a hotbed of Sentinelliste agitation.

All this took place in the atmosphere of nativism and militant Americanization of the early 1920s. *Les Croisés* (the Crusaders), a secret society led by Elphège Daignault, had been formed to resist these pressures, but it came to focus its efforts on diocesan centralization, leaving other issues to more moderate voices like those of Eugène Jalbert and Élie Vézina. In 1923 Daignault appealed to the apostolic delegate in Washington to curb Bishop Hickey's fund-raising activities, the first in a series of unsuccessful appeals to higher ecclesiastical authorities: he always believed that if only Rome knew the true story it could not but decide in his favour. In 1924 he founded *La Sentinelle* as an instrument for his views, and hired J.-Albert Foisy, an editor of *L'Action Catholique*, organ of the Archdiocese of Quebec, to run it. But Daignault and Foisy soon had a falling out: *La Sentinelle* dismissed Foisy, and under Daignault's direction it became considerably more strident in tone. Many of its articles displayed a curious mixture of invective and religious erudition, especially the ones written by Henri Perdriau, who came to *La Sentinelle* in 1925, having been a member of the Action Française in Paris in his youth. Foisy, after a stint with *Le Bulletin* of Fall River, came back to Woonsocket to edit *La Tribune*, which he turned into the principal voice of the anti-Sentinellistes.

The anti-Sentinelliste campaign was launched in earnest in December 1924 by Eugène Jalbert in his capacity as president of the Fédération Catholique Franco-Américaine, an umbrella organization grouping fifteen Franco-American societies. In his presidential report, Jalbert disavowed "this whole campaign of injuries and insults carried on for almost a year against His Excellency Monsignor the Bishop of Providence." In the ensuing debate, Daignault and his lieutenants in the Association Canado-Américaine all but pulled the Canados out of the Fédération. Bishop Guertin, whose diocese contained the head office of the Canados, was disturbed at what he considered their "complete disrespect for religious authority" and "strange liberty of thought and action", and he demanded a retraction of their stand; when there was no retraction, he removed their chaplains. At the 1925 congress of the Union St. Jean Baptiste the Sentinellistes mounted a slate of challengers against Vézina and the other incumbents but the challenge was rebuffed. The battle lines were now clearly drawn: newspaper against newspaper, society against society. Each side had support inside the church and out, in New England and in Quebec.

The Sentinelliste campaign reached its height in 1927. Enthusiastic public meetings were held in Lowell, Worcester, Manchester and other Franco-American centres, while in Woonsocket large rallies were a regular occurrence. A contribution strike was launched—a complete refusal to contribute to the church for any purpose. The Sentinellistes brought twelve parish corporations before the Rhode Island Superior Court, challenging their right to use parish funds for non-parish purposes—and skating close to the edge of a church prohibition of involving bishops in civil suits. Bishop Hickey disciplined two Sentinelliste priests, Father Prince of Woonsocket and Father Béland of Central Falls, further arousing the anger of Daignault and his supporters. In November 1927 Daignault left for Rome to take charge of his appeals there; he decided that all that was needed was a clear demonstration that the Sentinellistes had Franco-American opinion on their side, came back to Rhode Island to collect fifteen thousand signatures on a petition, and returned to Rome in April 1928. If a contest for public opinion had been all that was involved, the Sentinellistes probably would have had a fighting chance, but the controversy had grown to the point where it involved issues much larger than the Franco-American community. Forces external to that community, aided by some serious strategic errors on the part of the Sentinellistes, were now arrayed to crush the movement.

Right-wing nationalism flourished in diverse forms in the 1920s: National Socialism in Germany, Fascism in Italy, Action Française in France, Action Française in Quebec, the Sentinelle movement in New England, and many others. Early in the century the Catholic Church had tolerated and in some cases even encouraged these movements as bulwarks against openly anti-religious philosophies such as liberalism and socialism, but the church was also disturbed by their tendency to put nationalism before Catholicism: in the church's eyes, you were a Catholic first and foremost or else you weren't a real Catholic at all.

In 1926 Pope Pius XI publicly condemned the Action Française in France and put its newspaper on the Index. The same year Henri Bourassa, the most respected French-Canadian nationalist leader, was on a visit to Rome when intermediaries approached him with an unsolicited offer of an audience with Pope Pius. Bourassa listened while the pope delivered a long lecture against nationalism:

> At the present time, the main obstacle to the action of the papacy and the church in the world is the predominance of racial passions in all countries, the substitution of nationalism for Catholicism.

Bourassa took the pope's words to heart, and later described the experience as the most powerful lesson of his life.

Elphège Daignault, on his second visit to Rome in 1928, picked up a copy of *L'Osservatore Romano* and read that he and other members of his movement had been excommunicated because of their civil suits against the bishops. *La Sentinelle* of Woonsocket joined *L'Action Française* of Paris on the Index. By this time both the Superior Court and the Rhode Island Supreme Court had also decided against the Sentinellistes on the key question of the use of parish funds for non-parish purposes. Despite these setbacks the leading members of the movement remained defiant. Renamed *La Vérité* to escape the papal condemnation, the Sentinelliste organ reappeared. In a St. Jean Baptiste Day speech to three thousand supporters in Woonsocket Daignault pledged to continue the struggle, and the Association Canado-Américaine, taken aback by the excommunication of its president, decided to hold its 1928 convention in the friendlier territory of Quebec City. The Canados, including those who had been excommunicated, were warmly received by civic leaders and even by sympathetic priests, and Daignault was easily elected to another term.

Nevertheless the influence of the Sentinellistes was waning, and their decline became evident in the November 1928 American presidential election. Daignault had been an active Republican, but after the Peck school language bill, a Republican initiative, Daignault like many other Rhode Island Franco-Americans had switched to the Democrats. The Democratic presidential candidate in 1928 was Al Smith, an Irish Catholic and a Wet. Daignault was a prohibitionist—he liked to refer to Smith as "Al...coöl" (from the French for alcohol)—and he hated Irish Catholics more than he hated Protestants; he decided to enter the campaign on the side of Republican candidate Herbert Hoover. *La Vérité* became virtually a Hoover campaign sheet, but Daignault only alienated some of his own supporters without winning friends in the regular Woonsocket Republican organization (whose president was Eugène Jalbert, the prominent anti-Sentinelliste). Smith not only won a statewide majority but also carried Woonsocket, Central Falls, and other Franco-American centres.

The end of the Sentinelle movement, if not of the ideas that underlay it, was at hand. *La Vérité* was condemned by the pope, but continued to appear as *La Bataille*—the name change was so hasty that it did not extend to the inside pages of the paper—and finally as *La Défense*. Henri Perdriau, the most virulent of the Sentinellistes, took advantage of Daignault's absence in Quebec to produce a pamphlet entitled *Fiat Lux*—"Let There Be Light" —which recommended that Franco-Americans leave the Roman Catholic Church to become members of the Orthodox or American Catholic Church and bore an *imprimatur* from Casimir Durand, bishop of that church. "The Catholic Church, yes," it said, "the Roman Church, no!" Daignault seized and burned all the copies he could lay his hands on and read Perdriau out of the movement, but one copy found its way to Élie Vézina, who mailed it to his friend in Montreal, Henri Bourassa.

So far, Bourassa had been silent on the Sentinelle question. Daignault had once hoped for support from the nationalist leader, but more recently Bourassa had been in frequent correspondence with Vézina. He was now ready to make a pronouncement on the affair, and his series of five articles appeared in his Montreal newspaper *Le Devoir* in mid-January 1929. They dismissed the legitimacy of the Sentinellistes' complaints, blamed a world-wide "hatred of authority" for the rise of the movement, and cited Perdriau's pamphlet without mentioning that Daignault had disassociated himself from it. The articles were controversial, but Bourassa's influence was still considerable and his stand had the effect, in Robert Rumilly's words, of a "new excommunication". The Sentinellistes were now forced to admit that they had lost, if not that they were wrong. In February most of them announced their submission to papal authority, allowing the excommunication to be lifted. *La Défense* was quietly put to rest.

The passions took a while to cool, and left after-effects when they did. Bishop Hickey was not a gracious winner, and returned from a trip to Rome in the summer of 1929 with some very pointed papal decorations for Monsignor Dauray, Vézina, Foisy, and other leading anti-Sentinellistes. Daignault remained president of the Association Canado-Américaine until 1936, when some of his onetime supporters forced him out to pave the way for a return of the Canados' chaplains and a reconciliation with the Union St. Jean Baptiste. The former Sentinelliste leader died in 1937, a broken man.

There are still vast differences between Sentinelliste and anti-Sentinelliste versions of many of the key incidents of the struggle. Franco-American recollections of the period are often tinged with shame and guilt. For although not everyone acknowledged it at the time, the end of the Sentinelle movement effectively meant the end of the Franco-Americans' efforts to remain an essentially French-speaking community. And inevitably, once that began to sink in, people began to wonder whether they had all along been pursuing a mirage. "Was it all worth the effort in the end?" one third-generation Franco-American has asked:

> It is possible that in the process of resisting assimilation, Franco-Americans held up their economic and educational progress, a part of necessary acculturation to American life. There may have been so much emphasis on religion, ethnicity, the French language, and *survivance*, that economics and education became secondary.... Walking through some of the decaying textile cities of New England today, one wonders if the Franco-American elite made the

wrong choice; now there is little *survivance*, and little educational and economic growth to offset the loss.[40]

Although their opponents won the battle, it was the Sentinellistes who proved the more prescient: what prevailed after 1929 was not a moderate version of *survivance* but Americanization. Without commitment to the old values there was little basis for preserving the language and culture.

The Sentinellistes were also right about the relationship between developments in the Franco-American archipelago and developments in Quebec. After 1929 the French Canadians of Quebec and the Franco-Americans of New England have essentially separate histories, but it was only a matter of time before the forces that the Sentinellistes were fighting in New England would reach Quebec as well. The advance guard of these forces, in the form of Alcoa, International Paper, Shawinigan Water and Power, and the rest had already come in through the open gates. Economically, Quebec was already being integrated into the rest of North America. For those French Canadians who had gone to the United States, economic integration had eventually led to cultural integration; those French Canadians who had stayed in Quebec were protected from a similar fate only by a political border. That might ultimately make all the difference, or it might make no difference at all.

IMPORTING U.S. DOLLARS

The transformation of Quebec into an industrial society, already under way in the late nineteenth century, quickened at the beginning of the twentieth. U.S. investment played an important role in this process, especially in industries that required large amounts of capital to get off the ground, such as asbestos, aluminum, hydroelectricity, and pulp and paper. Enterprises in these industries were often bought out by Americans when the original owners ran out of money. U.S. investment also contributed to the growth of Montreal as a manufacturing centre, and the fifty-three branch plants, affiliates, and major warehousing operations of U.S. companies in Montreal in 1913 were exceeded among Canadian cities only by Toronto's ninety-four.

The asbestos industry, although oriented from the start toward the U.S. market, was initially owned by small local producers; but beginning in 1891 a series of market crises, accompanied by technological changes that increased capital requirements, drove out most of the small producers and left most of the industry in U.S. hands. Total Quebec production grew from under 50,000 tonnes in 1900 to 100,000 tonnes in 1910 and almost 200,000 in 1920.

The asbestos industry became the main source of employment in the area of the Eastern Townships where the asbestos deposits were found. The process of consolidation continued, culminating in the formation of the Asbestos Corporation from eleven separate companies in 1925.

But Quebec's most important natural resource is its rivers and waterfalls, and much of the industrial development of the province has been shaped by the hydroelectric power that could be generated from them. Quebec encouraged the growth of private hydroelectric companies, and until 1907 private entrepreneurs could buy power sites in Quebec outright. As early as 1895 A. Carignan and H. Mailhot of Trois-Rivières were prepared to buy Shawinigan Falls for $10,000, but before the deal was final a new Liberal government had come to power in Quebec City. The Liberals set much stiffer terms for the sale of the falls: a price of at least $50,000, and a commitment to spend at least $4 million within two-and-a-half years, to pay $200,000 in wages, and to produce electric power within twenty months. These terms were out of the reach of Carignan and Mailhot or any other local entrepreneurs, and the way was open for John Joyce and T.E. Aldred and their Boston group. With some important Montreal allies, this group raised the necessary capital and began construction in 1899, and successfully transmitted electric power to Montreal, 150 kilometres away, in 1903. They also developed a local industrial market for both water power and electricity, and major aluminum, chemical, and pulp and paper plants came to the new town of Shawinigan in the first decade of the twentieth century.

Industrial development was closely tied to the development of hydroelectric power sites elsewhere as well. In the Eastern Townships, the Southern Canada Power Company encouraged the growth of industries based on cheap and plentiful labour, both to develop an industrial market for its electricity and to enhance its residential market. Between 1920 and 1939 an estimated 137 new firms, many of them U.S. branch plants, located in the company's territory; textiles, woodworking, metalworking, and boots and shoes were the main industries represented. In the Ottawa valley, the Gatineau Power Company was established as a subsidiary of the U.S.-owned International Paper Company in 1926, primarily to serve its new paper mill in Gatineau and to sell power to Ontario. The hydroelectric resources of the Saguenay were first developed by U.S. tobacco magnate James Duke in alliance with Sir William Price, a representative of the family that had dominated the region's forest industries since the middle of the nineteenth century. In 1925 the Duke-Price Power Company was acquired by the Aluminum Company of America which used it as the basis for a huge new aluminum smelter.

Among Quebec's new industries none was so closely linked to hydroelectric development as the reduction of aluminum, which required large quantities of electric power. When Shawinigan Water and Power opened for business its first customer was Northern Aluminum, a subsidiary of U.S. banker Andrew Mellon's Pittsburgh Reduction Co. Out of the Pittsburgh Reduction – Northern Aluminum complex grew two of the great aluminum multinationals, the Aluminum Company of America (Alcoa) and the Aluminum Company of Canada (Alcan). The two were separated in the 1920s after the completion of the great smelter at Arvida on the Saguenay, but Alcan remained the property of the owners of Alcoa for another thirty years.

Bauxite for the aluminum industry had to be imported from tropical countries. Wood for the pulp and paper industry, however, was available right in Quebec, and the presence of hydraulic and later electric power was just another spur to the industry's growth. A third factor was government policy in both Canada and the United States. Federal and provincial governments in Canada adopted measures to discourage the export of raw timber and thus encourage U.S. capitalists to process Canadian pulpwood in Canada; in Quebec this took the form of an outright ban on raw timber exports after 1910.

Pressure from the newspaper publishers, an increasingly influential lobby, resulted in a removal of all U.S. tariffs on Canadian newsprint in 1913, and low wage rates were yet another inducement to produce in Quebec. A common labourer in the newsprint industry in Quebec earned an average of thirty-one cents an hour in 1923, as compared with thirty-nine cents in New York State and Maine, forty cents in Ontario and the Great Lakes states, and forty-six cents on the Pacific coast. The result was that most of the headlong expansion of the north U.S. newsprint industry in the 1910s and 1920s was concentrated in Canada, and especially in Quebec, and by 1929 fifty-seven per cent of the newsprint available for consumption in the United States was imported from Canada.

In Quebec the company that led the way in this expansion was U.S.-owned International Paper. In addition to its mills at Gatineau it had another at Trois-Rivières which, with the completion of additional facilities in 1926, became the largest newsprint mill in the world. At Grand Mère, on the St. Maurice a few kilometres above Shawinigan, U.S. capital was involved in a pulp mill in alliance with a Scottish Montrealer named John Forman as early as 1887. Another U.S. group came in, squeezed out Forman, and added a paper mill to the complex by 1900. Still farther up the St. Maurice at La Tuque, a pulp mill was built by the Brown family, which had a paper mill at the largely Franco-American town of Berlin, New Hampshire. The La

Tuque mill opened in 1910, shipping most of its pulp to Berlin for further processing. As the industry grew, few French Canadian entrepreneurs were able to compete with the U.S. giants. An exception was Alfred Dubuc, who established a successful pulp mill at Chicoutimi on the Saguenay, but even Dubuc could not do without U.S. capital forever, and he merged his enterprise with two U.S. companies in 1915.

In the early years of the century there seemed little danger that industry would ever challenge the traditional basis of Quebec's economy. What industry could be had was welcomed by most sectors of society; the government encouraged industrial growth to provide jobs and was generous to a fault toward foreign entrepreneurs. Quebec nationalists devoted little attention to economic matters. Henri Bourassa, the giant among the nationalist leaders of the era, was far more concerned with constitutional and religious developments. Even Errol Bouchette, who believed industrialization could secure the economic independence of French Canada and feared the effects of U.S. control, argued that industry could be built up without destroying the primacy of agriculture.

After the First World War, however, the direction and magnitude of economic change in Quebec were both clear and, to many people, disturbing. The 1921 census was a death-knell for the agricultural vocation of French Canada. While nearly forty per cent of the labour force had worked in agriculture in 1901, less than thirty per cent did so by 1921. The same census revealed that Quebec had become a largely urban society: fifty-six per cent of its population lived in urban areas compared to forty-eight per cent in 1911 and only forty per cent in 1901. At the same time the ills that industrialization was designed to cure continued to plague the province. Quebec underwent a short, sharp depression in the early 1920s, and large-scale emigration continued throughout the decade; it finally came to an end in the 1930s as a result not of economic growth in Quebec but of economic crisis in the United States.

For the Liberal government of Louis-Alexandre Taschereau, if industrialization and U.S. capital weren't having the desired results it was only because there weren't enough of them. Lip-service was still paid to agriculture and colonization, but government policy in the 1920s was, as before, directed toward bringing in foreign investment, and some of the more spectacular incursions of U.S. capital, like the hydroelectric and pulp and paper complex on the Gatineau and the aluminum smelter at Arvida, occurred in this decade. "I prefer importing American dollars," said Premier Taschereau on more than one occasion, "to exporting Canadian workers."

This approach found favour with most Quebec voters, who kept

Taschereau in power with convincing majorities, but their enthusiasm was not shared by nationalist intellectuals for whom economic issues had begun to acquire a new importance. "The national question," wrote Edouard Montpetit, a trained economist and one of the most clearheaded of the nationalist thinkers of the time, "has become an economic question." This equation summed up the priorities of many post – First World War nationalists, especially those grouped around *L'Action Française* in which Montpetit sounded his warning. This journal and the group that put it out borrowed their name from the fascist organization in France headed by Charles Maurras, but they borrowed Maurras's ideas only up to a point. Like the Action Française in France, they were authoritarian-minded, antidemocratic, anti-Semitic, and oriented toward the past; but they were not faced with the task of reversing the French Revolution, of which only faint sympathetic vibrations had reached Quebec. The ideology of the Quebec Action Française was free of some of the harsher aspects of Maurrassian doctrine, and it represented a certain continuity with the dominant conservative nationalist thought of post-1837 Quebec. Since this thought was largely based on the vision of Quebec as a predominantly rural and agricultural society, the dramatic economic changes of the early twentieth century represented a serious challenge to it.

There were several levels on which nationalists could criticize government economic policy and the industrialization it engendered. On the simplest level, they could criticize the government's unstinting generosity toward foreign capitalists and suggest that Quebec could at least get a better deal. On another level, they could argue that profits from the exploitation of Quebec's resources, human and natural, should stay in Quebec: that while industry was not in itself a bad thing its ownership by foreigners was. On a third level they could oppose the importation of values inimical to Quebec's traditions and priorities. Finally they could say that industrialization was evil in itself, and that Quebec policy should be directed not toward encouraging it but toward stopping or at least severely limiting it.

All these ideas were, in some measure, contained in the nationalist thinking of the 1920s. Abbé Lionel Groulx, the editor of *L'Action Française*, wrote in 1927,

> We accept foreign capital, but we accept it as an associate and a temporary assistance, not as a master and a despot.

Writing in *L'Action Française* in 1921, Olivar Asselin said:

If the intensive industrialization of Quebec doesn't suit us, it is only to the extent that is presupposes the loss of our last remaining natural resources to foreigners.

But industrialization brought with it urbanization, and that entailed such ills as movies and the yellow press. Abbé Groulx considered movies "an instrument of degradation" and a "vast school of demoralization". And many writers in *L'Action Française* kept alive the old vision of Quebec as a predominantly rural society. L.-O. David wrote in 1917:

The settler and the farmer have been the major artisans of our national destiny. More than ever we must count on them to ensure our happiness, our prosperity, and our influence in Confederation.

The economic events of the early twentieth century were a turning point in Quebec's development, and Quebec's response to them has therefore been of much interest to later observers. Antinationalists wishing to demonstrate the irrelevance of traditional Quebec thinking have pointed to the romantic and backward-looking aspects of the nationalist writing of the 1920s; more recent nationalist thinkers point to their farsighted critique of foreign investment. Probably the most important exponent of the first viewpoint has been Pierre Elliott Trudeau, who wrote in 1956 that French Canadian nationalists have "shown hostility to all change (even progress) coming from without" and quoted the Book of Ecclesiastes as "the finest comment on our social ideas in general" in the first half of the twentieth century: "Vanity of vanities, all is vanity." The second viewpoint is represented by the nationalist economist François-Albert Angers, who said in a 1969 essay:

Those who have put forward the "agriculturalist" hypothesis to explain the economic problems of our nationality and have accused traditional nationalists of being responsible for it, have formulated a gratuitous hypothesis, one that is not founded on the facts, and that serious history will never ratify.

There is much to be said in favour of the nationalist thinkers. It is difficult for an unbiased observer to interpret their ideology as primarily attacking industrialization as such, and in their awareness of the potential dangers of foreign investment they anticipated a line of thinking that would find wide acceptance some two generations later. Moreover, the social disruption that accompanied industrialization was real enough to give "agriculturalism" an appeal that was by no means confined to Quebec: Progressives in western Canada glorified agriculture, and there were "agriculturalist" elements in the liberal Catholicism prevalent in the United States. Closed-minded and narrow as the Quebec nationalists may have been in their rejection of modern culture, there is nevertheless lasting value in their insistence that material goals are not ultimate goals and that attention should be paid to moral issues. But the tide the nationalists were trying to hold back proved too strong for them. Even when they supported industrial growth, asking only that it take place under French-Canadian control, the nationalists acknowledged that the means for this did not yet exist and that limiting foreign investment would mean postponing industrialization.

> The day when our race has the technical knowledge, the administrative experience and the necessary capital to succeed in large-scale industry, it shouldn't hesitate to engage in it,

wrote Olivar Asselin, but that day had not yet come. Henri Bourassa, writing in 1923, was even blunter:

> It is better to stay poor longer, and free, than to get rich in giving up the best part of one's *patrimoine*.

Staying poor but free is not a decision that peoples generally make voluntarily. It was not the decision that French Canadians made in the 1920s.

5

Old Structures and New Realities

1929-1960

As QUEBEC WAS enveloped by the international economic catastrophe that began with the Wall Street crash of 1929, the ideas of its agriculturalists suddenly seemed worthy of new respect. Their worst fears about industrialization and the economic dependence of Quebec on the rest of North America had evidently been realized, while the optimistic visions of the industrial promoters had been shown to be without foundation. Enterprises established a few years earlier with such high hopes fell on rocky times and their closing brought unemployment and hardship to many. The pulp and paper industry, seriously overcapitalized in the twenties, suffered a particularly devastating blow.

The principal response to the Depression from French Canada's social theorists was the *retour à la terre* — the return to the land. Esdras Minville told a royal commission in 1939:

> The present economic instability is rooted in the desertion of the countryside
> and the extreme congestion of the cities, particularly Montreal.

Other nationalist thinkers, including Henri Bourassa, expressed similar views. The provincial government increased its efforts to promote colonization and the number of occupied farms grew by fourteen per cent during the 1930s, but unfortunately the best agricultural lands had almost all been taken when the *retour à la terre* began. Many of the new colonists were sent to the rocky Abitibi, the less fertile parts of the Gaspé, and other unsuitable areas where their efforts to scratch a living out of the ungenerous soil ended badly.

The Depression also shook the seemingly permanent Liberal domination of provincial politics, as it shook incumbent governments everywhere. In the provincial election of 1931 the Liberals retained seventy-nine of the ninety seats in the Legislative Assembly, but the opposition Conservatives won an ominous forty-four per cent of the popular vote. Three years later a group of dissident Liberals, a disparate collection of progressives, nationalists, corporatists, opponents of the electricity trust, and others dissatisfied with the regime, broke away and formed their own movement, the Action Libérale Nationale. This group and the Conservatives formed an electoral alliance, the Union Nationale, to contest the 1935 election and won forty-two seats. Sensing the imminence of power, the crafty Conservative leader Maurice Duplessis moved to press his advantage against the crumbling Liberals and to establish firm control over the Union Nationale. Revelations of corruption, carefully stage-managed by Duplessis in the public accounts committee of the legislature, forced Premier Taschereau's resignation in 1936. His successor, Adélard Godbout, immediately called an election, and Duplessis and the Union Nationale swept to power.

The new premier was from a traditional milieu. He was born in 1890 in Yamachiche, a village near Trois-Rivières, the same village that produced another politician of extraordinary skill, Governor Aram Pothier of Rhode Island. His father, Nerée Duplessis, was a lawyer and Conservative politician and a disciple of the ultramontane Bishop Laflèche. Maurice grew up in Trois-Rivières, received a seminary education, and followed in his father's footsteps. He was first elected to the Assembly as member for Trois-Rivières in 1927; he became Conservative leader within six years and premier within nine, and the circumstances of his coming to power and the breadth of the coalition he led created diverse and extravagant hopes for his administration.

The Quebec over which Duplessis presided for eighteen of the next twenty-three years continued to be a society between two worlds. It still contained many traditional elements, but even these elements were not unaffected by the imminence of change and influences from the outside world. Sociologist Horace Miner of the University of Michigan, who in 1936–37 spent a year in St. Denis de Kamouraska, downriver from Quebec City, in search of the "old rural French-Canadian folk culture in its least-altered existent form", was forced to conclude that:

> In every phase of life in St. Denis one finds cultural changes which have come about in the last one or two generations. Every society becomes altered through the years, but rural French Canadian culture has changed more in the last forty years than it did in the preceding century.

In more urban settings, change was not only part of life, it was central to it.[41]

After the Depression the last attempts to promote colonization as the cure for Quebec's economic ills gradually died away. The ministry of colonization remained in existence to the end of the Duplessis period but its useful days were behind it. The Second World War brought on a new wave of industrialization, and the number of wage-earners in Quebec more than doubled between 1939 and 1943. With massive loans from the Allied governments, the Aluminum Company of Canada expanded its capacity by a factor of five, undertaking new construction at Arvida, Shawinigan and other locations in the province. Industries such as chemicals and aircraft grew to a significant size for the first time. After the war the process continued and the industrial economy penetrated to previously untouched parts of Quebec, including the vast northern wilderness of the Ungava region.

Duplessis was able to survive all these changes because he himself embodied many of the contradictions of the society he governed. Despite the economic and social transformation it was experiencing, Quebec exhibited a remarkable political stability, especially after Duplessis returned to power in 1944 following a term in opposition. The premier's authoritarian and highly personal rule became one of the constants of the society. He by no means fulfilled all the hopes that he had aroused in 1936: progressives in particular were rapidly disillusioned, and Duplessis and his allies from the Action Libérale Nationale soon parted company, but he did manage to keep together a remarkably diverse alliance—conservatives, nationalists, priests, farmers, French-speaking professionals, and English-Canadian and U.S. business people—and to have something to offer all of his supporters.

In many ways he appeared to be the voice of traditional Quebec. He upheld the privileges of the church in the fields of education and health, and he constantly accused the opposition Liberals of plotting to set up a provincial department of education if they came to power—that is, to put education under secular control. He sponsored measures favouring farmers, ranging from agricultural credit and rural electrification to the banning of margarine (this last measure was so popular that the Liberals criticized it only for being carelessly enforced). His nationalism was expressed through strong stands in favour of Quebec's autonomy and against the encroachment of the federal government, a concern inherited from Honoré Mercier, and by providing Quebec with national symbols, notably its *fleur-de-lys* flag. He was a fiscal conservative, wary of state intervention, and stridently anticommunist: not even Joe McCarthy attempted to emulate the Padlock Law by which a home or office could be padlocked if it was being used to promote communism—or was deemed to be so by the attorney-general, a portfolio Duplessis retained for himself.

But even as Duplessis upheld the values of Quebec's traditional society he was steadily undermining the material basis of that society. Conrad Black said in his biography of Duplessis:

> Under him Quebec ceased to be a backward place in every respect except, perhaps, political methodology.

Black points out that church control of education and health was prolonged but the church became more and more dependent on public money in these areas, making eventual secularization virtually inevitable; and Duplessis's measures to aid farmers had the effect of tying them more closely to a larger economy beyond their control and chipping away at their fabled self-sufficiency.

Business people, both domestic and foreign, found in Duplessis as good a friend as they could want. He was on excellent terms with J.M. McConnell, reigning king of the English Montreal business community; Colonel R.R. McCormick, head of the Chicago *Tribune* empire; R.E. (Rip) Powell, president of Alcan, and many others. Another admirer was Lord Beaverbrook, whose London *Evening Standard* praised Duplessis as "the most remarkable Prime Minister [sic] in the Empire." With some business people, such as McConnell, the relationship went beyond common interest to mutual understanding. Duplessis appreciated power and therefore felt comfortable with these powerful individuals, while the business people were soothed by the thought that, with Duplessis in charge, an alien, complicated, and potentially troublesome province was in safe hands. The payoffs for Duplessis from these relationships were immense, and included side benefits ranging from the unwavering support of the two large Montreal English dailies, the *Star* (owned by McConnell) and the *Gazette* (owned by another of Duplessis's close friends, John Bassett), to seats in the owner's box at Duplessis's favourite sports spectacle, the World Series.

Many spectacular industrial schemes were undertaken during Duplessis's premiership, but none was more significant than the opening of northern Quebec to U.S. capital. The penetration of the north began in 1938 with the building of a paper mill and its town of Baie Comeau on the north shore of the St. Lawrence four hundred kilometres down river from Quebec City, all owned by Colonel McCormick. This was accomplished largely through the good offices of the Bishop of the Gulf of St. Lawrence, Monsignor Napoléon Labrie. Among the employees of the mill was an electrician named Benedict Mulroney, whose son Brian would sing Irish ditties for Colonel McCormick during the colonel's summer visits: indeed life in a company town built by paternalistic U.S. capital would help to shape young Brian's vision of the world.

But Baie Comeau was only a prelude to an even vaster and more complex project: the development of the iron ore resources of the Labrador Trough, in an area straddling the jurisdictions of Quebec and Newfoundland, hundreds of kilometres from useful transport facilities. Despite the difficulties involved in their exploitation, these resources began to attract the serious attention of U.S. steel manufacturers in the 1940s when the high-grade ore of the Mesabi Range near Lake Superior, until then their main source of supply, showed signs of exhaustion. Immediately upon his return to power in 1944 Duplessis received a letter from the Canadian-born Cleveland steel magnate Cyrus Eaton, proposing not only iron ore development but also the use of electric power to develop a steel industry in Quebec. Since the proposal involved nationalization of Quebec's existing private power-generating companies, which Duplessis opposed, it was never implemented. No steel mill would be built in Quebec during the Duplessis years, although the iron-mining part of the project was revived after the war.[42] By the mid-1950s the U.S.-owned Iron Ore Company of Canada (whose future presidents would include Brian Mulroney) had a mine and company town, Schefferville, on the Quebec–Newfoundland border, a terminal at what had until then been the sleepy village of Sept-Iles on the Gulf of St. Lawrence, and a 580-kilometre railway linking the two sites. The total investment ran to hundreds of millions of dollars.

The deal between the company and the Quebec government was a matter of some controversy, and became a major issue in the 1952 provincial election. Liberal opposition leader Georges-Émile Lapalme claimed that the Iron Ore Company's payments to the province represented "one cent a ton" of iron ore extracted, and went so far as to suggest that Iran, which under Prime Minister Mohammed Mossadegh was then challenging the hegemony of the multinational oil companies, might prove a useful model for Quebec.[43] An important side effect of the Iron Ore deal was a major upgrading of the transportation connections between Quebec and the United States. Proposals for the canalization of the St. Lawrence River between the head of navigation at Montreal and Lake Ontario had been under discussion since the early years of the century, but since such a project required an international agreement as well as a huge investment these proposals had never been able to overcome the various political and economic objections to them. Among the most consistent centres of opposition had been Quebec, which feared the effects of a St. Lawrence seaway on the port of Montreal, and one of the most vehement critics of seaway proposals was Maurice Duplessis. The prospect of exporting Quebec iron ore to the United States changed the equation. Quebec, firmly behind the Iron Ore deal, dropped its opposition to the seaway. Even more important was the addition to the pro-seaway forces of the powerful steel lobby in the United States. Congress approved the seaway in 1954, and it was completed five years later at a cost to the two countries of almost half a billion dollars.[44]

Perhaps the most modern aspect of Duplessis's Quebec was the opposition engendered by the premier's firm and somewhat arbitrary rule. Parts of this opposition bore some resemblance to earlier groups of French-Canadian social thinkers who had spun theories, published journals with small circulations, and had an uncertain and at best indirect effect on the society they were trying to influence. Some of the more prominent members of the anti-Duplessis opposition were to be found in the same circles that had produced these earlier movements: the élite newspapers, the universities, the professions, and certain sectors of the church; but these new journalists, intellectuals, professionals, and clerics differed from their predecessors in two fundamental respects — in the nature of the ideas they espoused, and in their relationship with the labour movement which now gave them the beginnings of a mass base. Despite the presence of clerics in their ranks their ideas were essentially secular; and although there were many nationalists among them, nationalism was not their unifying force. They tended to be open to ideas from outside Quebec and outside the church, to be liberal or social democratic in their political thought, and to accept industrialization without necessarily accepting the dictates of powerful industrialists. In short, Quebec was developing a social and intellectual movement more appropriate to what it was becoming than to what it had been. Pierre Elliott Trudeau, who had studied at Harvard and the Sorbonne and travelled around the world, represented the wider horizons of the new generation, and so did a rising young journalist who saw the Second World War as a propagandist for the U.S.A. and who went to Korea as a war correspondent for Radio-Canada, René Lévesque.

Trudeau wrote in 1956:

At the present conjuncture of events in Quebec... we are clearly aware of the
fact that the only powerful medium of renewal is industrialization; we are also
aware that this medium will not provide us with liberty and justice unless it is
subject to the forces of an enlightened and powerful trade union movement.[45]

In that context, the union movement became the rallying point for the forces
of opposition to Duplessis. The labour movement was by no means new in
Quebec: as in the rest of North America it had been around since the
nineteenth century, but its evolution differed in important ways from that of
the movement elsewhere on the continent, and after the Second World War
its very peculiarities helped to put it in a position to catalyse and focus the
progressive forces developing in Quebec.

Part of the Quebec labour movement consisted of international unions
with their headquarters in the United States and a smaller number of
Canadian unions with headquarters elsewhere in Canada. While the Quebec sections of these unions might enjoy a certain amount of autonomy, they
generally accepted the overall philosophy of the North American union
movement: this was by no means Marxist or revolutionary, but it envisaged a
challenge to established authority by working men and women through
collective, and if necessary militant, action on their part to achieve their
aims.

It was inevitable that such a philosophy would soon arouse the opposition
of the Roman Catholic Church in Quebec: as we have seen, in the 1880s
Cardinal Taschereau attempted to suppress the Knights of Labor, an early
manifestation of North American trade unionism. Quebec affiliates of the
American Federation of Labor and the Congress of Industrial Organizations
were no more pleasing to the church hierarchy, but it used a subtler strategy
to combat them. The church organized its own unions, which by 1921 had
grown big enough to form their own labour federation, the Canadian and
Catholic Confederation of Labour. This was a somewhat delayed implemen-
tation by the Quebec hierarchy of the social doctrine of the church, first
propounded in 1891, according to which workers had the right to organize
but were encouraged to organize in unions of which only Catholics were
members, and in which ideas of class collaboration rather than class conflict
held sway.

In Quebec before the Second World War the Catholic unions fitted in
well with the prevailing ideologies: their openness to co-operation with
management was exemplary according to the corporatist social thinking
popular at the time, and their opposition to affiliation with U.S. unions

endeared them to nationalists. In their early years the Catholic unions saw international unions rather than management as their main enemy, eschewed the strike weapon, and often played the role of company unions by replacing or forestalling international unions that might act more militantly in defence of the employees' interests. In the tumultuous late 1930s and early 1940s, however, membership losses led the Catholic unions to adopt many of the ideas and methods of the internationals: they fought and won a strike at Alcan in 1941 and participated in the Montreal municipal workers' strikes of 1943–44. Moreover, progressive tendencies were developing within the church itself under the guidance of liberal clerics such as Father Georges-Henri Lévesque, dean of the new faculty of social sciences at Laval University in Quebec City, and Monsignor Joseph Charbonneau, archbishop of Montreal. The leadership of the Canadian and Catholic Confederation of Labour was changing too: it became anything but a tool of the companies.

By 1948 the forces of change in Quebec were beginning to crystallize; "the worm-eaten remnants of a bygone age," in Trudeau's words, "were beginning to come apart." A group of artists issued the *Refus global*, their "complete refusal" to accept the traditional constraints on thought and action in Quebec. The labour movement fought energetically, and for the moment successfully, against the Duplessis government's labour code which would have banned the closed shop, limited the right to strike, and authorized the attorney-general to withdraw the certification of unions that had "Communists or Marxists" on their executives.

But all this was to be overshadowed by a conflict taking shape in the asbestos-mining region of the Eastern Townships. Early in 1949 negotiations over wages and job safety between a Catholic-affiliated union and the Canadian subsidiary of the U.S.-based Johns-Manville Company at the town of Asbestos were broken off. A month later union organizer Jean Marchand told a meeting of workers at Asbestos that the union had a choice between arbitration, where it was unlikely to get a fair hearing, and an illegal strike. The workers voted unanimously to strike, and employees of other asbestos-mining companies quickly followed their lead.[46]

A few days after the strike began Duplessis sent the provincial police into Asbestos to keep order. Since they were hardly even-handed enforcers of the law—even observers favourable to Duplessis reported "abuses" and "excessive" acts—this intervention changed the nature of the conflict: the provincial government had become involved on the company side, on the side of a U.S. corporation against a Quebec union. The police became even more provocative by protecting strikebreakers sent in by Johns-Manville to reopen the mine, and this led to frequent incidents of violence and numerous arrests.

The developing anti-Duplessis coalition mobilized in support of the strikers. The crusading newspaper *Le Devoir*, then owned by the Montreal archdiocese, sent reporter Gérard Pelletier to the strike area; his friend Pierre Trudeau, back from his world tour, came as a freelance agitator. A young nationalist lawyer, Jean Drapeau, represented the strikers in court. Rival labour federations rallied to the support of the strike. Father Lévesque was in frequent communication with the strike leaders, and Archbishop Charbonneau said in a May Day sermon in Notre Dame Basilica in Montreal that:

> The working class is a victim of a conspiracy which seeks to crush it, and when there is a conspiracy to crush the working class, the church has a duty to intervene.

Eventually the dispute went to arbitration (the arbitration award had to be modified before the unions would accept it), but the struggle between Duplessis and his opponents continued. Conservative elements in the church, with Duplessis's backing, launched a campaign in Rome against Monsignor Charbonneau and he resigned in 1950. Trudeau and Pelletier started a journal, *Cité Libre*, that provided a forum for anti-Duplessis intellectuals. Jean Drapeau was elected mayor of Montreal in 1954, but Duplessis put up a candidate against him at the next election three years later and, with questionable electoral methods, secured his defeat.

On September 2, 1959, accompanied by members of his caucus and officials of the Iron Ore Company of Canada, Duplessis paid a visit to Schefferville. It was billed as a fishing trip but there was speculation that the business people and politicians might also be discussing a new power deal for Iron Ore's mining operations. Soon after their arrival Duplessis collapsed with a cerebral hemorrhage; he died on Labour Day, and Schefferville town lore has it that he might have been saved if the town had had the hospital which Duplessis had refused to build when Schefferville's citizens refused to vote for the Union Nationale. Paul Sauvé, the minister of youth and social welfare and the most independent-minded member of Duplessis's cabinet (it was said that Duplessis had three categories of ministers: those who said "yes, Chief", those who said "yes, Maurice", and Paul Sauvé) succeeded to the premiership. In his inaugural speech Sauvé pronounced the portentous word "désormais"—henceforth. Henceforth things would change. Indeed they would, but under premiers other than Sauvé, who suffered a fatal heart attack after only three months in office.

LITTLE CANADA TO PEYTON PLACE

In the Franco-American archipelago, as in Quebec, the old assumptions and the traditional culture were on increasingly shaky ground and, as in Quebec, economic changes were at the root of the new questions and patterns of thinking; however the mill towns of New England were not contending with industrialization but with the departure of the industry that had been their reason for existence. The decline of the New England textile industry, which had begun early in the century, was well under way in the 1920s and was virtually completed in the Depression. In 1927 alone $60 million of New England's cotton capital headed for the more attractive — from an employer's viewpoint — territory of the South.

There were various reasons for this migration, but probably the most important was the growing unwillingness of New England textile workers to accept the paternalistic direction of the mill owners. By the beginning of the twentieth century discontent was rife even in places where paternalism had worked best in the early years, such as Lowell and Lawrence. Largely ignored by the craft unionists of the American Federation of Labor, the textile workers of these towns were natural recruits for the militant Industrial Workers of the World. In 1912 the IWW led successful strikes in both Lowell and Lawrence; the Lawrence conflict, highlighted by the clubbing of women and children by police in a railway station, became famous in the annals of U.S. unionism. Although the power of the IWW was short-lived, its achievements and its memory were lasting: the days of low wages and docile immigrant workers were clearly over.

Southern chambers of commerce advertised proximity to the cotton fields, cheap labour, U.S.-born but used to an existence no less circumscribed and difficult than that of most immigrants, and the open shop. The appeal of their campaigns to the mill owners of New England was evident. Places such as Fall River, where the cotton industry evaporated as quickly as it had been put together, Lowell, where eight of the "Big Eleven" textile mills had closed by 1940, and Manchester, where the giant Amoskeag company, once the largest textile operation in the world, went out of business in 1937, were forced to search for new industries to fill their acres of abandoned mill space. In Manchester the search met with some success, largely as a result of the efforts of a former mayor, Arthur Moreau. Some other towns had already developed a diversified industrial structure and were thus able to weather the new situation: one such was Southbridge, originally a textile centre, where textiles had for many years taken second place to the optical industry. But in many New England towns the departure of the mills was a disaster with which people were simply unable to cope. Thomas F. McMahon, president of the United Textile Workers of America, told writer Louis Adamic in 1930 that:

> There is, perhaps, more destitution and misery and degradation in the mill towns of New England today...than anywhere else in the United States.

The effects of economic change were already felt by the Franco-Americans in the early 1920s, when the first waves of mill departures helped produce the climate of uncertainty and fear in which the Sentinelle movement flourished. After 1930, reinforced by the disarray in which the defeat of the Sentinellistes left the Franco-American élite, these effects were felt with increasing force. Perhaps the most ominous development was the absence of new immigration: a flourishing textile industry had brought a continuous flow of immigrants across the border and encouraged close ties between the Franco-Americans and Quebec, but now, with the textile industry in sharp decline, the immigrants stopped coming and ties with Quebec began to loosen. The textile industry had also provided the economic base for the concentrations of Franco-American population in which the growth and survival of community institutions was possible; with the loss of that base at least some dispersion of the population and some weakening of the institutions was inevitable.

These changes were neither sudden nor complete. The Franco-Americans of the 1870s had moved from town to town in search of jobs, but in the 1930s they were settled in their communities; besides, there wasn't much work anywhere else either. A neighbourhood druggist in Lowell told Louis Adamic that the textile workers were

> stuck in Lowell. They probably own a little property or have some old parents who can't be moved. Some of those who were foot-loose back in 1928 and had a little money cleared out soon after the mills closed down for good. Some stayed, thinking the mills would open up again soon. They waited. Then it was too late for them to clear out. Now they're stuck.

The Franco-American communities thus tended to survive the erosion of the economic base that had created them, and all through the 1930s and succeeding decades there were continuing manifestations of Franco-American cultural vitality, resistance to assimilation, and attachment to Quebec. This was the period of maturity of the most distinguished Franco-American poet, Rosaire Dion-Lévesque; his most enduring work, a translation into a finely cadenced French of Walt Whitman's *Leaves of Grass*, was published in 1933.

> J'ai fait un rêve!
> J'ai vu une cité invincible aux attaques du monde;
> J'ai rêvé que cela était la Cité des Amis.
> Rien n'était supérieur, là, que la qualité de l'amour sain et robuste; ce sentiment conduisait tout.
> Il enveloppait chaque heure au cours des actions des hommes et des femmes de cette ville.
> Il se traduisait par leurs regards et par leurs mots.[47]

In 1937 four thousand Franco-Americans attended the second Congress of the French Language in Quebec City. As late as 1947, John Gunther could write in *Inside U.S.A.* that:

> Probably this unique minority group, almost unknown to the nation at large, is the most tenacious in the entire country.... The French Canadians now in this country almost never intermix; they hold with the utmost stubbornness and obstinacy to their own folklore, customs, language.

And another decade after that, Robert Rumilly, winding up his history of the Franco-Americans, found some black spots in the state of Franco-American *survivance*, but he also found reasons for hope and he concluded that the two more or less balanced each other.

Neither the defeat of the Sentinellistes nor the departure of the mills wiped out the Franco-Americans as a community, but both helped to weaken that community and left it with inadequate defences against the onslaught of Americanization that was to come. This new advance of Americanization was not a deliberate campaign like the one undertaken by the "hundred per cent Americans" during and after the First World War. It was less intentional, more insidious, and, in the end, more effective. By 1930 a series of technological and social changes that would engulf all but the most protected cultural islands had already begun. Radio, the movies (especially after they began to talk—in English), and eventually television were powerful new instruments of Americanization. The automobile facilitated communication, reduced distances, and brought previously isolated communities into the U.S. mainstream. The Second World War, in which

Franco-Americans participated wholeheartedly, brought young men from different cultural backgrounds together in the barracks and gave everyone a sense of working for a common cause.

In the postwar era the mass movement toward the suburbs depopulated the Jewish ghettoes, the Little Italys, and the Little Canadas of the central city cores. A home in the suburbs, a car, and a television set: redefined in these terms, the American Dream—less a dream, perhaps, than a shopping list—was available to more people than ever before, and most Franco-Americans wanted in on it. Interest in the struggle for *survivance* and energy to carry it on were attenuated. Questioning of the value of maintaining the French language and Franco-American cultural distinctness had previously come from the outside, but now it came from the Franco-Americans themselves. In 1930 a sixty-five-year-old Franco-American priest, Abbé Hormisdas Hamelin, published his explosive *Lettres à mon ami sur la Patrie, la langue et la question franco-américaine* (Letters to My Friend Concerning Country, Language and the Franco-American Question) in which he took Franco-Americans to task for trying to maintain their traditions, attacked the central thesis that the French language was a guardian of the Catholic faith, and concluded that "our great fault lies in foolishly opposing the laws of natural evolution by refusing to Americanize ourselves."

Abbé Hamelin's *Lettres* were a little premature, and were roundly condemned by leading Franco-Americans, but in the years that followed the actions of the mass of Franco-Americans provided much better support for Abbé Hamelin's theories than for those of his critics. The institutional structure that had provided the framework for Franco-American community life began to crumble. While the mutual benefit societies and most of the national parishes survived, it was in changed form, robbed of much of their original meaning. The cultural and national activities of the mutual benefit societies increasingly took a back seat to their insurance business, and the community leadership function they had once served became less and less significant. The national parishes, responding to the needs of younger parishioners, began to introduce Masses in English—first one each Sunday, then two, until eventually there were more Masses in English than in French.

The two other key institutions of *survivance*, the press and the schools, fared even worse. One by one, daily newspapers in the major Franco-American centres ceased publication, and now there were no new papers being founded to replace the ones that went under. *L'Avenir National* of Manchester, reduced to five issues a week, survived until 1950, while *L'Etoile* of Lowell went to thrice-weekly publication in 1943 and survived in that form to 1957. The last of the dailies, *L'Indépendant* of Fall River, finally gave up in 1963. There were still seven French-language weeklies in New England in 1960, but they showed few signs of continuing vitality. Only former Sentinelliste Wilfrid Beaulieu's *Le Travailleur* remained sure of its *raison d'être*. It was more a polemical tool than a newspaper in the strict sense: always ready for a fight, Beaulieu turned *Le Travailleur* into a virtual propaganda sheet for the Free French during the Second World War, when much of the Franco-American leadership was sympathetic to Vichy.

Rising costs and declining enrolment caught the parochial schools in a squeeze. A survey of thirty-three Franco-American schools in Massachusetts found that enrolment in twenty-four of them dropped between 1939 and 1956; two of the schools had closed by 1960 and nine more would close by 1971. In the schools that remained, less and less time was devoted to teaching in French: from half the day, to an hour a day, until in many schools French was taught only as an elective subject. Even the crowning institution in the Franco-American educational system, the Collège de l'Assomption in Worcester, underwent a transformation. In 1950 the Collège had only 182 students, while there were 125 Franco-American students at the Irish-run College of the Holy Cross in the same city. The need for change was evident, and the directors of the Collège moved quickly after a tornado destroyed its downtown campus in 1953. A new campus was built in the suburbs, students unfamiliar with French were admitted for the first time, and an increasing number of courses were taught in English. Twenty-five years later a Maison Française donated by the Union St. Jean Baptiste, an active French department, and a few courses in Canadian history were among the few reminders of the original purpose of Assumption College. In 1979 a new Institute of French and Franco-American Studies was established, an indication that at least something might remain.

The least perceptible change, but perhaps the most important one, was the drawing away from Quebec. Claire Quintal of Central Falls, later one of the leaders of the new generation of Franco-Americans, felt as a student in Montreal in the 1950s that she was in a foreign country and that the people who surrounded her were different and slightly behind the times. Ambitious and talented Franco-Americans tended more and more to seek fulfilment of their ambitions in a U.S. context rather than in a French Canadian or Franco-American one. But the cultural transformation of the Franco-Americans held more perils and fewer rewards than were accounted for in the mythology of the melting pot. Economic advance led most of them out of Little Canada but left them somewhat short of the snooty suburbs of Boston or New York; overwhelmingly, they remained in the working and lower middle classes.

There was, for instance, Urbain Ledoux, who was born in Ste. Hélène de Bagot, Quebec, in 1874 but soon afterward came to Maine with his parents, and who moved from a career in French-language journalism into the U.S. consular service, advancing from the consulate in Trois-Rivières to the one in Prague. In 1912 he returned to the United States as a journalist (in English this time) and lecturer, espousing the cause of world peace. But he soon found his true calling, as a champion of the unemployed, and led a demonstration in Boston that culminated in an "auction sale" of young unemployed men, stripped to the waist, on Boston Common. This did not make him popular among the better classes in Boston and so he moved on to New York where, in 1921, he bought meals for groups of unemployed veterans; since he refused to tell them his name, one of them dubbed him Mister Zero, a name that stuck. In 1922 he led a march of unemployed from New York to Washington and was received by President Harding; on another occasion he picketed the world disarmament conference, claiming to be "searching for a true Christian among the delegates." But Mister Zero became best known for The Tub, his basement cafeteria in New York where for a penny—eventually upped to a nickel—meals were served to those whom prosperity had passed by in the 1920s and to the victims of the Depression in the 1930s. He died in 1941, but The Tub survived him.

Or Father Armand Morissette, "Father Spike", a short, rotund priest whose varied interests and activities took him far beyond the modest Lowell rectory where he still lived in the late 1980s. Contrariness and rambunctiousness in early childhood developed into an irresistible sense of humour, a capacity for self-promotion, and a spirit of nonconformity as an adult, and Father Spike came to hold very unpriestlike views on such matters as abortion and mixed marriage. He remained more comfortable in French than in English, a partisan of French and Franco-American patriotic causes, and a holder of at least some traditional Franco-American attitudes ("the Irish are good at cheap authority, anything with a uniform—they make good policemen and good bishops"). He also began to move easily in the world of U.S. bluebloods and celebrities. He became a friend of the Lodge family, the pinnacle of Massachusetts Protestant aristocracy, and especially of Ambassador Henry Cabot Lodge (grandson of the nativist senator), but equally friendly with their Catholic rivals, the Kennedys. Presidents Eisenhower and Kennedy called on his services as an interpreter. An inveterate joiner, he became associated with a wide variety of organizations and causes, and was perhaps best known as the chaplain of French sailors in the U.S.A. and as co-chair of Americans for Expo 67, the International Exposition in Montreal (the other co-chair, until his death, was Walt Disney).

And then there was Grace de Repentigny, from a not particularly happy

home in Manchester, married at seventeen to George Metalious, whose
high-school dates with Grace had aroused the ire of her mother because he
was Greek. Grace had a baby, George was drafted into the army and fought
in the Second World War, and when he got back they both got jobs in the
mills. But they were ambitious: George went to the University of New
Hampshire and became a teacher, and Grace, with three children now, wrote
novels. In 1955 she finally sold one of her manuscripts, and it was published
a year later. It was called *Peyton Place*.

Written in prose that could most charitably be described as pedestrian,
Peyton Place portrayed and commented on small-town New England's social
structure and code of behaviour, which Grace Metalious knew from the
underside and had never escaped. It was billed as "the explosive best seller
that lifts the lid off a respectable New England town" and its subject turned
out in the telling to involve lots of sex; mostly as a result of this feature, *Peyton
Place* outsold all previous U.S. novels. Hollywood turned *Peyton Place* into a
movie and later into a highly lucrative television series dry-cleaned of both
sex and social criticism. Hollywood also turned Grace Metalious into a
wreck. An unauthorized sequel, *Return to Peyton Place*, was a "novelization" of
a movie script, and she called a press conference to denounce it. She
divorced George Metalious, married a New Hampshire disc jockey, divorced
him and married George again. She wrote another novel, *No Adam in Eden*,
recapitulating some of the themes of *Peyton Place* but set even closer to
home, focusing on a twisted and loveless Franco-American family and
containing snippets of dialogue in New England French. She drank heavily,
and in 1964 she died, not yet forty, a few months before *Peyton Place* went on
prime-time TV. Her estate, at first estimated at more than a million dollars,
eventually turned out to consist of a debt of $170,000 to the United States
Internal Revenue Service.

AMERICANIZATION ON THE BAYOUS

The forces that transformed the islands of the Franco-American archipelago
were also bringing change to an even more isolated corner of French America. John Gunther, who was so impressed by the tenacity of the French
Canadians of New England, nevertheless found that:

> this tenacity is as nothing compared to that of the French Canadians in
> Louisiana. Some parishes (the term county is not used) hardly seem to be part
> of the United States.

But when Gunther wrote these words the process of Americanization in the Louisiana bayou country was already well under way.

The state of Louisiana, admitted to the Union in 1812, consisted of the southernmost part of the Louisiana Territory purchased nine years earlier, the rest being largely unpopulated. In subsequent years the state followed the familiar southern pattern of King Cotton, slavery, planter aristocracy, secession, Civil War, and Reconstruction, but with variations that were peculiar to Louisiana. It had in New Orleans the only genuine urban area in the South: a cosmopolitan city, a point of attraction for immigrants, a port that gave it access to Europe, the Caribbean, and Latin America as well as to the rest of the United States, and a wide-open haven for gambling, prostitution, violence, and municipal corruption unparalleled elsewhere in the country. Louisiana was also unique in its continuing cultural pluralism, for in addition to "Americans" there were Creoles, centred in New Orleans; Cajuns, whose domain stretched westward along the bayous from the Mississippi and spilled over the Sabine River into eastern Texas; Creolized Germans; a pocket of Filipinos; Irish, Jewish, German, and other immigrants; and blacks, both English- and French-speaking. It was of course the French-speaking Louisianians who contributed most to the state's distinctiveness. Both Creoles and Cajuns played their separate parts in this, and each had its own importance.

The Creoles made up a large part of the state's political élite (there was also a Cajun political élite, but it was neither as large nor as powerful) and thus were instrumental in securing a high degree of official bilingualism in nineteenth-century Louisiana, especially in the period immediately preceding the Civil War: the French text of Louisiana laws had equal status with the English, French was recognized as a language of instruction in the public schools and a language of debate in the legislature, and the state constitutions of 1845 and 1852 required that the secretary of the Senate and the clerk of the House of Representatives be bilingual.

The Republican carpetbaggers who ruled Louisiana after the Civil War eliminated these provisions—perhaps because French-speaking Louisianians had been among the most outspoken secessionists—and when the Democrats regained control of the state's political apparatus in 1877 official bilingualism was only partially restored, for by this time the use of French among the Creoles had begun to decline. The proportion of "Americans" in New Orleans had been growing steadily and, despite the Creoles' notorious haughtiness and disdain for "inferior races", the influence of the newcomers was eventually felt as railroads improved communication between New Orleans and the rest of the United States and the Creoles' historic ties with

France became comparatively less important. By the 1920s French had all but died out as a spoken language among the Creoles.

Among the Cajuns, on the other hand, language loyalty was of a sort that does not depend on constitutions, legislatures, or, for that matter, schools. Sheltered from the world outside their swampy homeland, the Cajuns hunted and fished, told stories, developed their own music and cuisine, and tried not to take things too seriously. To the few outsiders who came in contact with them they were exotic specimens indeed. Richard Taylor, a Confederate general and a son of U.S. President Zachary Taylor, described the Cajun soldiers in the Civil War:

> A home-loving, simple people, few spoke English, still fewer had ever before moved ten miles from their natal *cabanas*; and the war to them was "a liberal education". They had all the light gaiety of the Gaul and, after the manner of their ancestors, were born cocks. A capital regimental band accompanied them, and whenever weather and ground permitted, even after long marches, they would waltz and "polk" in couples with as much zest as if their arms encircled the supple waists of the Celestines and Melazies of their native Teche.[48]

Poverty, illiteracy, ignorance and disease made up the darker side of their carefree existence. In Evangeline and St. Martin parishes, in the heart of Cajun Louisiana, the illiteracy rate among native whites was forty-four per cent or more in 1920. After English had begun to make inroads it was said that to be a Cajun was to be illiterate in two languages. The conservative alliance of rich planters and New Orleans machine politicians that ruled the state in the half-century following Reconstruction did little to change the situation.

In 1901 oil was discovered near Jennings in Jefferson Davis parish in southwest Louisiana. The oil industry soon became the most important in the state, and Louisiana came to occupy second place to Texas in oil production and first place in the production of natural gas. From Jennings the oil industry spread to all parts of the state, from the Protestant north to the Gulf of Mexico. To the Cajun southwest, where it had started, the industry brought increasing numbers of English-speaking Americans, most of them from Texas, whom the Cajuns nicknamed *cous rouges* (red necks). It also brought new jobs—in an English-speaking environment. In the 1930s oil was discovered near Lafayette, the unofficial Cajun capital, and in the 1950s, with the construction of the Heymann Oil Center, Lafayette became the administrative headquarters of the industry for the whole state.

While oil transformed the economic face of Louisiana, the complex political equations that allowed the state to be run by a conservative élite remained unchanged, at least for a while. Because Louisiana has such an extraordinary array of distinct groups and because one of the few things they all share is a passion for politics, political mastery in the state has always depended on maintaining a delicate balance. In the 1920s the balance that had held for fifty years was upset by Huey Long, a man who stood out even in a state so richly endowed with creative and original practitioners of the political arts.

Parallels have been drawn between Huey P. Long of Louisiana and Maurice Duplessis of Quebec; it was a comparison used on the hustings by Duplessis's political opponents. There was indeed a similarity in the ruthlessness of the political machines they built, but there were also crucial differences: while Duplessis's politics were essentially backward-looking, Long's were not; while Duplessis tried to perpetuate old-style conservative rule in a society where it had outlived its usefulness, Long introduced modern services and amenities to a society where they were long overdue; and while the political structure built by Duplessis was destined to crumble almost immediately upon his death, the one built by Long survived him, and for decades after Huey died the distinction between Longs and anti-Longs continued to be the most important political division in the one-party state of Louisiana.

During the gubernatorial campaign of 1927–28 Huey Long stood under the famous Evangeline oak in St. Martinville and told his Cajun listeners:

> And it is here, under this oak, where Evangeline waited for her lover, Gabriel, who never came. This oak is an immortal spot, made so by Longfellow's poem, but Evangeline is not the only one who has waited here in disappointment. Where are the schools that you have waited for your children to have, that have never come? Where are the roads and the highways that you send your money to build, that are no nearer now than ever before? Where are the institutions to care for the sick and the disabled? Evangeline wept bitter tears in her disappointment, but it lasted only through one lifetime. Your tears in this country, around this oak, have lasted for generations. Give me the chance to dry the tears of those who still weep here.

Long had run for governor before, in 1924, and the Cajuns had not voted for him, but now they responded to his appeal. He carried the Cajun south with as heavy a majority as he won in his redneck north Louisiana stronghold, and a hostile vote in New Orleans, where the machine was bitterly opposed to him, was not enough to keep him out of office.

More than most politicians, Huey Long delivered on his promises. He increased the severance tax paid by the oil companies and other resource extraction interests and used the proceeds to provide free school books, making education more accessible to poor Louisianians. Free night classes were established for adult illiterates and more than a hundred thousand people enrolled. The state university was expanded and greatly improved in quality. Louisiana had little more than five hundred kilometres of paved road when Long became governor, but there were over six thouand kilometres at the time of his assassination in 1935, and instead of three major bridges in the highway system there were forty. The changes Long initiated were continued by his successors, notably his brother Earl, and even when anti-Longs reached the modern governor's mansion that Huey had built they found it impossible to undo his work.

For the Cajuns, Long's roads, schools, and other novelties meant the beginning of an end to their isolation. The Long program was intended to benefit the poor, and the Cajuns were the poorest Louisianians except for the blacks. But one of the effects of modernization was linguistic. Learning to read and write meant learning to read and write English. Going to school meant going to school in English. Roads meant greater contact with Americans who spoke English. The Second World War had a further acculturating effect, as it did for the Franco-Americans of New England, and unlike the New England Franco-Americans the Cajuns had no institutional structure to protect their culture from these influences: there were no French-language newspapers, no national societies. As the knowledge of English increased among the Cajuns the knowledge of French declined. By the 1960s few Cajuns of the younger generation could speak the language of their grandparents.

During the years of their isolation, the Cajuns had lived apart not only from English-speaking North America but also from the French-speaking pockets elsewhere on the continent. People were astonished when a delegation of Acadians from the Maritime provinces and New England that visited Louisiana in 1924 returned with tales of a large and self-contained French-speaking society on the bayous. This gap too was about to be bridged, and the person who started this process was another remarkable politician and promoter and the acknowledged leader of his generation of Cajuns, Dudley J. LeBlanc.

Like Huey Long, Dudley LeBlanc began his working life as a travelling salesman, and like Long he entered politics at an early age, but while Long was unquestionably the greater politician, LeBlanc was probably Long's superior as a salesman. He sold shoes, burial insurance, and, most spectacularly, patent medicines. In the late 1940s and early 1950s a tonic called

Hadacol invented and introduced by LeBlanc became a national fad: it was one of the first popular vitamin supplements (alth some of the curative properties attributed to it may have been due to its twelve per cent alcohol content). Its success was undoubtedly helped by LeBlanc's innovative promotional schemes, the most lavish of which was the Hadacol caravan, a travelling variety show with an admission price of two Hadacol box tops. The caravan featured Hollywood and Nashville stars as well as Dudley LeBlanc himself and was pervaded by Cajun high spirits, which so intrigued country composer Hank Williams, one of the stars of the 1950 tour, that he put them into words and music in a hit song, *Jambalaya*. But Hadacol, like most of LeBlanc's ventures, was undone by the informality of its financial management: "Never," according to his biographer Floyd Martin Clay, "was such a large operation so devoid of explicit bookkeeping." LeBlanc's sales manager once pointed out to him that in the previous month the operation had lost $150,000. "That's okay," LeBlanc replied, "we'll catch it back next month."

Through all of this LeBlanc pursued his political career. Although his populism was in some respects similar to Huey Long's, the two were early opponents: LeBlanc's election to the state Public Service Commission broke Long's domination of that body, and LeBlanc made three unsuccessful tries for the governorship as an anti-Long. Then, in one of the turnabouts typical of Louisiana politics, he accepted the presidency *pro tempore* of the state Senate in 1948 under Governor Earl Long, a position that allowed him to enact his pet legislative project, an old-age pension. He continued to serve on and off as a state senator until his death in 1971.

There was yet a third side to LeBlanc's career: he was a proud Cajun and worked hard to promote and preserve Cajun heritage and culture. He always remained close to his Cajun constituency, especially through weekly bilingual radio broadcasts that became almost as much a part of Cajun Sundays as Mass, and he served as a link between that constituency and the outside world. His books, *The True Story of the Acadians* and *The Acadian Miracle*, helped to popularize Cajun history, particularly its more romantic aspects. In 1930 he organized a pilgrimage of fifty Cajuns, twenty-five of them young women dressed as "Evangelines", to their ancestral Acadian homeland; in addition to New Brunswick and Nova Scotia, they visited Quebec City and Montreal. The visit was returned the next year by twenty-five Acadian Evangelines, along with twenty-five male Acadians and a hundred other Canadians, and in 1936 LeBlanc organized another pilgrimage of Cajun Evangelines. More formal contacts with the French-speaking north were initiated the next year when Louisiana sent an official delegation to the second Congress of the French Language in Quebec City, and the enthusiasm generated by this meeting was partly responsible for restoring the teaching of French in Louisiana schools in 1938.

The immediate effect of these new contacts was small compared to the torrent of influences from Anglo-America, but they were important for the future. While "American" influence did not seem to be having much impact on the Cajuns' insouciance, sense of humour, and love of a good time, it was clearly making inroads in their ancestral language, and French in Louisiana appeared to be in the process of dying a natural death. If French was to be preserved, it could be done only by a conscious effort at language maintenance, and it was the growing mutual awareness of Louisiana and the rest of the French-speaking world that would make such an effort possible.

TI-JEAN

In 1957, a year after the publication of *Peyton Place*, another new novel captured the mood of a very different but no less significant part of the American public. Although it never matched *Peyton Place* in sales, *On the Road* had perhaps a greater impact and certainly a more lasting one, for it brought to wide public attention for the first time what its author, Jack Kerouac, described as "the sordid hipsters of America, a new beat generation that I was slowly joining." It was not the first piece of Beat literature to surface— John Clellon Holmes' novel *Go* had appeared in 1952 and Allen Ginsberg's long poem *Howl* had enjoyed success in limited circles since its publication in 1956—but it was the first one to capture the public imagination and the one that turned the Beat Generation into a media phenomenon.

Jack Kerouac was born Jean-Louis Lebris de Kérouac in Lowell in 1922, and he died in St. Petersburg, Florida, in 1969. The life he lived in those forty-seven years was a strange one by almost any standards, but it was especially strange for a person who was taken as a symbol of the rebellion of alienated youth in the United States. The curiosity seekers, hero worshippers, and vultures who came to his door after *On the Road* made him a celebrity were generally surprised to discover first that he was so old, second that he did not look like a "beatnik", and third that he still lived with his mother. There were some who lionized him as the King (or as the Quebec writer Victor-Lévy Beaulieu has perhaps more aptly put it, the "pope") of the Beats, and others who attacked him as a glorifier of moral degeneracy, but few who took him seriously as a writer; yet he always insisted that he was a serious writer, and in the autobiographical introduction to *Lonesome Traveler*, a collection of stories published in 1960, he wrote that he "always considered writing my duty on earth," and he continued:

> Also the preachment of universal kindness, which hysterical critics have failed to notice beneath frenetic activity of my true-story novels about the "beat" generation. Am actually not beat but strange solitary crazy Catholic mystic.

Not very many people took that seriously either, and the cover of the paperback edition of *Lonesome Traveler* trumpets Kerouac as "the wildest child of the Beat Generation".[49]

The fading of the Beat Generation from recent memory has allowed at least some of what is essential and universal about Kerouac to rise to the top, but the whole man is still not widely appreciated, and what is chiefly missing is an understanding of the forces that shaped his unique perspective on the world. His life was rich, varied, difficult, and ultimately tragic. In his childhood he imbibed both the rigid Catholic morality of the Franco-Americans and their new longing for U.S.-style success. His parents urged him to be good like his pious, saintly brother Gérard, who died at the age of nine when "Ti-Jean" was four; they also wanted him to become an insurance salesman and pushed him into being a star athlete at Lowell High School.

Kerouac went to Columbia University on a football scholarship, but he broke his leg in a freshman game, dropped out, tried to join the Marines, the Coast Guard, and the Navy, and finally ended up in the merchant marine. He shipped out, came back to New York, returned to Columbia, was benched by the football coach, quit school and shipped out again. On his return he lived with his parents, who had moved to Brooklyn, and began to meet the people who would become the nucleus of the Beat Generation — Lucien Carr, William Burroughs, Allen Ginsberg. He got married and moved to Michigan with his wife, but the marriage lasted only a few months and he hitched a truck ride back to New York. By this time his father was ill, and before he died in 1946 Léo Kérouac exacted a promise from Jack that he would take care of "Mémère" forever and one from "Mémère" that she would not let Allen Ginsberg into the house.

A year after his father's death Kerouac met Neal Cassady and took off with him on the cross-country adventures that would be the material of *On the Road*. Between rides he lived with Mémère and wrote his first novel, *The Town and the City* (the town was Lowell, the city New York), which was published in 1950 and praised by some critics but otherwise had little impact. In the next few years he was constantly moving—from New York and North Carolina (where his sister Nin lived and Mémère spent much of her time) and Florida to San Francisco and Mexico and Morocco and back again. He was also writing prolifically in the spontaneous-composition manner that let loose his best voice, typing at top speed on rolls of teletype paper, but nothing he wrote after *The Town and the City* could find a publisher. When he was broke, which was often, Mémère sent him money from her earnings at a shoe factory.

The publication of *On the Road* in 1957, six years after it was written, eased Kerouac's financial difficulties and made him a celebrity but it also brought new problems. Fame was not synonymous with appreciation or understanding: Kerouac's new audience had ears for only part of what he was saying, just as his public image corresponded to only part of what he had ever been and to even less of what he had become by 1957. The energy that had infused the Beat Generation had largely dissipated by the time it became a public phenomenon, and its principals were going their separate ways. Kerouac contributed to the confusion by being cryptic and facetious in most of his public appearances; he found these appearances difficult and could generally face them only if he was drunk.

More of the manuscripts written between 1950 and 1957 were published but they did not sell as well as *On the Road* and were savaged by most critics. By 1960 Kerouac's travels were behind him and he more or less settled down with Mémère, in New York and later in Florida where Nin was living. Ginsberg and other Beat writers evolved along with the movement they all had spawned, but Kerouac found himself increasingly out of sympathy with the movement and without a place in the counterculture of the 1960s. He continued to write, but his books were out of fashion with both the critics and the public. He spent more and more of his time drunk. By 1966 he had entered the last period of his life: Nin had died, Jack and Mémère had moved to Cape Cod, Mémère had suffered a stroke, Jack had taken his third wife. The three of them moved back to Lowell, then to Florida again. Kerouac told the *Paris Review* in 1967 that:

> The beat group dispersed as you say in the early '60s, all went their own way, and this is my way: home life, as in the beginning, with a little toot once in a while in local bars.

Jack Kerouac died in Florida in 1969. His body was taken back to Lowell, where Father Spike delivered the oration at his funeral; his gravestone in the Catholic cemetery is inscribed " 'Ti-Jean'... he honored life." In 1988, trying to rise above its grimy proletarian past, Lowell dedicated a small downtown park to his memory with passages from his novels carved onto the sides of granite obelisks. The project was bitterly opposed by some members of city council whose last memories of Jack Kerouac were of a deranged creature stumbling about in a drunken stupor.

Kerouac's books are really a record of his vivid inner life in a world whose limits were defined only by his extensive imagination. "I was a scared kid," he wrote in *Doctor Sax*, one of his novels about his Lowell childhood, and later he said,

> I... want everybody to know that my childhood years were fantastic flights of beauty into a world populated by saints and incredible monsters.[50]

Those saints and monsters were an important part of his adult life as well; Heaven intervened to tell him what to write and direct his hand at the typewriter. Zen was part of the vocabulary of the Beat Generation, but Kerouac always saw his mysticism as grounded primarily in the Catholicism he was born into. He told the *Paris Review* that Buddhism "has influenced that part in my writing that you might call religious, or fervent, or pious, *almost as much* as Catholicism has" (emphasis added) and that he saw "no difference" between Jesus and Buddha. When it was suggested that he wrote about Buddha but not about Jesus, he took offence and said "I've never written about Jesus?... All I write about is Jesus."

He had both the immigrant's chip on his shoulder ("I ain't going to take no shit from nobody") and the immigrant's gratitude ("the country gave my Canadian family a good break, more or less, and we see no reason to demean said country"). Like so many immigrants he was a political reactionary, especially in his later years when he supported the U.S. war in Vietnam, expressed admiration for the conservative journalist William Buckley, and gave vent to his own prejudices against Jews and blacks. He was always the Canuck from Lowell, with a strong family attachment and streaks of fatalism, moral rigidity, otherworldliness, and peasant practicality. (In *Vanity of Duluoz* he recalls having to make up credits in French and mathematics at a New York prep school before he could go to Columbia: "Big deal, I couldn't speak anything but French till I was six, so naturally I was in for an A right there. Math was basic, a Canuck can always count.") So while other critics have found precursors for Kerouac in Fenimore Cooper, Emerson, Thoreau, Whitman, Melville, Dreiser, and Thomas Wolfe, Victor-Lévy Beaulieu suggests that he cannot be fully understood without also taking into account the

Sentinelle movement and <u>Marie-Rose Ferron</u>, the Woonsocket woman whose stigmata and visionary powers were acclaimed throughout the Franco-American archipelago.

The very conflicts that made him the quintessential Franco-American of his generation also gave him some common ground with many other Americans, and especially young Americans, of the 1950s. But if Kerouac was able to make the world of the Beats accessible to his readers, none of the worlds that he sought was, in the end, accessible to him. The roads to the past—

> I'm writing this book because we're all going to die. In the loneliness of my life, my father dead, my brother dead, my mother far away, my sister and my wife far away, nothing here but my own tragic hands that once were guided by a world, a sweet attention, that now are left to guide and disappear their own way into the common dark of all our death, sleeping in me own bed, alone and stupid: with just this one pride and consolation: my heart broke in the general despair, and opened up inwards to the Lord, I made a supplication in this dream.... [*On the Road*]

and to mainstream America—

> Tho' sometimes I'd just look out the window of the mad world and watch a little dirt road that wound westward into the woods of Maryland leading to Kentucky and the rest, on misty days it had a particularly nostalgic look that reminded me of boyhood dream of being a real "Arkansas Railbird" with father and brothers on a horse ranch, myself a jockey, none of this drunken sailor shot and especially none of this cute and wise guy attitude toward the Navy.... I saw that little winding dirt road going west to my lost dream of being a real American man. [*Vanity of Duloz*]

and even to rejection of mainstream America—

> At lilac evening I walked with every muscle aching among the lights of 27th and Welton in the Denver coloured section, wishing I were a Negro, feeling that the best the white world had offered was not enough ecstasy for me, not enough life, joy, kicks, darkness, music, not enough night.... I wished I were a Denver Mexican, or even a poor overworked Jap, anything but what I was so drearily, a "white man" disillusioned. All my life I'd had white ambitions.... I was only myself, Sal Paradise, wishing I could exchange worlds with the happy, true-hearted, ecstatic Negroes of America. [*On the Road*]

were all closed to him.

Victor-Lévy Beaulieu suggests that there might have been a fourth road, the road to a Quebec that in his lifetime had already begun to change, but Kerouac could not even see the opening to that road, and when he came to Montreal in 1967 the Québécois laughed at the way he spoke French. Most Franco-Americans were not aware of what was happening in Quebec; they were far removed from it, had lost interest in it, and to the extent that any sense of the changes that had begun to take place seeped down to their archipelago they were mildly threatened by it. But it was happening nonetheless.

6

Wider Horizons, Power Connections, and Dreams Re-Examined

1960-1980

WHEN ANTONIO BARRETTE was sworn in as premier of Quebec in January 1960, the second new premier in four months, he took over a troubled and demoralized government. In quick succession the Union Nationale had lost its revered *Chef* and his only credible successor, Paul Sauvé. Keeping the crumbling machine together was beyond Barrette's modest capabilities, and the provincial election he called a few months later gave a narrow victory to the Liberals under Jean Lesage. The 1960 election marked not only a change of government in Quebec but a change of era. Lesage's government was every bit as strong as Duplessis's had been, but it was determined not to restrain the forces of modernization rampant in Quebec but rather to shape them and allow them to develop in an orderly fashion. For all the government's efforts those forces sometimes got out of control. It was soon labelled the "Quiet Revolution", although Laval University sociologist Gérard Bergeron thought it was more accurate to call it a "noisy evolution". He was probably right, but that term never caught on.

Few areas of life were unaffected by the changes of the early sixties. The role of government was redefined and expanded, the educational system was restructured, the influence of the church declined precipitously, cultural life showed a changed orientation and a new vitality. The secularization of society, which Duplessis had simultaneously paved the way for and prevented from happening, was perhaps the most dramatic development, and it underlay many of the others. While the church did not disappear overnight as a force—and still has not disappeared—its effect both on the direction of the province as a whole and on the daily lives of its citizens became increasingly marginal. Two thousand Quebecers entered seminaries in 1946, but barely a hundred in 1970. The French-Canadian birthrate declined from nearly thirty per thousand in 1959 to about fifteen per thousand in 1970.

The changes in education were in the same direction: the provincial Department of Education that had been held out as a threatening spectre by Duplessis was set up by the Lesage government, and its first minister was Paul Gérin-Lajoie, one of the powerhouses of the cabinet, ensuring a substantial government voice in education policy. New comprehensive schools were built, and the curriculum was reoriented toward producing technicians and planners instead of classical scholars. The ultramontane idea of the supremacy of the church over the state was finally laid to rest. The Quebec government, under the direction of a few key cabinet ministers such as Gérin-Lajoie and René Lévesque and aided by a group of capable and innovative technocrats attached to the civil service, showed unprecedented vigour and replaced the church as the central institution in Quebec society. The government broadened its presence in areas where it already had a foot in the door and entered entirely new ones. It set up countless new economic, social, and cultural agencies, among them the Société Générale de Financement as an investment vehicle, the Régie des Rentes to run a new pension plan, and the Ministry of Cultural Affairs. Instead of jealously guarding powers that it didn't use, as Duplessis had done, the government began to use the powers it had. Government expenditures grew by twenty per cent a year. In short, Quebec was becoming a society more like the others in North America.

The economic changes that had been going on since early in the century and had accelerated since the Second World War were finally having their political and social consequences. The disharmony between an economy based on advanced capitalism and a national ideology based on traditional Catholicism and reverence for an agrarian past could not last forever, and it was the ideology that was more easily disposed of. But the new harmony between how French Canadians thought of themselves and what they actually were did not produce social peace and political stability. When change came, there were some who thought it was going too quickly, others who thought it was going too slowly, still others who thought they weren't getting a fair share of its benefits. A hundred flowers bloomed in the new Quebec, and the atmosphere in the garden was not always peaceful or orderly.

One of the victims of the prevailing instability was the Lesage government itself, which fell to a revitalized Union Nationale in 1966. Daniel Johnson, leader of the Union Nationale since 1961, was a conservative nationalist, but once he became premier he could only slow the process of change, not reverse it. Indeed, one of the most important educational reforms, the establishment of a network of state-run junior colleges known as CEGEPs, was carried out by the Johnson government. Johnson was a skilled politician and manipulator with a Duplessis-like ability to keep a wide variety of groups, each with its own interests and inclinations, relatively satisfied, and he succeeded in keeping the lid on Quebec's social ferment during a particularly delicate period. In September 1968, however, he died of a heart attack the night before he was to have inaugurated the great dam at Manicouagan, the vast hydroelectric project that he had initiated as minister of hydraulic resources under Duplessis.

The years following Johnson's death were among the most turbulent in Quebec's history, for the energy unleashed by the Quiet Revolution was by no means confined to the government. It penetrated the trade unions, the universities, the arts, even the church. To the dismay of liberal antinationalists like Pierre Trudeau much of this energy took a nationalist direction, but it was a new kind of nationalism, or at least one with new elements. One of the paradoxes of the Quiet Revolution was that Quebec nationalism, now stripped of its seemingly indispensable allies of Catholicism and conservatism, nevertheless showed more vitality than ever before. Not that there were no conservatives and Catholics among the post-1960 nationalists — there were — but there were also liberals, social democrats, Maoists, anarchists, fiercely anticlerical secularists, and representatives of yet other colours on the spectrum of political thought. Quebec nationalism was no longer the virtual monolith it had been in the early twentieth century. If some still identified it with French Canada's Catholic mission in the New World, others identified it with anti-imperialism, Third World solidarity, and the liberation of oppressed peoples. If there could be said to be a dominant mindset in the new nationalism, it was mildly reformist, procapitalist, and based in the middle class.

Both the Lesage and Johnson governments tried to assume the nationalist mantle. Lesage fought with the federal government as vigorously as had Duplessis, but he fought for things his government insisted on doing and not just against things Ottawa wanted to do. When Prime Minister Lester Pearson tried to introduce a contributory pension plan in 1964 the Lesage government countered with one of its own, so clearly superior that the federal plan was modified to conform to Quebec's rather than the reverse.

Johnson campaigned on the slogan of "equality or independence", and although he died before he had a chance to put it to the test the threat was not forgotten. After Johnson's death the nationalist struggle took to the streets, where it remained throughout the unhappy nineteen-month premiership of his successor, Jean-Jacques Bertrand. Liberal premier Robert Bourassa, elected in 1970 on a platform of "profitable federalism" and economic growth through foreign investment, was no more able than his predecessors to ignore nationalist pressure. He had to rediscover "cultural nationalism" and introduce a language law that was a step in the direction of French unilingualism.

Many of the major threads in post-1960 Quebec society came together in 1968 with the formation of the Parti Québécois. It was the heir both to the Quiet Revolution, with its faith in modernization through state intervention, and to the extraparliamentary "separatists" with their goal of a sovereign Quebec. It incorporated the conservative nationalists of the Ralliement National, the eager militants of the Rassemblement pour l'Indépendance Nationale, and much of what had been the activist wing of the Liberal Party, and it attracted substantial support among civil servants, intellectuals and trade unionists. But not all of these diverse elements carried equal weight: the dominant tendency in the new nationalism was also the dominant tendency in the Parti Québécois, and it was this that gave the party its direction and turned it into the force that it became.

René Lévesque, once a flamboyant Liberal minister, was the leader and heart of the party. Two of his chief lieutenants were Claude Morin and Jacques Parizeau, both of whom had served on the task force that prepared the Lesage government's pension policy in the early 1960s. Under the direction of these and other leaders the party evolved an economic policy that gave a greater role to the state but otherwise did not unduly disturb existing structures, an activist but not radical social policy, and a constitutional policy that softened the blow of sovereignty first by linking it to an economic association with the rest of Canada and later by promising that it would not be implemented without a referendum. It was a successful electoral strategy, and carried the PQ from twenty-four per cent of the popular vote in 1970 to thirty per cent in 1973 to forty per cent and power in 1976. For the first time a party committed to a sovereign Quebec occupied the government benches in Quebec City.

But the success of the PQ and the strain of nationalism it represented left some deeper questions unanswered. When Quebec opened itself up to new influences it had little control over what came in, especially when the chief source of innovations, the United States, was itself becoming increasingly open to new ideas and ways of life. According to Quebec political scientist Denis Monière there was

> a transformation of individual and collective morals: change became a value in itself. An infatuation with novelty and new experiences opened the door to U.S. cultural influence.... Québécois put their daily lives in step with the advanced capitalist societies and with directed consumption, abandoning moral rigour and legitimizing immediate gratification through the consumption of things. Young people cheerfully violated the traditional taboos relating to marriage, sex, and drugs and joined the currents of liberation flowing through Western societies.[51]

Both the technocratic strain of Quebec nationalism embodied in the Parti Québécois and the anti-imperialist strain are products of these new currents. While some took their inspiration from General Motors and the Harvard Business School, others took it from Black Panthers, Algerian guerrillas, and Vietnam's National Liberation Front. It was not uncommon for marchers in Quebec demonstrations to chant in the same breath, "Le Vietnam aux Vietnamiens—le Québec aux Québécois". The parallel seemed a natural one to those shouting it, as did Pierre Vallières's characterization of the Québécois as "white niggers of America" in one of the most influential Quebec books of the 1960s. Like the old conservative nationalism, anti-imperialist nationalism gave Québécois a cause, an explicit reason for maintaining a society separate from the rest of North America; but for a variety of reasons this form of nationalism has been able to rally only a small minority. Identification with the Third World has limited appeal, and any course that might involve armed struggle, always an unpopular activity in Quebec, has even less. In the Quebec of the 1960s and 1970s anti-imperialism, like old-style conservatism, occupied only a margin of the nationalist movement. It involved choices that were too hard, a future that was too uncertain, and a denial of too much of what Quebec had become.

Technocratic nationalism, on the other hand, was seen to have no such faults. It envisaged no change in Quebec's status as a Western country. Its goals were to be achieved through bargaining and political persuasion. It did not expect material sacrifices, even in the short term. For all these reasons it appealed to thousands of Québécois who shunned both conservative and anti-imperialist nationalism. To be sure, it added to its legitimacy by borrowing icons and symbols from older forms of nationalism and situated itself in the Quebec nationalist tradition. Lionel Groulx (he was referred to as "Abbé Groulx" less often now) became something of a hero to the new

Quebec nationalists. A statue of Duplessis, commissioned right after his death, conveniently "lost" by the Lesage Liberals, and left in its crate even by the Johnson government, was dusted off and put up by the Parti Québécois. But in fact the Quebec envisaged by the Parti Québécois bore little resemblance to that of Abbé Groulx. The Quebec of the technocratic nationalists did not seek to preserve values different from those of Protestant, pleasure-seeking, materialistic North America. The difference between this Quebec and the rest of the continent was to be primarily one of language: thus it was no accident that the more open Quebec became to outside influence the more it seemed necessary to regulate linguistic affairs through legislation. Both the Bourassa government's Bill 22 and the more forceful Bill 101 of the Parti Québécois were armour to protect the position of French.

Nineteenth-century Irish nationalists wanted an "Ireland, not free only but Gaelic as well; not Gaelic only but free as well." The Quebec of the 1970s came to desire similar goals: French as the dominant language, and freedom — whether in or out of a confederation with the rest of Canada — to make its own decisions on a wide range of economic, social and cultural matters. But for Quebec nationalists of the 1970s to have adopted this slogan, it would have had to be rephrased: "Quebec, not free and French only, but modern, secular, open, capitalist, consumption-oriented, urban, Western, and on friendly terms with the rest of North America as well."

THE ARABS OF ELECTRICITY

As agriculture's place in Quebec political folklore declined, electricity rose to take its place: virgin lands awaiting colonists to make them fruitful had symbolized the old vision of what Quebec could be, and virgin rivers awaiting dams symbolized the new one. No one was more aware of the connection between electricity and politics than Maurice Duplessis, who had a taste for puns and frequently played with the similarity between *electrical* and *electoral*.

An important difference between the new symbol and the old was that the Québécois were not alone in their enthusiasm for Quebec's electricity. It had also interested Americans since the early years when they set up Quebec's largest generating company, Shawinigan Water and Power, and other power concerns. Shawinigan was eventually controlled by English-Canadian capital and closely allied with the English-Canadian-owned distribution company Montreal Light, Heat and Power: together they were the most visible manifestation of corporate power in Quebec, and in the eyes of many Québécois they remained a foreign intrusion. For years Sir Herbert

Holt was the dominant figure in Montreal Light, Heat and Power, and he became one of the most hated figures in the province. When his death was announced at a baseball game at Montreal's Delorimier Stadium in 1941 the crowd erupted into cheers.

English-Canadian domination of the Quebec electric power industry persisted through the Duplessis decades. Direct U.S. interest in it was relatively small, although U.S.-owned industries continued to be among its most important customers. (In the 1960s and 1970s Quebec hydroelectric resources and U.S. investment capital would once again be brought together, but in a vastly different context fashioned by growing government involvement.) Before the 1940s the Quebec government's participation in determining the direction of hydroelectric development was timid and limited. The outright sale of waterfalls ended in 1907, but power sites remained easily available on long-term leases. Electric power in Quebec was still a high-profit industry for its private owners, characterized by low rates for industry, high rates for consumers, neglect of unprofitable rural areas, and low wages in construction projects.

There were many Québécois who thought this should be changed, but little was done until 1944, when one of the last acts of Premier Adélard Godbout's Liberal government was to set up the Quebec Hydro-Electric Commission—Hydro-Quebec—which took over the assets of Montreal Light, Heat and Power, including the great generating station at Beauharnois southwest of Montreal. The 1944 election gave control of Hydro-Quebec to Duplessis, who had opposed its creation but nevertheless appreciated this new government asset and administered it vigorously. Rural electrification was substantially achieved, the installation at Beauharnois was greatly expanded, and the Bersimis River on the north shore of the St. Lawrence was dammed to provide more than a million kilowatts of electricity. In 1959 Duplessis's new minister of hydraulic resources, Daniel Johnson, announced the start of the largest project yet, the damming of the Manicouagan and Outardes rivers, also on the north shore and even more remote from Quebec's main population centres than the Bersimis. By the time of Duplessis's death Hydro-Quebec generated more electricity than any of the province's private power companies. Nevertheless there were anomalies in the system. The plethora of companies led to duplication and waste, and opportunities for French Canadians in the private power companies were limited: in 1962 only forty per cent of the engineers at Shawinigan were French Canadian compared to eighty per cent at Hydro-Quebec. The continued existence of private power companies alongside an expanding state system was only one of the many contradictions that Duplessis bequeathed to his successors.

In 1962 Liberal Premier Jean Lesage called an election in which the government slogan was "maîtres chez nous" ("masters in our own house"), an old nationalist motto of which Abbé Groulx had been particularly fond. Now, however, it meant the nationalization of Shawinigan Water and Power and several other private utilities, bringing the province's hydroelectric network (with the significant exception of Alcan, which generates electricity largely for its own use on the Saguenay) under public control. The proposal was a popular one—even opposition leader Daniel Johnson, caught off guard, tried to jump on the bandwagon by promising to nationalize some of the smaller companies and hold a referendum on the rest—and the Liberals were re-elected with an increased majority. Nationalization was carried out with an alacrity unusual in the annals of election promises. The government's offer for Shawinigan was announced six weeks after the election and by the end of April 1963 nationalization was virtually complete.

Quebec's way of meeting the $600-million cost of the takeovers was almost as momentous as the nationalization itself. In the past Hydro-Quebec and the Quebec government had satisfied most of their borrowing needs on the Canadian bond market, but the size of the loan needed to finance the electricity takeover—$300 million—was beyond the limited sources of capital available to it in Canada. There were other reasons for raising the money in the United States: as a financial adviser to the Quebec government explained later,

> it would provide an investor seal of approval on the takeover, remove all doubts about Quebec's ability to finance the purchase, and quiet the concern of any of Lesage's colleagues... who might have some lingering doubts.[52]

Quebec had made its entry into the big-time U.S. bond market, and it had latched onto a source of capital that would grow in importance as the government and Hydro launched ever larger and more grandiose schemes. Especially significant for the long term was the involvement of the two largest U.S. insurance companies, Prudential Life and Metropolitan Life: Prudential bought $100 million of the $300-million issue and Metropolitan $50 million, the first substantial investment of either in Hydro-Quebec bonds. These two remained Hydro-Quebec's most important investors, and by the end of 1977 Prudential held $303 million in Hydro-Quebec bonds— its largest investment in the securities of any single institution other than the United States government—and Metropolitan held $161 million.

After nationalization, which doubled its size overnight, Hydro-Quebec faced a number of challenges. It had to weld the systems it inherited into a

coherent network and standardize an illogical and inequitable rate structure; but above all it had to continue to expand to satisfy a demand that in the
1960s and 1970s would double every nine years. Hydro-Quebec's answer
was conceptually simple, although it involved enormous engineering and
financial complications: it would roughly double its network every nine
years to meet the demand. This was not the only path Hydro could have
taken. It could have promoted energy conservation to slow the growth in
demand; it could have improved its load management and met at least part of
the increased demand by using its existing plants more efficiently instead of
by constantly building new ones. But the post-nationalization atmosphere at
Hydro-Quebec was a heady one. Quebec still seemed to have a limitless
supply of cheap hydroelectric power, and nuclear energy seemed to offer
another limitless supply of cheap power once all the rivers were dammed. It
would be another decade before the words "energy" and "crisis" would be
used in the same breath. The vast Manic-Outardes project in northern
Quebec was then under construction, and it had become a symbol of the
technological capability of the new Quebec. The growth of electricity
consumption promised yet more and bigger Manics. Well into the 1970s
Hydro not only did nothing to discourage growth but even encouraged it by
promoting consumption through its advertising.

Hydro-Quebec's relationship with the New York money market therefore
became increasingly important. There would be a steadily growing need for
capital, and the voices of those who were adept at raising it were listened to
with increasing attention at Hydro-Quebec. The most important of these
was Roland Giroux, president of Lévesque, Beaubien Inc., one of the few
significant French-Canadian firms in the Anglo-dominated field of Montreal finance. As a rising St. James Street power, Giroux was asked for
financial advice by successive provincial governments, and in 1969 he was
appointed president of Hydro.

At the same time, Hydro-Quebec was being looked at with new respect
on Wall Street and in other financial centres. Its succession of large projects
offered a continuing outlet for investment capital, and its source of revenue—
Quebecers' electricity bills—was a secure one that could be counted on to
grow: if it did not grow fast enough Hydro could, with government approval,
raise its rates. Finally, if all else failed, Hydro's status as a public utility meant
that its bonds were guaranteed by the government of Quebec. There were
other things in Hydro's favour as well. Its performance on the Manic project
had inspired confidence in its technical competence, and Quebec's proximity to New York aroused the hope that some of that cheap electricity might
be sent flowing south to be used by utilities like Consolidated Edison, which

supplied power to New York City and was closely allied to the very institutions that had begun to buy Hydro-Quebec bonds in large quantities. About the only risk was that the Quebec government might interfere with Hydro's priorites, its rate structure, its plans for growth, or some other aspect of its overall design; but by the late 1960s power relationships within the government were such that this was unlikely. The government had to depend for its evaluation of Hydro-Quebec's performance and plans on information supplied by Hydro itself. In addition, Quebec needed Roland Giroux's status as Quebec's unofficial "ambassador to Wall Street" and the trust he generated among the New York financiers. The fear of offending Giroux and his friends in New York was enough to prevent any effective regulation of Hydro-Quebec. The result of these dependencies began to emerge with the Churchill Falls deal, and became clear with James Bay.

That inveterate dreamer Premier Joey Smallwood of Newfoundland had initially conceived the harnessing of Labrador's majestic Hamilton Falls (Joey renamed them when Sir Winston Churchill died in 1965) as the beginning of the development of his province's northern territory. The vehicle for this development was to have been the British Newfoundland Company (Brinco), owned by a consortium of British investors, but the eventual realization of the Churchill Falls project involved U.S. financing, U.S. customers, and a Hydro-Quebec guarantee. Serious negotiations began in 1962 when the Wall Street house of Morgan Stanley interested Consolidated Edison in buying Hamilton Falls power through Hydro-Quebec. Agreement in principle was not reached until 1966, partly because of Brinco's status as a private company. René Lévesque and other Quebec government representatives thought that projects on such a scale should be developed by public entities, and the hardheaded financial people who were being asked to provide the money came to share that opinion. Hydro-Quebec had to demonstrate its commitment by investing $100 million in the Brinco-controlled Churchill Falls (Labrador) Corporation, entering into a long-term contract for all the Churchill Falls power, and promising to complete the project if Brinco was unable to do so. With these guarantees in place, Morgan Stanley was able to market a $500-million bond issue of which Metropolitan and Prudential each took up $125 million. Douglas Fullerton, who participated in the Brinco–Quebec negotiations on the Quebec side, wrote later:

> The irony of the final deal is that it was accomplished by turning Brinco in effect into a public utility.... Events showed that the Churchill Falls project could not really be carried out as "private enterprise".

Private enterprise did, of course, have a role to play at Churchill Falls — in the form of Morgan Stanley, Metropolitan, Prudential, and similar institutions — but it was private enterprise in a new kind of relationship with government bodies, one in which Hydro-Quebec became uncommonly skilled. The Churchill Falls deal was a good one for Hydro-Quebec. (Newfoundland, on the other hand, later claimed that it had been bilked.) Hydro had, in effect, increased the size of its own system by fifty per cent at a price that compared favourably with any of the other possible options. But Churchill Falls and the Manic-Outardes project could meet Hydro-Quebec's needs only through the 1970s. It was already time to be thinking about the 1980s and beyond.

In 1970 the government of Premier Robert Bourassa began to consider an integrated development of the James Bay region in which a hydroelectric project would be part of an overall economic plan. The advocates of the scheme conceived it as

> a project that could in some way galvanize the enthusiasm of the Quebec collectivity, stimulate the stagnant economy and recreate the spirit of the Quiet Revolution that had dimmed with the end of the impact of the work at Manic.[53]

A certain urgency was created by the political crisis that followed the kidnapping of British diplomat James Cross and Quebec Labour Minister Pierre Laporte by the Front de Libération du Québec in October 1970. The Bourassa government had been shown to be weak and at the mercy of Ottawa; James Bay might be able to restore the province's morale and the authority of its government. But the crisis was only a spur: the week of the Cross kidnapping Premier Bourassa was already in New York telling the Wall Street financiers of the possibility that cheap James Bay power might be available for export (blackouts and brownouts the previous summer had highlighted Consolidated Edison's need for new sources of power); and Paul Desrochers, Bourassa's chief adviser, was in San Francisco, where officials of the Bank of America introduced him to the president of the Bechtel Corporation, the giant U.S. engineering firm that built Churchill Falls.

In April 1971 Bourassa announced the James Bay project. He had managed to extract from Roland Giroux a letter expressing Hydro's support for the project, but control of it was to be given not to Hydro but to the James Bay Development Corporation, a new agency that would be responsible for all aspects of the region's development. Energy resources would be developed by a subsidiary called the James Bay Energy Corporation. Concern for the interests of the region was not Bourassa's only motive for this: he thought

Hydro-Quebec was too independent a power, he didn't trust Giroux, and he wanted to cut both the utility and its president down to size. Hydro fought back immediately and won substantial control of the James Bay Energy Corporation with three of the five seats on its board of directors and a majority of its shares. The president of both James Bay corporations, however, was to be Pierre Nadeau, a Bourassa loyalist. The struggle for control of James Bay was intense, and it ended in Nadeau's defeat and resignation, and an apparent alliance of Bourassa, Hydro-Quebec, and Bechtel, whose presence at James Bay with Hydro-Quebec's backing showed how closely Hydro was now tied to its U.S. connections. Bechtel's contract contained no incentive to control costs: on the contrary, as the project's costs went up so would Bechtel's fee. When the contract was leaked to the Montreal *Gazette* in 1974, public outcry over this provision was so great that it had to be scrapped and replaced by a fixed fee ($36 million) over cost.[54]

It was soon evident that the James Bay project had not turned out to be the inspiring symbol that Robert Bourassa wanted. The idea of integrated regional development had been abandoned: "James Bay" in its first phase had become simply a hydroelectric project with three large dams, enough to meet Hydro-Quebec's needs through 1985, and it generated opposition from a variety of sources: Cree and Inuit residents of the James Bay region, environmentalists, and labour unions caused so much trouble for the project in its early years that at times it seemed doubtful that it would ever be completed. In 1973 a maverick judge named Albert Malouf granted an injunction halting the project at the request of the Cree and Inuit, who argued that its continuation would destroy their historic way of life. This judgement was quickly reversed by an appeals court but it necessitated a costly settlement with the Native peoples. A few months later, a union official named Yvon Duhamel took a bulldozer and ploughed into the three electrical generators at the biggest James Bay construction site, LG – 2. Among the causes of his intemperate action were interunion rivalry, pent-up frustration among workers at the site, and the statement attributed to a Bechtel official and headlined in a regional weekly, the Val d'Or *L'Echo Abitibien*, that "you Canadians know fuck all."

By the time the Parti Québécois came to power in 1976 most of these kinks seemed to have been smoothed out. Labour unions and Native people might have the power to delay and harass a project backed by Hydro-Quebec and its New York friends, but they did not have the power to control or stop it, and they had by and large accepted that. There was also a widespread realization that, despite the mounting costs of the project, James Bay was probably the cheapest, most secure and environmentally least harmful way of supplying Quebec with electricity. While there were many things in Quebec that the new government intended to change, Lévesque quickly made it clear that the mutually profitable association between Hydro-Quebec and the financial community in New York was not among them.

The sale of Quebec hydroelectric power to the United States, talked about since the early 1960s, was an idea whose time seemed to be coming. A deal for 800 megawatts of Quebec summer surplus electricity was originally reached between Hydro-Quebec and Consolidated Edison in 1972; the first interconnection between the Quebec and New York systems was completed in 1977, and the cheap electricity started flowing south in 1978. The price for most of the power Hydro-Quebec sent south was considerably less than it charged its Quebec customers — and only a fraction of the cost to its U.S. customers of producing the same power themselves.[55] The link between Consolidated Edison and Hydro-Quebec's New York creditors was direct. Most of Hydro's connections were with the Rockefeller and Morgan groups of capital — which, according to some authorities, were so closely linked as to be almost inseparable. This capital nexus included, among other institutions, Metropolitan Life, the First Boston Corporation, and Morgan Stanley. It also included the Chase Manhattan Bank and Morgan Guaranty Trust, the two banks controlling the largest share of the pension funds that were large investors in long-term securities such as Hydro-Quebec bonds. Con Ed itself was generally identified as a Rockefeller or Rockefeller-Morgan company.

New York State was far from being the only potential customer for Quebec hydroelectricity. At the 1979 conference of the eastern Canadian premiers and New England governors Premier Lévesque delivered a strong sales pitch to the governors and took three of them and some energy officials on an aerial tour of James Bay. One of those officials was Edward Burke, energy adviser to Gov. J. Joseph Garrahy of Rhode Island, who told the Boston *Globe* that:

> they've got approximately a million lakes up there, all of which feed into rivers and pour out into some bay or other. You can read about it, you can imagine it, but then when you find out that there are 16,500 people hard at work up there, it's a can-do, it's not a pipedream — it's there.

The energy developments of 1979 highlighted the strength of Hydro-Quebec's position. The near-disaster at the Three Mile Island nuclear plant in Pennsylvania in April focused attention on the public nervousness about nuclear power, its mounting costs, and the unresolved questions it raised; and the gasoline shortage in June reawakened doubts that oil would continue to be available at prices people were willing to pay. In his energy message on July 15 President Carter called on U.S. utilities to reduce their dependence on oil for generating electricity—a dependence that was heaviest in New England, which generated sixty per cent of its electricity from oil, with New York State not much better off at forty-three per cent. The next day he told a Kansas City audience that "we will continue to share hydroelectric power and other energy sources with our neighbour to the North." He did not mention that this "sharing" was almost entirely one-way.

In October 1979 Hydro-Quebec inaugurated the first and largest of its James Bay generating stations, LG–2, amid general satisfaction. The labour troubles of 1974 had not recurred, the Native peoples had prospered under their agreement with the government, the runaway cost increases of the early construction period had cooled down after 1976, and, with yet another redefinition of the project in 1978, Hydro had even been able to reduce its cost estimate by a billion dollars. There were few naysayers left, and the opening of LG–2 provided a good opportunity to dramatize the existence of a utility that could generate enough power from hydroelectric sources to meet not only all its own needs but also some of the needs of a U.S. market that one Hydro official described as "a bottomless pit".

Jacques-Yvan Morin, who became minister of education in the PQ government but earlier was leader of the parliamentary opposition, had characterized Hydro-Quebec's managers at a 1976 meeting of the National Assembly's natural resources committee as "the Arabs of electricity". The comparison did not offend Roland Giroux. But, like the oil reserves of the Arab countries, Quebec's hydroelectric power is not unlimited. At the rates of growth recorded in the 1970s the province's actual and potential hydro-electric sites would be sufficient to meet its needs only into the mid-1990s. The imminence of the day when there would be no more rivers to dam began to have its effects on Hydro-Quebec's thinking. It no longer insisted that its 7.75 per cent annual growth rate was permanent and immutable. It began to pay more attention to talk of energy conservation and load management, the kind of talk Roland Giroux used to dismiss out of hand; and, whatever the doubts about nuclear power, Hydro-Quebec continued to believe it would eventually have to generate significant amounts of electricity from that source.

Despite its remarkable accomplishments and its contributions to Quebec's economic growth, Hydro-Quebec would no longer ride as high on the crest of the wave as it had done in the 1960s and 1970s. Its ambitious schemes to harness yet more northern rivers would be trimmed back and delayed because of slowing growth in demand, high interest rates, and environmental concerns in the United States. Moreover, the rise of a new class of Quebec entrepreneurs, along with evidence that Hydro was losing its magic touch, would knock Hydro-Quebec from the pedestal it had occupied in public opinion for a full generation.

WINNING HEARTS AND MINDS

Political instability brings little glee to institutional investors; even a vague whiff of uncertainty can worry them. Since the end of the U.S. Civil War North America north of the Mexican border has been just about the most stable region on earth, at least in geopolitical terms, but the election in 1976 of a Quebec government favouring independence raised the possibility that this tranquillity might be disturbed.

Even before the Parti Québécois government was sworn in, New York bond-rating agencies were urging René Lévesque to come down to New York to address investors: "He couldn't do better than that—come here and lay his cards on the table," John Pfeiffer of Standard and Poor told the Montreal *Gazette*. Still, this desire to hear Lévesque reflected only mild concern, said Jackson Phillips of Moody's agency: "If there was cause for alarm we'd be up there now to see if the ratings have to be adjusted."

Lévesque soon fulfilled the request. Before the election he had agreed to speak at a New York business seminar sponsored by Probe International; now that he was premier he decided instead to address the more prestigious Economic Club of New York a week later. He delegated the Probe assignment to his minister of state for economic development, Bernard Landry, who thus became the first cabinet minister to carry the PQ message to the United States.

The subject of the Probe seminar was "Does U.S. Business have a Future in Canada?" and it attracted representatives of a variety of large and medium-sized companies, along with the senior Canada hand at the State Department, who outlined U.S. policy toward Canada, and an economist from the CIA, who just listened. Bernard Landry was undoubtedly the star attraction, but the new government in Quebec was not the only thing on the business people's minds: there was general agreement that Canada was simply not as good a place to do business as it used to be. They pointed to the federal Anti-Inflation Board, the Foreign Investment Review Act, the nationalization of potash in Saskatchewan, and union militancy all over; but overriding all these specific worries was a more general and more serious one that they called "uncertainty". Business people profess to be able to deal with almost any eventuality so long as they know it's going to happen. They come to business seminars to be reassured about the future, and this time no one was of much assistance to them.

Bernard Landry was blunt on the subject of uncertainty: he said it was inevitable in a democracy, adding that if the business people were looking for a place where there was no uncertainty they might try the USSR, which under Leonid Brezhnev was very stable indeed. In the absence of prophecy, Landry outlined the PQ's plans in a way that reassured his audience. On the political level, he said, the government proposed sovereignty-association, and since Quebecers, being North Americans, were pragmatists, association could include a wide variety of things. He told them the government favoured social democracy, and by the time Landry finished defining social democracy almost everyone in the room was a social democrat. The government would be involved in the economy, but there would be room for the private sector as well. New foreign investment would continue to be welcome, sometimes in the form of joint ventures with the government, but not to the exclusion of fully private ventures. Not very much was planned in the way of new social programs because taxes in Quebec were already too high. The questions came mostly from the Canadians in the audience. What would happen to the rest of Canada? What if it fell apart? How could there be association if there was no Canada to associate with? "We deal south," answered Landry. Doesn't your government feel responsible for what happens to the rest of Canada? Of course we do, Landry said. If we didn't we'd have begun negotiations with Washington long ago. Afterwards an executive of one U.S. multinational said he thought business had nothing to fear from the PQ.

Considerably more attention surrounded Lévesque's visit to New York the next week. Regular pilgrimages to Wall Street had been part of a Quebec premier's job description since the days of Jean Lesage in the early 1960s, and, like previous premiers, Lévesque spent much of his time in private meetings with the city's financial community where, like previous premiers, he was accompanied by Roland Giroux whom the financiers knew and trusted. But René Lévesque was not an ordinary premier, and the Economic Club of New York, whose membership included the dons of the business community from David Rockefeller on down, was not an ordinary platform. They listened to Lévesque with a combination of curiosity, apprehension, and ignorance in potentially explosive proportions, but he could not concentrate on reassuring them even had he wanted to: his speech was carried in Canada by both French- and English-language television networks and he had to say not only what he thought the Americans wanted to hear, but also what he thought the folks back home wanted him to tell the Americans. He had to please everybody, and it is not surprising that he didn't.

Landry, with his nuts-and-bolts pragmatism, had made the independence of Quebec sound palatable to his audience of New York business people: nothing that affected *them*, he suggested, was likely to change much. René Lévesque in fact said many of the same things, but they were overshadowed by his message to his Canadian audiences: that he believed sincerely and passionately in the ideals of independence and social justice that had brought the Parti Québécois to power, and that he meant to act on them. It was the impression left by Lévesque that lasted. The immediate response to the speech was cool but not universally hostile; once what Lévesque had said sank in, however, it became clear that he had offended the sensibilities of the New York business people in some undefined but profound way. Where Lévesque mentioned the U.S. Declaration of Independence his audience was more likely to draw dark parallels with the U.S. Civil War. After their initial post-election jitters, the New York business circles had persuaded themselves that the PQ was not really serious about independence and had been elected only because of the unpopularity of the previous regime. "Lévesque's speech," said one knowledgeable observer, "which was certainly honest if not wise, changed that."

If the reaction to Lévesque's Economic Club speech was galling to the PQ, Prime Minister Pierre Trudeau's reception in Washington less than a month later rubbed salt in the wound. Quebec was not the only Canadian contender for the hearts and minds of the Americans: while the PQ was groping for signs that influential Americans might be amenable to Quebec independence, the governments of Canada and the United States were arranging a show of support for Canadian federalism. This was not entirely simple: too overt Washington support could be construed as interfering in the internal affairs of another country—something which, as everyone knows, Americans never, never do. Nevertheless a joint session of the U.S. Congress applauded Trudeau at numerous points during his address, never so loudly as when he proclaimed, "I say to you with all the certainty I can command that Canada's unity will not be fractured." The "chemistry" between Trudeau and Carter was judged to be just right, a new trouble-free era in Canadian-American relations was trumpeted, and the visit was declared a huge success. Piqued Quebec cabinet ministers, asked to comment, said they had been "too busy" to watch Trudeau's address on TV.

Some of the major skirmishes in Canada's federalism-versus-separatism battle were now being fought on American soil. There was occasional grumbling about this from the PQ side: on the eve of Lévesque's Economic

Club speech, Finance Minister Jacques Parizeau referred to pilgrimages to New York by Quebec premiers as "odious", and Tourism Minister Yves Duhaime's reaction to Trudeau's Washington visit was that "the decision will be made by Quebecers, and not by Mr. Trudeau or Mr. Carter." But most people saw the United States as an appropriate enough theatre for the battle because the United States would have so much say in its outcome: there are U.S. interests that have a large stake in what happens in Canada, and they have ways, not always subtle, of making their presence felt. Quebec's pursuit of U.S. opinion quietly continued. Cabinet ministers, notably Claude Morin, visited the United States and addressed U.S. audiences. At the post-election convention of the Parti Québécois its advocacy of withdrawal from the NATO and NORAD military alliances was abandoned with little controversy. On Roland Giroux's retirement the presidency of Hydro-Quebec passed to his chosen successor Robert Boyd, to the great satisfaction of Hydro's U.S. bondholders.

In 1978 Prime Minister Trudeau made another landmark speech, choosing Lévesque's platform of the previous year, the Economic Club of New York, and once again it was carried by Canadian TV; but this time the response of the New Yorkers was markedly different. The audience, much larger than the one that had come to hear Lévesque, gave Trudeau a standing ovation as he came in, and despite the lack of substance in his speech it gave him another one as he sat down. It was clear that the New York economic élite had come not so much to listen to Trudeau as to give him a vote of confidence.

The PQ did not appear to be discouraged by the evident odds against it. The Department of Intergovernmental Affairs let it be known that relations with the United States occupied second place on its scale of priorities, right behind relations with the rest of Canada, and that 1978 was its Year of the United States. (Relations with France, which had received so much publicity, were farther down the list.) This was reflected in Quebec's permanent missions in the United States. Their function was primarily economic: the pursuit of potential investors, tourists, and trade opportunities. The first had been opened in New York in 1940, and in 1969–70, others were added in Chicago, Los Angeles, Boston, and Dallas, as well as a cultural office in Lafayette to assist in the revival of French in Louisiana. Boston acquired a cultural officer in 1975. The PQ government added offices in Atlanta and Washington: the latter elicited unusual attention, and unfriendly newspaper and magazine articles described it as the beginning of a Quebec embassy. The office was extremely touchy about such allegations, and the delegate in Washington curtly refused a request for an interview.

Jean-Marc Blondeau, appointed First Consul of Quebec in the New York delegation in 1977, was much less guarded. Blondeau's mission was explicitly political (the Canadian consulate was said to have nicknamed him the "Quebec KGB"). His most pressing task was to establish closer communication with centres of power in the United States, but his job description also included reading and reacting to articles in the U.S. press and providing information to students, reporters, and business people. Information officers were appointed to several of the other delegations as well. (Evelyn Dumas, editor of the PQ newspaper Le Jour until its demise in 1978, was assigned to Boston; she had little hope that they could make much dent in the wall of U.S. indifference toward Quebec.) But while the political and public relations activities of the Quebec offices attracted more attention, trade and investment remained their primary concerns. Given the economic importance of the United States to Quebec it could hardly be otherwise; moreover, the offices were staffed largely by career civil servants, by no means all of them Péquistes.

The high priority attached to relations with the United States also led to a steady stream of visits south by Quebec cabinet ministers, including several by the premier. In a speech at Harvard University, his first in the U.S. since his Economic Club fiasco of a year earlier, Lévesque was blunt, entertaining, expansive, even—for him—relaxed, and the audience, less single-minded in its interests than the New York business people, gave him a much friendlier reception. He also took frequent advantage of opportunities to be interviewed on U.S. television, even accepting a guest shot on a segment of the Dinah Shore Show filmed at the Quebec Winter Carnival.

Lévesque described the dominant attitude of the Americans he had met as "genial skepticism", which was perhaps the best that could reasonably be hoped for; but the Montreal Star, an implacable opponent of the PQ, pronounced his U.S. campaign a failure. Star editor Gerald Clark reported complaints by influential Americans about everything from the government's "socialist" policies to the length of Lévesque's speeches. The PQ had held power for two years, but people Clark talked to still expressed a fear of "uncertainty" and a continuing resolve to "wait and see". The persistence of these attitudes was real, and the calm in U.S. business circles indicated a determination not so much to come to terms with the PQ as to outlast it.

A fact of life the PQ had to deal with was that Americans, even those with more than usual knowledge of and interest in Quebec, got little of their information from Quebec sources. Lévesque often alleged that most of the distortions about Quebec were of English-Canadian origin and that English Canadians had attempted to poison what would otherwise be friendly relations between Quebec and the United States. This allegation was self-serving, but it was not entirely without substance. Lines of communication between the United States and English Canada have always been much better than those between the United States and French Canada, whether in business, diplomacy, academia, or journalism. "When it comes to Quebec, American firms are captives of their Toronto management," said Guy Brassard, who in 1978 was Quebec's Delegate-General in Boston: more than one U.S. company's decision to invest in Quebec, he said, had been reversed on the advice of its Toronto office. Lévesque's theory was also supported by the number of negative articles about Quebec in the American press that were written either by English Canadians or by Americans from primarily English-Canadian sources: but his theory does not even come close to explaining the generally unfavourable U.S. view of Quebec after 1976. U.S. journalists did not need English-Canadian help in creating this: they did a good job of it by themselves. Features in U.S. newspapers and magazines ranged from reasonably balanced reports to anti-PQ diatribes.[56] Even the fairer ones started with a not unjustified assumption of their readers' total ignorance and thus could relate little more than the basics of the situation. Few Americans took the trouble to look beyond the jumble of half-truths and oversimplifications contained in such articles, and those who did were concentrated in the "foreign policy minority"—those who, usually as a result of business, academic, or government positions, took a serious interest in what goes on beyond the borders of the U.S.A. Those who were interested in Quebec were a minority even within this minority, but because of their positions these few people were disproportionately influential in determining U.S. policy toward Quebec.

In the State Department in Washington Canada's priority began to rise in 1977. Canada was long considered too bland and dependable an ally to merit much overt attention from top State Department officials, but an army of analysts nonetheless toiled diligently to keep abreast of happenings in the dull snowbound land to the north which was, after all, the U.S.'s biggest trading partner. While the rise of the Quebec independence movement had once sparked concern because of the Marxist and anti-imperialist leanings of some of the early *indépendantistes* and later because of PQ's neutralist stance on defence issues, the State Department gradually came to recognize that a movement dominated by the PQ's unmistakably moderate mainstream was unlikely to cause any grievous disruption to U.S. interests. In *In the Eye of the Eagle*, his admirable study of how U.S. policymakers perceived Quebec during the tumultuous years from the 1960s onwards, journalist Jean-François Lisée notes that some officials were frankly alarmed by the PQ's electoral triumph: this was especially true of Zbigniew Brzezinski, Jimmy

Carter's national security adviser and a former Montrealer who felt he understood Quebec better than some of the theorists in the State Department. The moderate behaviour of the PQ after it took the reins of power and its acceptance of an eventual Quebec role in the NATO and NORAD military alliances quickly calmed most of these fears.

As a show of good faith, and to lessen the chances that his government's positions might be misunderstood, Lévesque made a regular habit of confiding his intentions on a wide range of policy considerations to top U.S. diplomats. This was often done several weeks before they were revealed publicy (and sometimes even before members of his cabinet were informed, according to a former Lévesque aide): since the U.S. could count the premier himself among its sources of background information on Quebec, little the PQ government said or did came as much surprise. U.S. officials knew in advance, for instance, about the controversial nationalization of Asbestos Corporation, a mining company whose St. Louis–based parent General Dynamics fought the takeover bitterly.

Contrary to suggestions heard in some Toronto intellectual circles that the U.S. favoured the breakup of Canada because it wanted weak neighbours it could manipulate more easily, the U.S. government much preferred to avoid instability and uncertainty on its northern border. Thomas Enders, then U.S. ambassador in Ottawa, later said he had no doubt that, if the need had been felt, Washington would have been prepared to pull off the gloves and come to Trudeau's assistance. The situation never became that serious, he added, and Trudeau was not keen on the idea.[57]

Despite both the spectacularly ill-informed accounts that appeared in some U.S. news media and the common Canadian assumption that Americans tend to be blithely ignorant of anything north of the border, at least some State Department officials were producing analyses of a quality and prescience that put many Canadian commentators to shame. A secret State Department study entitled *The Quebec Situation: Outlook and Implications* is dated August 1977, but its conclusions seemed to anticipate the constitutional arguments that would rage in Canada more than a decade later:

> As long as the legitimate grievances and aspirations for safeguarding their ethnic identity are not resolved in a manner satisfactory to the francophone majority in Quebec, an unstable situation will continue that could result in damage to U.S. interests....
>
> It is therefore in our interest that Canada resolve its internal problems. How

this is done is of course primarily for the Canadians themselves to decide, but we have a legitimate interest in the result and must consider whether there is any positive policy in this regard that we can pursue.

Our primary concern is the protection of over-all U.S. interests in Canada — including Quebec. A devolution of powers to Quebec only, particularly in cultural and social affairs — which have a human rights aspect, could well be less disruptive to U.S. interests than a general devolution of powers to all the provinces. At the present time English Canada does not support a Two-Nation approach, but this could change. It should also be kept in mind that Quebec does meet generally accepted criteria for national self-determination in the sense of ethnic distinctiveness in a clearly defined geographic area with an existing separate legal and governmental system. There is also no question regarding the basic long-term viability of an independent Quebec in the economic sense or in regard to its ability to be a responsible member of the family of nations. The unresolved and determining factor is and must be the will of the people of Quebec.[58]

The view of Quebec outlined by State Department officials in 1978 confirmed that analysis. There was faith in the Canadians' ability to work it out. There was satisfaction that U.S. business had not yet given up on Quebec, and a belief that its hesitancy about investing stemmed as much from Canadian economic problems as from the Quebec situation. It also emerged that Washington was not particularly alarmed by the prospect of Quebec independence because it would be in the interest of an independent Quebec to maintain good relations with the United States.

Of greater concern to U.S. officials was the survival of a stable English Canada in the event of Quebec independence. Canada was good for the United States — especially a Canada with just enough internal tension to make anti-Americanism unlikely. They liked being able to count on Canada, not only as a source of raw materials, a market, and a place to invest capital, but as a reliable ally and supporter of the U.S. position in world affairs. An intensification of regional differences in Canada could lead to the United States being caught in the middle, to Canadian issues spilling over into state – federal problems in the United States, to having to consider applications from some of the poorer Canadian provinces for admission to the U.S.A. All this had crossed the minds of the people on the State Department's Canada Desk, and none of it was comforting.

Interviews with private members of the foreign policy élite at about the same time made clear that, while there was no unanimity on what Quebec independence might mean for the U.S.A., there was agreement that self-interest would prevail. If Quebec and English Canada worked out an agreement before the country broke up it would be because it was in their common self-interest to do so. If an independent Quebec chose to maintain friendly relations with the United States, that too could be explained by self-interest. What emerged even more clearly was that Americans would act in *their* self-interest, and that they would define that interest themselves, not leave it to Quebec City or Ottawa to define it for them.

One of these Americans was Alfred Hero, who grew up in Louisiana in a cultural milieu that was almost as French as it was American, and since 1954 had been director of the World Peace Foundation, a stately old Boston institution that conducts research and organizes seminars on international affairs. He felt that both the U.S. view of Quebec and Quebec's view of the United States were coloured by dubious assumptions: the belief on the U.S. side that "the Canadians will somehow shake this thing out," and the PQ government's conviction that "if the Americans really knew what we're up to they would be more sympathetic." The fact remained that the PQ had little U.S. support:

> I don't know anybody in the business community or in the U.S. federal government whose sympathies aren't with Ottawa.... If independence did seem imminent, then the relevant élites would sit down and scratch their heads and say, "What's our interest now?" Then the whole chemistry changes.

On Wall Street, a representative of one of the New York financial houses that underwrites Quebec government and Hydro-Quebec bond issues was predictably more optimistic: he saw few concrete causes for investors' apprehensions about the PQ government, which he described as "very competent"; he said PQ language laws had not caused much concern in the United States, and reaction to the nationalization of the Asbestos Corporation, then pending, had been diminishing:

> At first people thought, "That's the tip of the camel's nose, and pretty soon the whole camel will come under the tent." But it hasn't worked out that way.

The New York business community, he continued, had initially reacted less strongly than the Toronto community to the election of the PQ ("in the first months after the election, it was always good to phone Toronto for comic relief"), but it had also taken longer to settle down. As for independence, he said that if independence meant a language and a flag, then Quebec was already independent; if it meant being able to defend itself militarily, then it never would be.

James Lewis, although not an American, represented U.S. interests as president of the Canadian operations of the Prudential Insurance Company of America, one of the largest investors in Quebec government and Hydro-Quebec bonds and in Quebec real estate. Companies like his maintained and even increased their investments in Quebec during the PQ years only because they were reasonably sanguine about the future of those investments,[59] and James Lewis praised the PQ's approach toward business since it had come to office, although he disliked its "Buy Quebec" policy which sometimes made Prudential ineligible to quote on group life insurance. He felt that Quebec independence was something Prudential could live with.

William Diebold, a senior research fellow at the Council on Foreign Relations in New York, also saw the PQ's problems with American business as temporary:

> There are some terribly simplistic and ill-informed views in this country. The number of businessmen and bankers who had no idea what this was about was on the shocking side, and as a result there's been a lot of overreaction.

The best cure for overreaction is time, Diebold said. What the U.S. wants is "a unified Canada with whatever greater powers are needed to keep Quebec happy." And then he added:

> Canadians often complain that the United States doesn't pay enough attention to them. I've told some of my Canadian friends, "The moment will come when the U.S. will pay a lot more attention to you, and you're not going to like it."

VARIATIONS ON THE DREAM

The conventional definition of the American Dream was in trouble in the second decade after the Second World War. Young Americans were not living where they were supposed to live, studying what they were supposed to study, doing what they were supposed to do, or thinking what they were supposed to think. Many of them aspired to Haight-Ashbury, the East Village, or a rural commune, instead of to Scarsdale or Skokie. Higher education had been held out as the ticket to a golden future and there were more of them in college than ever before, but there were also more of them who were dropping out. They smoked dope and lived together in unmarried couples or even multiples. They thought there might be something to learn from people who lived in countries other than the United States and spoke languages other than English and had skins that weren't white and espoused Buddhism or Hinduism or even communism, and they were highly skeptical of the idea implicit in the American Dream: that their own society had found the one true way.

These doubts and heresies were not new: as far back as the 1830s Alexis de Tocqueville had noted the tension in the United States between the pressures toward conformity and the belief in individual liberty. In the twentieth century the tendency toward conformity had generally been dominant, and by the 1950s cultural and political dissent was restricted to the most courageous and the most fed up. Prevailing notions about the relationship between the individual and the collectivity made it increasingly unfashionable for Americans to identify themselves with any group other than "American society" as a whole. Then, in the 1960s, the old tradition of individual liberty was infused with a new vitality and, paradoxically, so was the equally old but even more submerged tradition of group identification.

One of the freedoms that began to be rediscovered was the freedom of non–Anglo-Saxon Americans to be different from their Anglo-Saxon neighbours. This new idea did not have an easy road ahead of it, because universality was one of the most firmly entrenched aspects of the American Dream in its postwar version. The belief had taken root that the American Dream could be applied not only to all Americans but to the rest of humanity as well: just as the Teaching was to go forth out of Zion and the Word of God from Jerusalem, so the word of the marketing analysts, missile technicians, and mythmakers was to go forth from New York, Washington, and Los Angeles. There was no more ardent believer in the universality of the American Dream than the man who stood at the centre of most of the controversies of the 1960s: as much because he symbolized what was being challenged as for his own undoubted achievements, President Lyndon Johnson became the dominant political figure of the decade.

When Johnson was a young school principal in Cotulla, Texas, in the late 1920s, his heart went out to the Mexican-American children who were the great majority of his school's pupils. He said later:

> I saw hunger in their eyes and pain in their bodies.... Those little brown bodies had so little and needed so much. I was determined to spark something inside them, to fill their souls with ambition and interest and belief in the future.

One obstacle to that was their limited command of English, so Johnson punished pupils who were caught speaking their native Spanish. A perceptive biographer commented that:

> his approach contained no awareness that his pupils' own cultural traditions and language might constitute an independent source of strength and fulfilment.

More than thirty years later, as vice-president of the United States, Johnson distributed ballpoint pens and cigarette lighters to the crowds that came out to see him on his numerous foreign trips; but the pens and lighters were only tokens:

> I felt a special rapport with all those Asians. I knew how desperately they needed our help and I wanted to give it. I wanted them to have all the dams and all the projects they could handle.

As president, Johnson wanted to extend his own version of the American Dream, the Great Society, not only to all Americans but to the rest of humanity as well. One of his pet schemes was the development of the Mekong River in Southeast Asia, a project that would bring water and electricity to millions of Asians and dwarf the wonders that Franklin Roosevelt had wrought in the Tennessee Valley. As he said in 1966:

> I want to leave the footprints of America in Vietnam. I want them to say when the Americans come, this is what they leave — schools, not long cigars.[60]

But in 1966 there were hundreds of thousands of U.S. troops in Vietnam and U.S. bombers were laying waste to both North and South. Before the Vietnamese could be made to appreciate Johnson's benevolence those who did not want an American solution imposed on their country had to be suppressed. There was, however, growing opposition to the U.S. war in Vietnam, and it was by no means confined to radicals and hippies. The antiwar movement drove Lyndon Johnson from office in 1968, and the National Liberation Front of South Vietnam drove the Americans and their clients from Saigon in 1975.

The whole adventure had a profound effect on the American psyche. There was no longer any doubt that there were forces in the world that were resistant to U.S. knowhow, U.S. wealth, and U.S. power. Manifestations of U.S. power abroad, whether in the form of ITT, the CIA, or the Sixth Fleet, were by no means at an end, but they were now subject to criticism, to an examination of their ends and a questioning of whether these justified the means, on a scale that had been rare before Vietnam. The rebellion against the idea that the values and standards of white Anglo-Saxon America were applicable to everybody began to call into question the internal composition of U.S. society as well as the foreign policy of its government.

As late as 1964 sociologist Milton Gordon could write that "the nature of group life...has received minimal attention on the American scene." Some groups, such as blacks, were patently not integrated into U.S. society, but this was viewed as a problem of discrimination: it was assumed that these people wanted nothing more than to become the same kind of Americans as everybody else. People speaking for minority groups generally confirmed this view of their situation and goals. Gordon interviewed representatives of twenty-five U.S. organizations concerned with group relations, and found that most of them had paid little attention to group life as such: there was a generally favourable attitude toward "cultural pluralism" in the abstract, but few coherent ideas as to what it meant. Only two years later, however, a new generation of black leaders was talking about Black Power instead of civil rights. They rejected integration—that is, cultural assimilation; the black movement, they said, must challenge white social and economic structures by building black structures that were independent of white influence. They preached pride in black culture and heritage and called on blacks to abandon the old notion that whatever was white was superior.

Blacks were not the only ones who had bought the American Dream but been denied a fair share of its fruits: Hispanics, Native Americans, and many "white ethnics"—the grandchildren of turn-of-the-century immigrants—were still waiting for the Dream's promise to be fulfilled; and more and more of these people were becoming aware of their common interests and potential power *as groups*. A *Newsweek* article in December 1970 described "ethnic power" as "the newest rallying cry in American politics," and quoted Barbara Mikulski, a Polish community leader in Baltimore (and later a U.S. Senator) as saying that:

> America is not a melting pot [but]...a sizzling cauldron for the ethnic American who feels that he has been politically exploited by both the government and private enterprise.

Like the black movement before it the ethnic movement acquired a cultural dimension, not only paralleling developments in the black community but taking inspiration directly from them. Alex Haley's 1976 book *Roots* and the spectacularly successful television series based on it strengthened black Americans' knowledge of their links with Africa and their pride in that connection; but it also sparked a similar awakening among the white ethnics, who showed a new interest in their almost-forgotten links with Poland, Italy, or French Canada. In the same year the celebration of the U.S. bicentennial encouraged people to become more aware of the ideals and traditions they had inherited from their ancestors, even if those ancestors didn't happen to be Mayflower pilgrims or Virginia aristocrats. Where it had once been a facile commonplace that "no one could resist the melting pot," by the late 1970s it was equally commonplace, and equally facile, to say that the melting pot hadn't worked. The popularity of *Roots* contained elements of fad, but it gave encouragement to Americans who were committed to cultural pluralism. One of their major concerns had always been the preservation—or revival—of almost-forgotten ancestral languages, and in the climate of the "roots" phenomenon they have been able to carry on their struggle largely within the framework of the federal government's bilingual education program.

The Bilingual Education Act, Title VII of Lyndon Johnson's omnibus Elementary and Secondary Education Act, had not, however, been intended to promote cultural pluralism when it was adopted in 1968. Quite the reverse: it was a recognition that pedagogical methods of the sort used by Johnson in Cotulla were not always effective in drawing minority-language children into the mainstream. The thrust of Johnson's education reforms was to provide equal educational opportunity to disadvantaged and handicapped children, and by assimilationist criteria there could be no doubt that minority-language children fit into that category. The theory was that if they were first taught to read, write, and figure in a language they could understand they would be more likely to get hooked into the school system than if they had to sink or swim in English. Children in the bilingual programs therefore had some of their lessons in their native tongue and spent the rest of the school day learning in English. The program was usually limited to the early school years and students were then switched to all-English classes.

Alliance with the federal Office of Bilingual Education, with its official goal of transition to English, was uncomfortable for many of the advocates of language maintenance. But they were newly emerged and unsure of the extent of their constituencies and they could not afford to say no to federal money: however much they mistrusted the bilingual education program, they also needed it. It was a choice between preserving their languages under compromising conditions and not preserving them at all. There was also uncertainty about ultimate goals within the cultural minorities themselves, a continuing confusion about what language maintenance should be *for*. In a sense, the difficulties facing U.S. language-maintenance activists were similar to those facing Quebec's technocratic nationalists. The crucial question was less "can it be done?" than "what does it mean?"

Early in the century, before Americanization had done its work, there had been no such confusion. Language and culture were not something apart: they were intrinsic to an attitude toward the world and a way of life; but attitudes and ways of life changed, and the decline of non-English languages was a part of those changes. There was a persistent feeling among non-Anglo-Saxon Americans that something valuable was lost in that process, but that feeling was not accompanied by a belief that what had been lost could be recaptured. Nevertheless there were some who thought it was worth trying to salvage something from the wreckage, and they had succeeded by 1976 in making the new movement for cultural pluralism a force to be reckoned with. Whether the pieces that were being picked up would have any independent life outside the structure that once gave them meaning remained to be seen.

A LEGACY OF PRIDE AND PAIN

Still only a generation or two removed from the fiercest battles in their doomed struggle to keep the influence of the larger U.S. society out of their archipelago, the Franco-Americans were inevitably affected by the new ethnic pride movements of the 1970s; but there were many who were not even aware of what they had left behind. A bust of Félix Gatineau, the most important figure in Southbridge's Franco-American history, stands at one end of the town's main intersection, but there were Franco-Americans living half a block away who knew nothing of the bust's significance and could not read the French inscription at its base.

Even those who were raised with more of the tradition intact might be ambivalent. "I grew up with a burden—Canada," said Julien Olivier, a product of the bilingual parochial school system in Manchester, New Hampshire, who had come by a roundabout route to work for the National Materials Development Center, preparing French-language materials for bilingual education programs. "French was an excessive demand on us. It prevented us from being modern, from being American, from blossoming. I wasn't prepared to fight the battle of the *ancien régime*." A conversation with Olivier in the late 1970s began in English, but when he started talking about what he had had to overcome, how he had had to work out a new attitude toward his heritage, and how he had finally become involved with an agency seeking to preserve Franco-American culture, he switched to a low-keyed but passionate French. A revival was under way, despite the obstacles and despite the indifference of most Franco-Americans. It has been a fragile revival, by no means a "movement", and it was slow to come to terms with the questions posed by Julien Olivier, questions crucial to its future.

Those fighting for a revival of French were aware that they had both to recognize their continuity with the Franco-American past and to make departures from that past, but doing that required a delicate balance that Franco-Americans sometimes found it difficult to strike. The revival was fuelled by the *Roots* phenomenon and by bilingual education, but it was kindled by unmet needs within the Franco-American community itself, needs whose continuing existence showed that the assimilation of the Franco-Americans was never as complete as it seemed and never carried with it the benefits it was supposed to bring. The attempt to divest themselves of their past left many Franco-Americans with psychological wounds, wounds in which feelings of guilt, inferiority, and stubborn pride festered, and which were constantly reopened by the insensitivity of the surrounding society to cultural differences and linguistic transitions. The cultural duality of the Franco-Americans, which had once seemed to offer them two worlds, now seemed to exclude them from both those worlds. They were "frogs" or "dumb Canucks", and in socially stratified New England that was the wrong thing to be. Montreal has been described as the only place where a French accent is not a social advantage, but the same could be said of Lewiston, Lowell, or Manchester—especially when in the French-speaking world your accent is condemned as inferior to "real French".

Some continuity has nevertheless been maintained, and those Franco-Americans still conscious of their heritage often retain more of the values traditionally associated with French Canadians than do the Québécois. Catholicism is still an important part of their collective self-conception, family ties are still strong, and there is still a prevailing conservatism. (One of the authors heard two prominent Franco-Americans engaged in a spirited discussion of which century represented the pinnacle of civilization, the eleventh or the twelfth.) There is also still an unashamed capacity for having a good time, even in adverse circumstances and in ways that some Québécois have cast off as "folkloric". After a 1978 Franco-American conference in Louisiana the flight taking the New England delegation back to Boston was delayed for several hours: impromptu singing and dancing broke out in the departure lounge—"Alouette", "Un canadien errant", "Au clair de la lune" and, in honour of the Franco-Americans' Cajun hosts, "Evangéline". Everyone joined in, some told funny stories, and the group boarded the plane in high spirits. But despite that lingering conservatism Franco-Americans are no longer a community led by priests, big wheels in insurance societies, and journalists with small newspapers and large ideas. The new leaders come largely from the universities: their organizations may not constitute a mass movement, but neither are they an exclusive élite. Perhaps they can best be described as a group of people with a common cause in search of one another and of themselves.

Among these leaders has been Claire Quintal, head of the French Institute at Assumption College in Worcester, Massachusetts, and editor of its publications, who grew up in Rhode Island but was educated in Montreal. Born in 1930, she belongs to a transitional generation of Franco-Americans, but more than most people of that generation she has been able to retain elements of the past and transmit them to Franco-Americans younger and less steeped in the tradition than herself. The Fédération Féminine Franco-Américaine, of which she is a past president, has been one of the largest and most vibrant Franco-American organizations. Her frequent speeches at Franco-American gatherings show a keen awareness of what Franco-Americans have inherited from the past and how it has been a source of both pride and pain.

Yvon Labbé is a decade younger than Dr. Quintal and did not come to the United States from his birthplace of St. Georges de Beauce, Quebec, until he was eleven. His suppressed feelings about that "overnight experience" only surfaced when, working with disadvantaged students at the University of Maine, he began to find out more about Maine's Franco-Americans. Labbé was the central figure in a discussion group that became the nucleus of the Franco-American Resource Opportunity Group—FAROG, pronounced of course "frog"—which sporadically publishes Le FAROG-Forum, a rough-and-ready bilingual tabloid leaning toward letters, poems, short stories, and articles recounting personal experiences. Labbé once described himself as "an agitator" who "tries to upset people", and those he has upset have included members of the old-style Franco-American leadership: "The traditional organizations had become unspontaneous. We were spontaneous."

Still, in the late 1970s it seemed unlikely that Franco-Americans would ever again form the self-contained, self-sufficient community they once had. Whatever the extent of the revival, there was probably no better indication of its fragility than the extent to which it became tied to the U.S. government's bilingual education program. Many of the hopes for a cultural comeback were pinned to that program, which across the United States had to contend both with an antibilingual backlash fuelled by a renascent "hundred per cent Americanism" and with the no-frills, back-to-basics movement in education. Heated debate arose over whether the program should take a language-maintenance approach or push for rapid transition to

English only. Some thought it should focus on children who didn't yet speak much English rather than on helping the grandchildren of immigrants to revive a dwindling tongue. Franco-American organizations, naturally, favoured the maintenance approach. These and other arguments were abruptly made irrelevant in the early 1980s by the budget cuts of the new Reagan administration: most bilingual education schemes in Franco-American communities ground to a halt, although one local program in northern Vermont survived until later in the decade. For many people involved in bilingual education, the limb they had gone out on was no longer attached to the tree.

The writer Antonine Maillet may be the most eloquent contemporary interpreter of what it is like to remain stubbornly French on an English-speaking continent. An Acadian, Maillet speaks for a people who were hard done by but who have survived through their own cleverness, courage, faith, and perseverance, and her words find resonance in Louisiana and New England as well as in Quebec or her native New Brunswick, because she affirms the right to be different and the need for people to be true to themselves, important themes for French-speaking Americans. She told an audience at the 1978 Fête du Retour aux Sources in Quebec City:

> We have only one word to say. It's our word. It's a *cri du coeur*—the song of a people. We don't have the right to say any other. We don't have the right to die before our last hour.

Episodes from Maillet's one-woman play *La Sagouine* were shown at a Franco-American conference in Lafayette the same year. The play is a series of monologues by an uneducated but wise and independent Acadian scrubwoman, and many of the French-speaking Americans in the audience must have asked themselves questions like those aroused in the scrubwoman's mind by a census form:

> Your nationality, they ask you. Citizenship and nationality. It isn't easy to say.
>
> We live in America, but we're not Americans. No, the Americans, they work in shops in the States, and they come here to walk on our beaches, in the summer, in white pants and speaking English. And they're rich, the Americans, and we're not. Us, we live in Canada; that means we must be Canadians, it seems to me.
>
> But Canadians have names like Dysart and Carroll and Jones, and they speak English too—
>
> ... while us, we're French.

No, we're not really French, I can't say that: the French, they're the French from France. Ah! for that matter, we're even less French from France than we are Americans. We're more French Canadians, that's what they told us.

But that can't be either. French Canadians, they're people who live in Quebec. They're called *Canayens*, or Québécois. Now how can we be Québécois if we don't live in Quebec? For the love of God, where *do* we live? [Authors' translation]

By giving voice to such conflicts, doubts, yearnings, and articles of faith, Antonine Maillet had probably come closer than most of her contemporaries to uncovering what is truly common among French-speaking North Americans outside Quebec. No Québécois had been able to strike so deep a chord, but it was significant that Maillet's speeches at the Fête du Retour aux Sources and the Lafayette conference, and the showing of *La Sagouine* there, should have been sponsored by the government of Quebec, which now saw Quebec's presence on the North American continent as central to the fate of French-speaking Americans.

And yet the emergence of the new Quebec failed to fire Franco-American imaginations: even New England Franco-Americans, Québécois by heritage and still living within a few hundred kilometres of Montreal, seemed largely indifferent to it. A woman in Newport, Vermont, was undoubtedly speaking for most of them when she told a Vermont Public Radio reporter:

It seems so far away to me. I was only five when I moved here. That's not my country—this is my country. I'm not really interested in Quebec. Maybe I should be but I'm not.

Newport is just ten kilometres from the Quebec border.

There were compelling, if perhaps unconscious, reasons for not taking too lively an interest in the new Quebec. As they let the old values slip away from them many Franco-Americans took comfort in the belief that those values continued to be maintained in Quebec. Whether this belief corresponded to reality—and increasingly it did not—was of little importance. Julien Olivier in Manchester, New Hampshire, said that:

Franco-Americans have a very old image of Quebec. They think of a rural, idealized Quebec. They're horrified by the changes that are going on in Quebec. If the church is gone, what's left? They don't know the Quebec of the Quiet Revolution, the Quebec of the PQ.

Indeed the idea of Quebec independence often strikes a chord of horror. "Because the rowboat isn't getting you to where you want, you throw away the oars," said a Maine woman at a conference of Franco-Americans in Lewiston. Nevertheless, some Franco-American leaders began to see Quebec's vitality as a positive force for their own community. Claire Quintal said in a speech at the same conference:

> There will be near us a renewed Quebec, a Quebec rediscovered by us, where all sorts of creative energies will be encouraged. It can encourage and inspire us.

There was beginning to emerge a sense of belonging to a French-speaking North American community that, despite its divisions, despite its dispersion, has never entirely come apart, and a realization that the path Quebec takes will have profound repercussions for this community as a whole. One sign of renewed ties with Quebec was the increasing availability of French-language television from Quebec on cable in places with large Franco-American populations — even if it was true that people turned to the French channels only for hockey games and dirty movies.

If some Franco-Americans had the feeling that Quebec would be important to them, they were not yet sure just how. They were wary of being used by Quebec for its own cultural and political ends, which might not correspond with their own, and of cultural paternalism on Quebec's part; and if their attitude was slow in changing, the same could be said for Quebec's attitude toward French-speaking Americans. The Quebec government's self-appointed role as the defender of French culture in North America should in theory have led it to show interest in French minorities outside Quebec, but in practice these minorities, especially in the United States, offered far too little direct political advantage to excite many people in Quebec City. Louis Falardeau, a *La Presse* reporter who covered the Fête du Retour aux Sources, found signs of life among the French minorities in the other provinces of Canada and especially among the Acadians, but he wrote that:

> The Franco-Americans are despair, even death. Those who are here are mostly over fifty years old, and many of them are over sixty. They tell the story of their defeats, of their failures, the only victories they report being new failures that they know are inevitable but that they have succeeded in delaying until later.

He didn't seem to have bumped into Yvon Labbé.

The Fête was the centrepiece of Quebec's renewed expression of interest in the minorities outside Quebec and provided an opportunity to dramatize what Premier Lévesque called "a far-flung community whose dignity is tied to Quebec." Lévesque was an almost constant presence at the Fête and missed few chances to point out its political meaning. "The more Quebec is French and sure of itself, the more the French-speaking people of America will feel the benefits," he said, and he appealed to Franco-Americans "to understand and, if their hearts tell them to, to support the evolution of Quebec."

The idea that Quebec and the French-speaking minorities could work to their mutual advantage was an ideological departure for the Parti Québécois, which viewed "normal" countries as unilingual and unicultural, in contrast to Trudeau's vision of a bilingual Canada. The PQ view had a certain appeal to Québécois who liked to feel that they had a monopoly on Frenchness in North America. Jules Poisson, Quebec's delegate-general in Lafayette from 1976 to 1978, told an interviewer:

> I used to think to hell with the Francophones outside Quebec. Quebec should be a Promised Land for all North American Francophones and they should come to us.[61]

After arriving in Louisiana Poisson changed his mind, as have many other Québécois who have had first-hand contact with minorities outside the province. Poisson told of a visit by Quebec Intergovernmental Affairs Minister Claude Morin to a rural Cajun parish where the old language and culture were holding up fairly well. Morin shook his head and said:

> It's not for us to decide the fate of minorities outside Quebec — it's for them to decide. And it's for us to help them, according to their needs and our means.

In fact, with much of their traditional culture gone, the Cajuns were nevertheless enjoying something of a renaissance in the 1970s. The previous decade had seen continuing changes in the Cajuns' self-image and in their relations with other groups in Louisiana. French was still on the decline as a spoken language among them, but now there were stirrings of official interest in saving it. There was also the beginning of a new pride in being Cajun, a sense that Cajuns might be able not only to share camaraderie and good humour among themselves but elicit respect from other people as well. Like virtually everything else in Louisiana society, this new spirit among the

Cajuns was bound to have a political expression, and it brought to the fore two new Cajun champions: Edwin W. Edwards and Jimmy Domengeaux.

No Cajun had been governor of Louisiana since Alexandre Mouton in the 1840s, although not for want of trying; but by 1971 Edwin Edwards was not only running a strong campaign but running it with the slogan "Cajun Power". Edwards seemed an unlikely person to implement Cajun Power. He is Welsh on his father's side (though his mother's maiden name was Brouillette), and he was raised as a Protestant, converting to Catholicism only in later years. Before his gubernatorial campaign he did not flaunt his Cajun background. But he is a clever politician and he knew that to win the governorship he had to run up a heavy majority in south Louisiana. He campaigned in French and promised to appoint more Cajuns to state positions, his campaign culminated in a triumphal tour through the bayou parishes, and when he took the lead in a primary election he picked up a microphone and shouted "Cajun Power!" to his supporters; but once in office Edwards ignored his pledges: broken promises are not foreign to Louisiana politics, and "Cajun Power" became the latest on that long list. Few Cajuns were appointed to important positions, and although Edwards easily won re-election in 1976, a 1977 poll showed that his popularity in the Cajun parishes had declined significantly.

The position of Jimmy Domengeaux (in the local speech the name comes out sounding like DiMaggio) as a Cajun representative has been more lasting. Not that he wasn't controversial: differing opinions can be found on everything from the efficacy of his programs to whether he was a Creole or a Cajun. Whatever questions have been raised about Domengeaux, there is no doubt that he poured a great deal of energy into a difficult and perhaps impossible task: preventing the French language from dying out in Louisiana.

Domengeaux was born in Lafayette in 1906, the son of a crawfish dealer. He became a lawyer and served a brief term in the state House of Representatives (highlighted by a fist-fight with Dudley LeBlanc and a subsequent court case) and then moved up to the U.S. Congress in 1941. He ran for the U.S. Senate in 1948, but at that point no Cajun could win in a statewide campaign. Jimmy withdrew from elective politics, and turned his attention to Louisiana's state crustacean: he built up his father's crawfish business until it was worth millions while retaining both his law office and his political connections.

In 1968 the Louisiana legislature created the Council for the Development of French in Louisiana (CODOFIL) and Jimmy Domengeaux was appointed its chair, a position he held until shortly before his death in 1988. It was frequently charged that CODOFIL had become his personal instrument, and clearly there was some substance to the allegations. A visitor's request to talk to someone about the CODOFIL program sent the office into a tizzy. There were little huddles and hurried meetings behind closed doors. "Jimmy won't like it if we talk to him," someone was overheard to say. "We'd better send him to Jimmy." Around the corner at Domengeaux's law offices, the Chairman of CODOFIL received the same visitor graciously, if not modestly:

> My temperament and disposition is that I have somewhat of the crusader's characteristic.... There are few people in my position of having financial independence, political knowhow, and broad acquaintanceship throughout the state. There were people much more qualified in the language than I, but they didn't have the same combination of circumstances.

(His French was in fact laboured, and it was jokingly said that CODOFIL was a multimillion-dollar program of the State of Louisiana to try to teach Jimmy Domengeaux to speak French.)

Domengeaux's main role was as an ambassador on behalf of French both inside and outside of Louisiana, and he became so thoroughly identified with the French-language movement that sometimes it was difficult to discern where Jimmy ended and the movement began. There were CODOFIL posters in store windows and office buildings in Lafayette with messages such as "*Soyez à la mode — parlez français*" (be fashionable — speak French) and "*Parlez français avec vos enfants à la maison*" (speak French with your children at home) and "*Ici on parle français — faites votre demande en français*" (French is spoken here — make your request in French). The posters identified themselves as coming from the Conseil pour le développement du français en Louisiane, James Domengeaux, Chairman. Jimmy could be counted upon to be a telephone guest on Montreal radio programs. He went to Paris to negotiate a cultural agreement with President Georges Pompidou and to Quebec City at the head of the Louisiana delegation to the Fête du Retour aux Sources, where the Quebec government awarded him its *Prix du 3 juillet 1608* for "the exceptional quality of his participation in the French life of America."

But if there has been a great deal of show to the CODOFIL program there has also been some substance, most of it concerning the teaching of French in elementary schools, and by 1978 it was estimated that 45,000 elementary students were enrolled in French-language classes. Training is also provided for Louisianians who want to become French teachers, but the demand for French teachers well outruns the local supply and teachers have been brought in from France, Belgium, Quebec, and most recently New Brunswick. These programs have emphasized standard French, as opposed to the Cajun dialect, and have been aimed at all Louisianians: the same program of second-language instruction is used in both Anglophone and Francophone settings. Standard French has been one of the most controversial aspects of the program, and some heavily Cajun districts, notably Terrebonne and Lafourche parishes, resisted going along at first because they didn't think French should be taught as a foreign language and they didn't like the implication that Cajun French was inferior. Sister Anne Catherine Bizallon, a nun from France and a long-time resident of Louisiana, told Ross Munro of the Toronto *Globe and Mail* in 1973 that "CODOFIL is a phony.... To import somebody to teach them French French—it's an insult. It helps kill what was left." It was unlikely in any case that CODOFIL could re-establish French as a spoken language among the Cajuns; but Jimmy Domengeaux was probably not exaggerating when he listed the agency's greatest accomplishments as:

(a) the re-establishment of pride in the culture and language of the native Louisianians of French ancestry, and (b) the accomplishment of this without conflict, misunderstanding or irritation from the Anglo-Saxon Protestants of the State.

Quebec's interest in international affairs and Louisiana's interest in a planned program of language maintenance began to grow at about the same time, and they were a good match. Spurred by such people as Bona Arsenault, a longtime student and partisan of the Acadians and a cabinet minister under Jean Lesage, and Guy Frégault, a historian who became deputy minister of cultural affairs in the mid-1960s, Quebec began to establish contact with Louisiana, and the formation of CODOFIL in 1968 was followed by negotiations between Quebec and Louisiana officials, a visit to Quebec by Louisiana Governor John McKeithen, and the opening of a Quebec delegation in Lafayette. In the early years the new Quebec office in Lafayette and the equally embryonic CODOFIL worked closely together: Léo LeBlanc, Quebec's first delegate-general in Lafayette and former press secretary to Premier Daniel Johnson, would sometimes write CODOFIL press releases. There have been exchanges of students between Louisiana and Quebec, and Quebec became a steady supplier of French teachers to Louisiana schools.

A less formal manifestation of cultural ties between Quebec and Louisiana was the successful Montreal-based singing career of Zachary Richard, a Cajun from Scott, Louisiana, who built his own style of popular music on

Cajun foundations and found an audience for it in Quebec. Another Louisiana musician who built an enthusiastic following in Quebec was the late Clifton Chenier, the great exponent of zydeco (from a corruption of the French word *haricot*, meaning bean), a musical style developed by black Creoles that bears some resemblences to Cajun music.

Formality has never been a Cajun hallmark. At one conference in Lafayette, when Madeleine Giguère, a prominent Franco-American, was introduced to lawyer and machine politician Walter Landry as "a professor of sociology at the University of Maine at Portland–Gorham," he replied, "I'm a Cajun." He travelled all the way to New Brunswick in 1977 to attend an international gathering of Landrys, and he was somewhat put out that Quebec's economic development minister Bernard Landry had not done the same. Walter Landry struck his most substantial blow for cultural pluralism in the United States in 1974 with an amendment to the Democratic party constitution making any language with official status in at least one state an official language of the National Democratic Party.[62] It became known as the "coonass amendment", after a popular designation for Cajuns. This greatly distressed Jimmy Domengeaux who, preferring the term "Acadian", had learned to live with "Cajun" but drew the line at "coonass".

(Walter Landry can muster some basic Spanish, but he speaks hardly a word of French.)

7

Political Retrenchment, Business Advance, and the Lure of the South

1980-1991

RARELY ARE VOTERS in the Western democracies consulted directly at the ballot box on matters as fundamental as breaking up a venerable federation and carving out a separate nation-state. With the 1976 election that brought René Lévesque and his Parti Québécois to power, Quebec voters were preparing to allow themselves that option; but, when they were confronted four years later with the opportunity to say yes to independence, a majority shied away.

Independence had, of course, been the PQ's initial *raison d'être*, but it had not been easy to win the support of the many citizens who felt the time had come to dump the increasingly unpopular Liberal government led by Robert Bourassa but who hesitated to take the radical leap of voting for a frankly separatist PQ. Keen to reassure such voters, Lévesque and Claude Morin, who would be his minister of intergovernmental affairs, devised a strategy of *étapisme*, a step-by-step approach to independence. The first step was of course to get elected. Many Péquistes were reluctant to admit that a vote for the PQ did not necessarily mean a vote for Quebec independence, but serious splits within the party were avoided, and voters were promised they could elect the PQ and decide later about independence in a referendum. Even the word "independence" had long been too strong for the PQ: Lévesque coined the term "sovereignty-association" for his concept of a politically sovereign Quebec in economic association with what would remain of Canada; moreover, even a Yes vote in the referendum would not automatically bring sovereignty: voters would merely be asked for a mandate to negotiate a new arrangement. The question that appeared in French and English on the ballot on May 20, 1980 asked for a Yes or No to the following:

> The Government of Quebec has made public its proposal to negotiate a new agreement with the rest of Canada, based on the equality of nations; this agreement would enable Quebec to acquire the exclusive power to make its laws, levy its taxes and establish relations abroad—in other words, sovereignty— and at the same time to maintain with Canada an economic association including a common currency; no change in political status resulting from these negotiations will be effected without approval by the people through another referendum; on these terms, do you give the Government of Quebec the mandate to negotiate the proposed agreement between Quebec and Canada?

In the acrimonious and electrifying campaign leading up to the referendum the Yes side was led by Lévesque, who was personally popular and ran a reasonably popular government. The No side was headed by Claude Ryan, editor of *Le Devoir*, who had been drafted to replace the unpopular Bourassa as Quebec Liberal leader. Ryan was respected for his moral integrity, but the image he projected was dour and austere and he was utterly incapable of matching Lévesque's charismatic appeal; he also had to contend with constant sniping from his federal Liberal partners in the makeshift coalition that was cobbled together to fight the PQ. But with the help of the formidable oratorical power of federal prime minister Pierre Trudeau, along with a dose of fearmongering, the No side carried the day.

Trudeau took the high road, promising constitutional reform within Confederation if voters gave Canada another chance, while his justice minister, Jean Chrétien, took the low road, scaring Quebecers about the price of "la tanque de gaz" if they separated from Canada, and health minister Monique Bégin warned them that federal old-age pensions could vanish. The pro-sovereignty forces made skilful use of Quebec's national symbols and at times they stooped to some subtle intimidation of their own, but when the votes were tallied close to sixty per cent of the Quebec electorate had chosen to stick with the devil they knew. Even assuming that all non-Francophones had voted for the No side (which must have been very nearly true), there was little doubt that a slim majority of French-speaking voters wished to remain within Canada.

Both sides were wary of any U.S. involvement in the referendum campaign, but for very different reasons. Strategists in the No coalition feared that noisy U.S. support for Canadian federalism or implied U.S. threats against a sovereign Quebec would create a backlash. Claude Morin and his PQ colleagues feared just the opposite: for them the possibility of U.S. intervention in favour of the No side was a nightmare: "Were this to have occurred the least bit loudly and clearly, the support of Quebecers for sovereignty-association would, in my opinion, have been greatly reduced," Morin later told Jean-François Lisée. PQ strategists knew from the contacts they had been cultivating in the U.S.A. that the best they could hope for from Washington was neutrality, and this they largely attained. Some U.S. officials even appeared to backtrack slightly: Secretary of State Cyrus Vance, who in 1978 had emphasized his government's preference for a united Canada, in 1980 insisted to journalists that Quebec independence was and would remain a matter to be settled within Canada.

On the day after the referendum Daniel Latouche, who had played a part in formulating the question, interpreted the result to an audience at Harvard University. He saw it as a defeat for the vision promoted by Quebec's poets and chansonniers:

> I think Quebec as the homeland of the French in North America survived until 1960 for a variety of very peculiar reasons which had nothing to do with its internal dynamism as a society. After 1960 we got into the business of existing as a nation, slowly at first; in a way we lived way above our heads in terms of our real position of power and security in North America. We are not as strong as our culture makes us look.... I think we were overextended culturally. In other words, reality has caught up with us.

The public mood during the referendum period had tingled with emotion: gestures and arguments conveyed an agitated sense of historical destiny, and for Quebec society as a whole it proved highly divisive. Thousands of families were split down the middle; mother was pitted against daughter and friend against friend. When it was all over, the winning side felt more a sense of relief than a surge of triumph and the losing side was engulfed in bitterness and gloom, but both were aware that the margin of victory was not overwhelming. The vote had not buried the independence option as deeply as some had hoped. What did seem overwhelming was a feeling of collective trauma, a mood of political exhaustion that seemed to affect nearly everyone. For two decades Quebec had been reverberating to more than its share of political turbulence. The referendum marked the culmination of this turbulence, but it would also prove to be a watershed. As the baby-boomers who had helped to sustain years of political hyperactivity began creeping toward middle age, and as they and their elders became more preoccupied with economic concerns or with "alternative" movements like environmentalism and feminism, grand affairs of state would retreat from centre stage and Quebec society would rest its weary political bones.

The re-election of the Parti Québécois in 1981, on the heels of the 1979 and 1980 federal elections in which Trudeau's Liberals won nearly every Quebec seat in the House of Commons, underlined the paradoxical nature of Quebec politics. Even before becoming prime minister in 1968 (a post he would hold for most of the next sixteen years) Trudeau had been the high priest of Canadian unity, the foremost advocate of a strong central government, and the scourge of Quebec nationalists. How, then, could so many voters support both the arch-centralist Trudeau and the independentist Lévesque? It may have been that Quebec voters subconsciously sought an equilibrium between these two positions: they needed Lévesque to offset Trudeau, and vice versa. A more obvious answer was that they saw Trudeau as the best defender of their interests at the federal level while Lévesque upheld their interests most effectively at the provincial level. Or, as one humorist put it, what voters really wanted was a proud and independent Quebec within a strong and united Canada.

Lévesque's second term as premier would be very different from his first. With independence on the back burner and the bulk of its reformist legislation already in place, day-to-day housekeeping began to loom much larger for the PQ government; and a steep North American recession that hit Quebec especially hard had trimmed its revenues and limited its room for manoeuvre. The PQ began to draw away from its earlier social-democratic creed and undergo a perceptible shift toward the pro-business outlook that would pervade the 1980s. This was, after all, the era of Margaret Thatcher and Ronald Reagan, and the PQ was not slow to catch the drift. As before, however, Lévesque missed few opportunities to pick fights with Ottawa, and his government continued to show great zeal in protecting and seeking to expand its jurisdictional turf.

Trudeau meanwhile began to deliver on his promise of constitutional reform, but what he promised and what he delivered were perceived by many Québécois to be rather different. His vision of renewed federalism included the "patriation" of the constitution (by an absurd anachronism it had been an act of the British Parliament) and the adoption of a Charter of Rights, but those who had hoped that Trudeau would allow Quebec greater autonomy within Confederation were not pleased with the revised constitution, and Quebec's signature did not appear on the document, a fact that would return to haunt the Canadian political scene. North America was in its worst economic slump in half a century, and Quebec saw its commodity shipments sink, its unemployment soar, and its budget deficit spiral out of control. The PQ was split on the issue of *étapisme* versus "independence now". By 1985 the PQ government was visibly worn out and falling apart, and the Quebec Liberal Party under a resurrected Robert Bourassa swept to an easy electoral victory. Bourassa's return to the premier's office came soon after the stunning 1984 election triumph of the federal Conservatives under Brian Mulroney. The Mulroney–Bourassa team was in sharp contrast to the quarrelsome duo of Trudeau and Lévesque. It reflected a subtle but unmistakable shift in Quebec's political values: relations between Quebec and Ottawa would be warmer than at any time in decades, and one of the fruits of this cosy ménage would be closer ties with the U.S.A.

Trudeau and Lévesque had disagreed fundamentally on how the federal structure of Canada should evolve, but both had an ideological approach to politics that predicated a large role for the state in public affairs. Trudeau favoured a strong central government, and his most controversial economic initiatives, such as the creation of the Foreign Investment Review Agency and the adoption of the National Energy Program, were meant to protect and augment Canadian control of an economy largely dominated by foreign owners. Lévesque's primary goals were promotion of the French language and the independence of Quebec, and he made little distinction between English-Canadian and other "foreign" ownership. His major initiatives lay largely outside the economic realm, although they had economic repercussions: investors often had little sympathy for a style of politics that deviated from North American concepts of business as usual.

With Mulroney and Bourassa that would change. Mulroney had grown up in a small town dominated by a U.S.-owned newsprint maker and had been president of the U.S.-owned Iron Ore Company of Canada. He never hesitated to proclaim his pride in Canada, but his vision for Canada was of a broader opening for business and a narrower role for government. When he announced just days after taking office that "Canada is open for business again," his words were greeted cheerfully on Wall Street and in Washington. In short order the Foreign Investment Review Agency was replaced by an agency with even smaller teeth and the National Energy Program was scrapped to a roar of oil company applause.

Bourassa's views on the role of the private sector and his keen interest in luring foreign investment were in line with the conventional thinking of the 1980s, and as a mainstream economist he understood instinctively what motivated U.S. investors and policy-makers. His was a quiet approach, quite unlike the effusive pro-Americanism of Mulroney or the alternate seduction and nose-thumbing of Trudeau (who understood the Americans better than his critics gave him credit for). Lévesque never really learned to penetrate the U.S. mind, as had been proved by his disastrous Economic Club performance and on several subsequent occasions. Bourassa was a dull speaker and he may not have wowed his U.S. audiences, but he spoke their language.

Mulroney and Bourassa stumbled badly in their attempt to remake the constitution in a way acceptable to Quebec through the Meech Lake Accord (which collapsed in 1990), but they had greater success with the 1989 Canada–United States Free Trade Agreement. Mulroney might conceivably have pushed ahead even without Quebec's approval, but Bourassa's enthusiastic support made its success almost inevitable even though, outside Quebec, polls showed majority support for the deal only in Alberta. Elsewhere there was considerable opposition: critics said, among other things, that it would force Canada's policymakers to kowtow to multinational investors and traders, and that closer ties to the U.S. colossus would render Canadian culture even more vulnerable. In Quebec the cultural argument did not wash. To defenders of the French language, Toronto's influence was as threatening as New York's; they were all part of North America's vast Anglophone sea.

Free trade with the United States was especially appealing to the Parti Québécois, which could henceforth argue more convincingly that an independent Quebec would enjoy the benefits that went with membership in a large trade bloc. The interest of PQ economic thinkers in free trade, in fact, went back a long time. In 1970 Rodrigue Tremblay had published a small book called *Indépendance et Marché Commun Québec–E.U.* (Independence and a Quebec–U.S. Common Market) in which he dismissed Canadian nationalism as "the attachment to British institutions of a certain political élite and the preponderant influence of Bay Street financial circles," an attachment that prevented English Canadians from seeing that their true interests lay in a common market with the United States. The idea had a brief vogue, and was adopted by Union Nationale finance minister Mario Beaulieu as his platform in that party's 1971 leadership race; but Beaulieu was defeated and the proposal gradually faded away. The Parti Québécois continued to advocate sovereignty and economic association with the rest of Canada. Nevertheless Rodrigue Tremblay joined the PQ in 1976, but he had not changed his mind about where Quebec's economic destiny lay. After being elected to the National Assembly and named to Lévesque's cabinet as Minister of Industry and Commerce he told the CBC Radio program *Sunday Morning*:

It's obvious that we are in North America. We need to catch up with the rest of the continent on the economic ground. And we start off, mind you, with a good base. I think the Quebec economy is very strong — potentially strong. We have a lot of resources.... And our location is not too bad. Within the Canadian common market which is a strip of 200 miles 3,500 miles long, we are not well located compared to Ontario. But if we have a sort of North American common market which I think we are going to evolve toward in the next quarter century, then the Quebec–Montreal area, the St. Lawrence area, is well located. Our natural market is not Vancouver, of course. It is mainly Boston, Pittsburgh, Cleveland, Washington, Philadelphia and New York.

If Tremblay had accepted the PQ idea of a Quebec–Canada common market, it was only as a prelude to a larger arrangement that would involve both Quebec and Canada in a common market with the United States. The next week, again on *Sunday Morning*, the new minister of finance, Jacques Parizeau, confirmed that this was the scenario PQ economic strategists had in mind.

It's possible, simply, that steps have to be taken one by one. We all know, in North America, that sooner or later there won't be much in terms of tariffs between the United States and Canada, since for the last thirty years these tariffs have fallen regularly.

Stressing the importance of Quebec's economic links with Ontario, Parizeau said that for the moment he was

talking about a customs union with Canada — largely because of Ontario, but with Canada — and then eventually that, shall we say, a free-trade area within North America will gradually take place. So it's one step after another.

And in 1983 Bernard Landry, who had just taken over the international relations portfolio, said in an interview with the Montreal daily *La Presse* that he was

in favour of natural economic circuits, tied as closely as possible to the major factors that determine competition — transportation costs, the concentration and proximity of markets. In a radius of 500 miles from where we're sitting, there are a hundred million solvent consumers, and I don't have to tell you that only a tiny minority of them are in Quebec or in Canada.... You have to remember that Canada is an artificial political creation set up by Britain in the late nineteenth century so that it could keep its North American empire. This prevents us from selling in Boston and New York and vice versa. This is the end of the National Policy [the protectionist policy of Sir John A. Macdonald]; since the Kennedy Round, the theory of John A. Macdonald has become an illusion, if not an absurdity.

PQ ministers were talking not only about making sure that Quebec's economic relations with the United States were undisturbed but about working toward making those relations closer. While in most parts of the world independence and national self-assertion were associated with a loosening of U.S. control, Quebec's peculiar circumstances had produced a nationalist movement that saw close relations with the United States as not only compatible with its independence project but indeed an essential part of it. In the PQ vision, there was no contradiction between the independence of Quebec and the vital interests of the United States.

THE EMERGENCE OF QUEBEC INC.

Like most of North America, Quebec entered the 1980s in economic distress. Unemployment remained near fourteen per cent through 1982 and 1983 and was only one per cent lower in the "recovery" year of 1984. The North Shore of the Gulf of St. Lawrence suffered more visibly than most regions: structural problems in the American steel industry and a sizeable drop in newspaper advertising throughout North America—and hence in the demand for newsprint—quickly reversed the boom times created there in earlier decades by U.S. investment. The port city of Sept-Iles lost close to a third of its inhabitants as iron ore shipments plummeted; Port Cartier's population was cut nearly in half by lower ore shipments and by the closing of a huge U.S.-owned pulp mill built only a few years earlier with the aid of heavy government subsidies. Even more dramatic, and more deeply symbolic, was the decline of iron ore production, heavily dependent on the troubled American steel industry. The U.S.-controlled Iron Ore Company of Canada closed its concentrator and pelletizing plant in Sept-Iles in 1981 and shut down its Schefferville mining operation in 1982. Schefferville was about to become little better than a ghost town, and a committee of the Quebec National Assembly met in the town's high school gymnasium to discuss the plight of the community. Its star witness was the president of the Iron Ore Company, Brian Mulroney, in his last act before returning to his first love, politics.

There were other places in Quebec where the seeds were planted for a very different turn of economic events. In the Beauce, long viewed as a sleepy, old-fashioned corner of Quebec tucked into a remote area along the border with Maine (and once the source of more than half the world's commercial maple syrup), local traditions of community solidarity and hard work had turned cottage industries into thriving businesses, several of them growing to multinational scope. The Beauce not only gave the world Vachon cakes and Dionne textiles but also spawned Canam Manac Group Inc., built by entrepreneur Marcel Dutil into one of the continent's top makers of steel joists for the construction industry. The company got its start selling to the New England market; its palindromic name is a contraction of Canadian-American spelled forward and then backward. "Those damn Americans have been coming up here for two hundred years, so we've never been afraid to do business down there," Dutil has been quoted as saying.

Despite its often low wage levels the Beauce began to achieve a modest prosperity, and newspaper and magazine articles in the late 1970s called attention to the phenomenon of this poor but self-reliant farming area suddenly bursting with a wide array of industries with only scant help from outside investors. It was a phenomenon that would grip Quebec as a whole in the 1980s as business, often viewed in the past with deep suspicion, achieved a respectability and acceptance in Quebec that it had long had in most of North America. In yet another respect Quebec was moving into the North American mainstream, but at its own pace and in its own distinct fashion.

The early days of the Quiet Revolution had seen a proliferation of *sociétés d'état*, or state corporations (as crown corporations are called in antimonarchist Quebec). While none came anywhere close in size or prestige to Hydro-Quebec, these corporations spread their tentacles into many sectors of the economy, including Sidbec in steel, Rexfor in forestry, Soquem in mining, Soquip in oil exploration, Soquia in food processing, the Société Nationale de l'Amiante in asbestos, and the Société Générale de Financement, a general investment fund. Besides the state corporations, the government also established the Caisse de Dépôt et Placement du Québec, a financially powerful administrator of tens of billions of dollars in public pension funds with significant holdings in many publicly traded companies. The state corporations, notably Hydro itself and the Caisse de Dépôt, were created largely to give Francophone Quebecers some of the economic control that had eluded them in the private sector. This nationalist thrust was in line with a trend toward wider state ownership of industry in much of the Western world in the 1960s and 1970s, and it also came at a time when youthful protesters were questioning social and political values, including capitalism itself. This was doubly so among Francophones, since English was still very much the language of Quebec capitalism.

Soon after the Parti Québécois took power in 1976, however—indeed partly by default since outside investment was dwindling—small locally owned businesses began to play a more important role in the Quebec economy. Little noticed during the years of tumult, significant change had occurred in the way many people perceived their economic destinies. Educational reforms begun in the early 1960s had led to great leaps in both the number and the qualifications of university graduates. Many of the dominant Anglo-run firms became less reluctant to hire and promote Francophones. Meanwhile the lustre had begun wearing off state corporations, which were no longer hiring in large numbers anyway, and the doors to the private sector were opened wider by the emergence and growth of a rising corps of Francophone-run firms.

Bombardier Inc. is often cited as a shining example, a Quebec firm that went from humble origins to break into the corporate big leagues. It is also an example of the way government promotion of economic nationalism can sometimes pay off. In 1973 the low bid for an order of subway cars for the Montreal Metro came from British-controlled Canadian Vickers, but the Liberal government of Robert Bourassa gave the nod instead to Bombardier, hoping that the home-grown snow-vehicle company would use it as a springboard to build an aggressive, export-oriented business in rail and transit equipment. The strategy worked: Bombardier would soon build or acquire manufacturing facilities in Vermont and in several European countries, and later its newly acquired Canadair aerospace division would buy out foreign aircraft makers including Kansas-based Learjet Corp. and Northern Ireland-based Short Brothers. Although still the biggest and best-known of Quebec's Francophone-run industrial multinationals, Bombardier is not alone. The heroes of Quebec's business breakthrough of the 1980s—and they have been hailed as such—have included people like Marcel Dutil of Canam Manac, Bernard Lemaire who turned Cascades Inc. from a collector of waste paper into an important producer of cardboard and packaging materials on both sides of the Atlantic, and Pierre Péladeau whose Quebecor Inc. printing and publishing empire grew to include sizable U.S. operations.

These three, and hundreds of smaller firms in virtually every area of economic endeavour, were able to finance their growth with the help of something known in English as Quebec Stock Savings Plans. This program, introduced by the PQ in 1979 and modified substantially in 1983 to favour smaller firms, provided generous tax writeoffs to purchasers of eligible shares in Quebec-based companies. Besides helping such companies raise capital, this defused some complaints about high taxation and whetted the appetites of people who had never before played the stock market. By the late 1980s some fourteen per cent of Quebec adults were shareholders in publicly traded companies, still below the Canadian average but nearly three times the five per cent of a decade earlier.

In Quebec, as in so many other places during the 1980s, government—even a PQ government—was learning to get along better with the corporate sector, and this was made easier by the growing proportion of Francophones in that sector. Big business no longer seemed so alien. Rather than objects of suspicion, home-grown millionaires who had made it into the big leagues were, for a brief period, cheered on and venerated almost like star athletes by a sizable portion of the public. Even the crime-and-sports tabloid *Le Journal de Montréal* began carrying stock tables. In keeping with the spirit of the times, the depositor-owned Desjardins credit union movement began straying from its populist roots to move into corporate finance, and the once-radical Quebec Federation of Labour established its own risk capital fund in 1984 with the stated goal of helping finance job creation, but also with the aim of providing a healthy return on investment.

When the Bourassa Liberals returned to power in 1985 after nine years in the political wilderness they found the pro-business economic policies put in place in the PQ's second term much to their liking. Unlike the PQ, however, they set about dismantling some of the government's holdings in the economy, although they retained a sizable and varied portfolio of industrial holdings. A position paper presented soon after the Liberals regained power argued that Quebec's new business dynamism made government involvement in the economy harder to justify and that the onus should be on the state to prove the need for public intervention; but this same paper argued that:

> privatization is not an end in itself. When it is required, privatization of a state
> corporation must seek to strengthen the economic structure of Quebec while
> assuring Quebec's presence in key economic sectors.

Even in the age of Margaret Thatcher and Ronald Reagan, a society that feared for its cultural survival was unlikely to give up what it saw as valuable collective tools.

Among the untouchable parts of this structure were the Caisse de Dépôt and Hydro-Quebec. Hydro-Quebec's glory days were clearly behind it, but its appetite for massive capital spending seemed barely to have been tamed, and Robert Bourassa never lost his enthusiasm for exploiting the economic potential of Quebec's northern rivers. Just before he regained the premiership, his 1985 book *Power from the North* once again brought hydroelectricity and power exports to the centre of Quebec political debate. Bourassa proposed that Quebec dam the remaining rivers flowing into James Bay, as well as a number of rivers on the north shore of the St. Lawrence, for the sole purpose of exporting the power to the United States. The billions of dollars required for these gigantic projects would also come from the United States on the basis of firm contracts to purchase the power. Bourassa launched the book with a press conference in Washington, and then announced his candidacy in a provincial by-election, campaigning with the book as his chief prop. The PQ retaliated with a book of its own, criticizing the feasibility of Bourassa's proposals—but not the principle of power exports. By 1988 Hydro had signed a series of new export contracts with power authorities in New York and New England that would run for up to thirty years and would involve annual sales of up to 14.6 billion kilowatt-hours of electricity.

The new James Bay project was opposed, however, by U.S. environmentalists concerned about both the aesthetic and the public health aspects of high-voltage transmission lines; by others, in both Canada and the U.S., concerned about the effects of new hydro dams on Native peoples and wildlife; and by the Quebec Cree, who alleged that the new project would violate environmental assurances in their 1975 agreement with the Quebec government. By late 1991 this opposition had grown to the point where Bourassa was forced to postpone the project and doubts existed about whether it would ever be built.

The growth of electricity exports was just one part of a tendency toward closer north–south economic ties. The Free Trade Agreement with the United States created a rare measure of consensus among Quebec's economic and political decision-makers. Support was especially enthusiastic among some of the ambitious and self-assured members of Quebec's new business élite who saw glorious opportunities in a tariff-free continental market.

The obvious affinity of many business people with the United States led inevitably to comparisons with Quebec's other major trading partner, Ontario. The feelings of Canam Manac's Marcel Dutil may not be shared by everyone, but they do point to a problem:

> I never like going to Toronto, but I have to because I have a plant there. I still notice a negative reaction to French Canadians in Toronto. They don't treat us like we are equal. Personally, I don't feel that I'm not equal, but that's the feeling they try to give me. The welcome is not there. We go to Missouri or Boston or Maryland and we are part of the game. In Toronto, that's not the case.[63]

Bombardier chief Laurent Beaudoin made similar observations:

> The United States has always been a more open market to us than the rest of Canada. In the U.S. if you give them a good product at a reasonable price, they'll buy it. In Ontario, we've always had trouble. Being French is always a problem there.[64]

Ontario investors have also run up against obstacles in Quebec. In 1989 a Toronto-based consortium made a vigorous series of offers for the shares of the Montreal-based Steinberg supermarket and real estate empire. The Quebec government made it clear that it wanted control of Steinberg to stay in Quebec, and the Caisse de Dépôt countered with a proposal of its own in partnership with a Montreal entrepreneur named Michel Gaucher. Owners of the family trust that controlled a majority of the voting shares found themselves under intense pressure to accept the Quebec offer, and the Ontario group was thwarted. At about the same time, Paul Desmarais, head of the Montreal-based holding company Power Corp. of Canada and the controlling shareholder in pulp and paper giant Consolidated Bathurst Inc., also of Montreal, agreed to sell Consolidated Bathurst to Chicago-based Stone Container Corp., and neither Quebec nor Ottawa raised a finger to stop the sale. The different treatment of the two cases hinged on more than the fact that one outside bidder was from Ontario and the other from the United States, but it did send a confused set of signals. Some financial writers in Toronto took to using the sobriquet "Quebec Inc." in alluding to the government's strategic co-operation with certain businesses: this was intended to draw a parallel with the formidable power once wielded by Japan's legendary Ministry of International Trade and Industry and the carefully co-ordinated attacks on foreign markets it devised in conjunction with Japanese private firms. But the notion that government and business in Quebec work in any sort of Japan Inc.–style lockstep is an exaggeration. Clearly the Quebec government has used the financial power of its agencies to promote the likes of Michel Gaucher, but such an approach has been far from systematic.

Despite the relentless rise of the Québécois business community only a handful of the largest corporations are under Francophone control; but as you go farther down in the corporate rankings the proportion of French names constantly increases, and this gives a clearer idea of what is happening in the Quebec economy. Its growth in recent times has been driven by its multiplicity of small and medium-sized firms, most of them French-speaking and many of them only a few years old.

University enrolments tell a similar story, one that would have been unimaginable a generation ago. Quebec in the late 1980s had only a quarter of Canada's population and slightly more than a fifth of its university students, yet it accounted for nearly half of all Canadian students enrolled in business courses. All four universities in Montreal offered well-attended graduate programs in management, and Francophones made up a hefty proportion of students in such programs at the two English-language institutions. It seems Quebec is going to have many more business people in the years to come, and this is bound to have its political and cultural consequences.

PRECARIOUS SURVIVAL TO THE SOUTH

August has not yet ended, but already Madawaska High School has been in full session for nearly two weeks. The school year starts early in northern Maine and then recesses in the latter half of September: potatoes are the agricultural mainstay of this part of the world, and student labour contributes mightily to getting the harvest in on time. Then it is back to the books. As the students queue patiently for lunch in the high school cafeteria they produce a low hubbub of conversation. Only one language can be heard, and it's not French. The surnames here are mostly French and, listening carefully, one may detect hints of a French accent here and there. But the chatter is all in English. This could be a high school cafeteria almost anywhere in the United States. The students gobble their food and rush off to afternoon classes. Then it is the turn of the custodians and the cafeteria staff to take their lunch. These people are mostly in their forties and fifties, the same generation as the students' parents, and the language they are speaking is not English. Their talk is larded with English terms and expressions, and to delicate ears it may not always sound very refined, but it is unmistakably French. Here one generation and gone the next: as in other French-speaking pockets of the United States, the language is receding, especially among the young.

The *Madawaskayens* of northern Maine have long had a special place in the history of the French in North America, and as recently as the 1970s it had seemed that if any French-speaking part of the United States had a chance of resisting full Americanization it would be this one. Although railways, roads, public schools, radio, and television had gradually reduced the St. John valley's isolation it was still on the periphery of their influence. In terms of economics and transport the valley's links with Canada have been much closer than those with the United States. A wide stretch of forest separates the valley from the population centres to the south, and while modern U.S. highways have put the valley in somewhat closer touch with the society on the other side of the forest they have not made it completely part of that society.

There are few places where the Canada–U.S. border is so patently artificial: geographically the valley is one, and it seems united rather than divided by the river from which green fields stretch out on both sides to the distant hills. The towns that dot the river banks at irregular intervals come in pairs, one on one side of the river and one on the other: Clair, New Brunswick and Fort Kent, Maine; Edmundston and Madawaska; St. Leonard and Van Buren; and so on. The bridges are staffed by customs and immigration officers, but townspeople cross back and forth regularly for shopping, entertainment, and sometimes employment. Many older residents remember when there were scarcely any border inspections at all.

The U.S. half of the valley shares many of the characteristics of Atlantic Canada: the quiet beauty, the subsistence economy, and the frequency with which people who grew up there have left for wealthier and faster-moving parts of the continent. Obituaries in the *St. John Valley Times* often report that the deceased is survived by sons or daughters in other parts of the United States, often as far as California but most likely in Connecticut: Geraldine Chasse of Madawaska says that there is "hardly anyone in the valley who doesn't have relatives in *le Conneckticut*." But the impact of U.S. political sovereignty on the south side of the valley is clearly visible. Mainstream U.S. culture is not indigenous or natural to the valley but it is there all the same, and the primary carriers of that culture have been institutions brought in by the governments of the United States and the State of Maine. Foremost among these is the educational system: Marcella Violette of Van Buren says the system "wasn't designed to produce French people who spoke English; it was designed to produce Americans and that meant Anglophones."

The town of Madawaska has an English face, but across the river the face of Edmundston is decidedly French. The English-language *St. John Valley Times* is published in Madawaska, the French *Le Madawaska* in Edmundston; Madawaska has the Madawaska Historical Society, Edmundston the Société Historique du Madawaska. The valley institutions that probably are least inconvenienced by the border are the twin mills of the Fraser Companies (since 1974 a subsidiary of Toronto-based Noranda Inc.): pulp is produced on the New Brunswick side and moves across the river through an elevated pipeline for conversion to paper at a mill on the Maine side. The pulp mill was built in 1918, the paper mill seven years later: at the time there was a high U.S. tariff on paper but pulp entered duty-free. Today, as in the past, pungent industrial odours waft indiscriminately across the international boundary.

The border may be of little consequence to the Fraser Companies but few *Madawaskayens* are in a position to treat it quite as flippantly. Those who live on the U.S. side tend to think of themselves as different from their neighbours who live "across". They also see the fate of their threatened culture as tied less to events in nearby New Brunswick or Quebec than to those farther away in Augusta or Washington. Valley particularism is common to both sides of the border, but the notion of the *République de Madawaska* is largely Canadian. Those on the U.S. side tend to romanticize their Acadian heritage, even though their ancestry is at least as much French Canadian as Acadian and probably more.[65] History professor Roger Paradis, whose elegant hillside dwelling in the forested Maine countryside overlooks the equally verdant New Brunswick side of the valley, ascribes this inconsistency to the neglect of regional history in school curricula, but he says many *Madawaskayens* are aware of it:

> The Quebec presence is stronger here, but people in the Valley identify more with their Acadian ancestry. The Acadian tragedy is such a tear-jerker— people can relate to things like that.

But, commenting on a state grant announced in 1989 for the establishment of a regional cultural archive, Paradis urged those responsible to hurry: "The old people are dying off. The tales and songs are almost dead."

Gérard Morin is the librarian at Wisdom School in St. Agatha, a picturesque hamlet that until recently was regarded as among the most heavily French-speaking in northern Maine. Morin laments the virtual absence of French books or newspapers in his library: "All we have in French are dictionaries and classic literature, but nothing contemporary." He enjoys speaking French, but the occasion arises less often now:

> Life here has really become very Anglophone. French is becoming something that is learned as a second language. It's strange, but at the same time there's a certain mistrust toward the Anglos who arrive here from outside.... You often find people who have the ability to speak French but lack the will. It's quite common to hear parents speak to their children in French and for the children to reply in English. The children have to be given reasons to speak French, and there aren't any.

In the 1950s there was a concerted attempt to keep French out of the schools: children were punished for speaking French in the playground. That gave way in the 1970s to a brief but intense show of enthusiasm for bilingual education. Gil Albert, who teaches in Fort Kent, says most French-speaking *Madawaskayens* are literate only in English, and this creates serious problems of self-image. He hopes the Canada – U.S. Free Trade Agreement will bring more contact with Quebec because "the economy controls culture and not the reverse." But Jim Pinette, a writer and teacher who lives near Caribou, a short distance southeast of the valley, says that

> We don't speak Québécois French. They learned to read French and update it; here we stick to eighteenth century agrarian French.

Although French is now spoken less widely, it still allows local people to communicate in a sort of code:

> Many find they still need French to be with their friends. It also gives them a "secret" language to "hide" from those in power. It prevents outsiders from getting a complete foothold.

In few places in the United States did the ethnic pride movement find as much resonance as in southwestern Louisiana. From being a label of shame and backwardness Cajun became downright trendy, not only in the triangular region that is now proudly called Acadiana but right across the U.S.A. Some writers and entrepreneurs have exploited Cajun stereotypes shamelessly, and the exotic image that many Americans hold of Cajuns as happy-go-lucky, beer-swilling, crawfish-devouring, pirogue-paddling swamp dwellers who dance to strange music and speak an unintelligible dialect has only a faint link to reality. In a sour little book called *The Truth About the Cajuns*, Lafayette journalist Trent Angers takes a swipe at certain magazine writers for

> their overemphasis upon the quaint, the offbeat, the outmoded—without putting these things in their proper perspective.... To read some of these stories, you'd swear that all the Cajuns do is eat, drink and dance!... The false impressions conveyed by some media to the American public are an annoyance and embarrassment to the Cajun people. They also tend to hurt south Louisiana's prospects for industrial expansion and job creation.

Angers is undoubtedly correct in pointing out that there has been a great deal of exaggeration. He celebrates both the distinctiveness of Cajun culture and the extent to which Cajuns have become absorbed into modern U.S.

society, but he seems to wonder why it is that many outsiders are so much more intrigued by what makes Cajuns different from other Americans than by what makes them the same. Once the myths and stereotypes are stripped away, Cajuns do look more like other Americans than some romantics like to imagine, but they have also kept alive a broad cultural tradition that is filled with reminders of the time not so very long ago when most Cajuns did indeed live on remote farms or near isolated swamps and when French was the dominant tongue. Today Cajun food, for instance, is as romanticized as all the rest of the mythology: in fact, the generous use of cayenne pepper, where it occurs, is a fairly recent borrowing from Creole cooking; crawfish étouffée, sometimes regarded as the Cajuns' national dish, was seasonal before modern aquaculture; and blackened red snapper is Cajun only insofar as master chef Paul Prudhomme, who invented the dish in 1970, grew up in a small-town Cajun household. A more authentic cultural export has been Cajun music. Barry Jean Ancelet, who has written extensively about Cajun music, describes it as "bluesy, born of a Euro-Afro blend that encompasses rock and roll and jazz, displaying great vitality and independence." Live radio broadcasts from venues like Fred's Bar in the town of Mamou have become part of the regional culture, and Lafayette is host to two annual music festivals. "People have been predicting the demise of Cajun culture since the 1930s," Ancelet says. "It's sure taking a long time to die, don't you think?"

If the culture remains vibrant, however, the same cannot be said of the language on which it is based. Even where the traditional ways have held on most persistently people have had to begin asking what form their Cajun identity will take if the French language largely disappears. Part of the answer may have been provided by a young man in a small town on Quebec's Gaspé peninsula. Although his surname was McBrearty he spoke only halting English, but one of his proudest boasts was "je suis irlandais." His family had lived for generations in the Gaspé; he probably never heard the Irish language spoken and had only passing contact with Ireland's adopted English tongue, yet he still felt some identity with his Irish ancestors. It is likewise not uncommon to hear Louisianians boast—in English—of their Cajun heritage. The loss of the language may render the heritage dilute and incomplete, but it is still there today and is likely to remain for generations to come, long after its current trendiness has worn off.

In 1987 a Cajun named Paul Hardy was elected lieutenant governor of Louisiana. Hardy grew up in a French-speaking family in the town of Cecilia in St. Martin parish, and he insisted that it was his ability to speak French that put him over the top in the election:

I still speak French with my high school friends. Fifteen years ago if we spoke French people would sneer at us and didn't envy our ability, but now they are envious and wish they could speak French too.

Toward the end of an interview, Hardy was asked whether Cajun identity could survive the loss of the French language. The answers to previous questions had sprung quickly to his lips, but now he took a long pause before giving a careful reply:

I don't know if we can retain our uniqueness and our authenticity if we lose our heritage, and our French language may well be the heart of our heritage. So we can't take a chance. We can't afford to lose our heart and expect to survive.

Claire Quintal has long contended that one of the obstacles to galvanizing New England Franco-Americans has been the absence in their history of anything comparable to the Acadian tragedy. "We have no Evangeline myth," she says, "no leaky boats to talk about." Madeleine Giguère is inclined to agree: "Even if we had our own Jimmy Domengeaux, I don't think we could ever be as trendy as the Cajuns."

Those who identify themselves as Franco-Americans are very clearly an aging group. Many younger people refuse to accept that label, either because they want to be termed simply Americans or because, to at least one person we came across, it sounded too much like a popular U.S. brand of canned spaghetti. Giguère, as a sociologist, paints a sombre picture of a people still heavily concentrated in menial or semiskilled jobs and with little upward mobility or ambition; many of the more ambitious have moved elsewhere. But the predicted demise of Franco-Americans as an identifiable group has not occurred, and Giguère's personal view as a Franco-American is less gloomy. "They have a sense of identity that is more stable and deeper than we think," she says. Here, too, questions arise as to what will remain of the identity once the language is gone. In the 1980 U.S. census, 410,000 New Englanders said French was spoken in their homes. In Manchester, New Hampshire, 51,000 of the city's 160,000 inhabitants had at least one French-speaking parent, and 22,000 lived in homes where French was spoken. Some instances could even be found of people speaking French at work, especially among older workers in the building trades, but the once essential link between language and religion has largely been lost. In many traditionally Franco-American parishes perhaps one Sunday Mass out of five will be offered in French, often at an inconveniently early hour, and most of those present will be elderly.

Lewiston native Paul Paré, who became a senior administrator with the Association Canado-Américaine in Manchester, says that Franco-Americans who have been assimiliated in terms of language are often the most deeply attached to other cultural traits and have stuck loyally to family and neighbourhood:

> To speak French or not to speak French is not something that is decided consciously: it is something that happens, like being born or dying.

In Woonsocket, Rhode Island, which was once "la ville la plus française d'Amérique" and in the 1920s had a higher proportion of Francophones than Montreal, the Union Saint Jean-Baptiste had only two bilingual secretaries left by 1989; it had not been possible to recruit new employees who could take dictation in French.

Whether in Woonsocket, in Berlin, New Hampshire, or in any number of other towns that make up their archipelago, Franco-Americans have not been immune to a common immigrant experience: the first generation often has only a shaky grasp of English; the second generation learns English at school and feels comfortable in both languages; the third generation may have at best a passive knowledge of the heritage language; by the fourth generation it is largely gone. What is perhaps more surprising is that this has also been happening among the Cajuns and *Madawaskayens*, who cannot be viewed in any sense as immigrants: their communities go back centuries, and it was Anglophones who were the intruders. From Louisiana to Maine, people born after the Second World War, with some noteworthy exceptions, are simply less likely than their elders to be fluent in French. Many younger people may understand French but do not feel comfortable speaking it. Nor is it uncommon to find adolescents or adults who speak a sort of baby French: they spoke French as young children and have retained their accent but can command only a childish vocabulary. Not so long ago it was also common to find young children who had difficulty communicating with French-speaking grandparents, but as the unilingual elderly dwindle to statistical insignificance this phenomenon is disappearing. The use of French has also suffered from mixed marriages: where one spouse is Francophone and the other Anglophone English nearly always becomes the language used in the home. This effect spreads beyond the immediate household: at large family gatherings, which ought to be one place where the French language prevails, people will often speak English to avoid excluding unilingual in-laws from the conversation.

It is also true, however, that a number of individual families scattered throughout the French-speaking archipelago of the United States still strive to preserve the use of French at home and have made sure their children also can speak the language. One such family is that of Robert Perreault, a writer, lecturer, and tour guide living in Manchester, whose 1983 novel *L'Héritage* was the first by a Franco-American to be published in French since 1938. Perreault argues that the Franco-American response to the ethnic pride movement proved weaker than the rebound of Cajun culture because it had not been as repressed:

> At a time when Cajuns were being punished for speaking French in school, we had parochial schools with half-days of instruction in French. We learned to read and write in French. We hadn't lost our culture enough to rediscover it.

Certainly some of the distinctions between the Cajuns of Louisiana and the Franco-Americans of New England revolve around the fact that one group was traditionally rural, the other predominantly urban; one group relied mostly on oral traditions, while the other was largely literate in French. But even these distinctions are becoming blurred as Cajuns become more urbanized and Franco-Americans lose their ability to read and write French. In Lowell, Massachusetts, Albert Côté, who put together the monthly *Journal de Lowell* as a labour of love, acknowledged that his readership was composed increasingly of elderly people. Robert Perreault was in the last graduating class of the École St. Georges in Manchester before bilingual courses were phased out in 1965: after that the courses had to be given in English because the children had insufficient knowledge of French. Perrault says sadly:

> The Irish see themselves as Irish and the Cajuns see themselves as Cajuns, but this is less so among the Franco-Americans. Children will say: "I'm not French, my grandparents are." Many others are almost totally unaware of their background.

Others, however, are less pessimistic. Raoul Pinette of Lewiston, an undertaker, says any idea of burying French is premature. He criticizes current Franco-American leaders — "they lack vision" — and some of those from the past — "they wanted to make us Canadians; their heart wasn't in the United States." Some people regard the language as an obstacle, but Pinette says it is no such thing: it didn't stop him from becoming national president of his professional association. Interrupting a French conversation to speak for a moment to his daughter in English, he said he still thinks it is possible to revive the French language in the United States. "We have to eliminate defeatism. We have to show more imagination. We have to sell the idea. We have to discover who we are."

TURNING DREAMS INTO GOLD

At Exit 5 on the Maine Turnpike the driver is suddenly confronted with a sign in French. It points the way not to Lewiston or to any of the other historic centres of French life in Maine but to Old Orchard Beach.

The Maine coast is the closest outlet to the sea for most of the thickly populated areas of Quebec, and its resorts have long been popular summer vacation spots for residents of Montreal and other cities in Quebec, but for French Canadians there is something special about Old Orchard Beach. It is a part of the United States where they can feel at home. Old Orchard's eleven kilometres of sandy beach brought summer visitors as early as the 1820s. A few Montrealers made the trip by coach, and more of them made the trip after the Grand Trunk Railway — the same Grand Trunk that brought thousands of mill workers to Lewiston — was completed between Montreal and Portland in 1853. In the late nineteenth and early twentieth centuries Old Orchard became part of the New England tourist circuit, boasting fashionable hotels and its famous pier. Since the Second World War things have changed. The handsome turn-of-the-century wooden hotels that once lined the beach have given way to functional but dreary motels; with its amusement area right on the beach, its streets lined with fast-food stands and souvenir shops, Old Orchard Beach today has a tackiness that makes some of its older residents wince. A pleasant, reserved elderly lady at the town's Historical Society prefers to reminisce about the days when Guy Lombardo and Rudy Vallee used to entertain wealthy visitors rather than acknowledge what Old Orchard Beach has become.

The Québécois who swarm across the border, on the other hand, seem to like it just as it is. Always a substantial minority of the tourists at Old Orchard, in July they almost seem to have the place to themselves. It takes neither much money nor much sense of adventure for a Québécois to spend a week or two in Old Orchard Beach in July. The town itself is as much an attraction as the sand or the ocean. Driving no more than six hours from Montreal, and speaking nothing but their native language, Francophones from Quebec can spend some time in a foreign country. Old Orchard Beach makes an effort to cater to what has become its most reliable market. Québécois are invited to use their own language by *Ici on parle français* signs in many store and restaurant windows, although some like to try out their

English when they are in the United States and others heed the rumours that places where French is spoken sometimes charge more than those where it is not. Some of the food stands stick resolutely to New England specialties like fried clams while several others cater to a recent Quebec fast-food fad and offer that viscous combination of french fries, cheese curd, and chicken gravy known as *poutine*. Bars at oceanside hotels feature entertainers like "Ti-Gars" Plante at the organ, playing a mixture of Quebec and U.S. popular favourites, and both the Town of Old Orchard Beach and the Chamber of Commerce have made a point of seeking bilingual employees.

This, fortunately, is a condition that a sizable number of people in the area can still fulfil, since the 6,500 year-round residents of Old Orchard Beach as well as the people of the nearby towns of Biddeford and Saco are largely Franco-American. Some local people have complained that visitors from Quebec tend to look down on them and treat them as poor cousins, but Norman Beaupré, who teaches literature at the University of New England in Biddeford, says Quebec visitors

> have always been part of the culture here. They have blended in very well, and people here are happy to have the chance to speak French to native speakers.

In the rest of the Franco-American archipelago activists seeking to preserve the language lament the absence of any economic advantage in knowing French, but this has not been a problem in Old Orchard Beach. A former town manager, Jérôme Plante (no relation to "Ti-Gars"), a third-generation Franco-American from Biddeford, said that "without the French Canadians coming here, I would have lost my French." Plante believes that the existence of a French-speaking host population has helped Old Orchard Beach maintain its position as the pre-eminent Québécois summer resort. "People go to Kennebunkport or Ogunquit or Hampton Beach once, for a change," he said, "but then they come back here." Jérôme Plante may not be entirely unbiased, but it is true that Old Orchard Beach seems in little danger of losing its Quebec clientele. Nevertheless Québécois can now be found in summer resorts all along the Atlantic coast, not only in Maine and New Hampshire but also on Cape Cod (where René Lévesque spent many summers and where he wrote the book *Option Québec* outlining his ideas on sovereignty-association) and in Wildwood, New Jersey (whose promoters sent an airplane flying over Montreal during the 1979 gasoline crisis with the message "Wildwood has gas" trailing behind it). In the winter the scene shifts to southern Florida and to the agglomeration of resort towns running north from Miami.

The attractions of Miami are more complex and diverse than those of its smaller competitors, for Miami does not survive solely on tourism but is also a centre for such related activities as banking and the buying and selling of real estate. It is one of those American cities, along with Los Angeles and Las Vegas, that lives by turning dreams into gold, and among the people who have been lured by the prospect of this conversion are a growing number of Québécois.[66] While parts of Miami are lavish others are every bit as tacky as Old Orchard Beach. It is, however, more varied. The rundown southern part of Miami Beach is Jewish, elderly, and bored. Downtown Miami, on the other side of Biscayne Bay, has largely been taken over by Cubans and other Spanish-speakers who are not enamoured of the changes that revolution has brought to their nearby homelands. Fort Lauderdale, a few kilometres north, acquired a reputation in the 1950s as the place "where the boys are" and for many years was known as a rowdy hangout for students on spring break. And in the beach resorts just north of Miami large pockets of Québécois have collected. None of these groups mixes particularly well with any of the others, but if Miami seems to be a segmented society, the same can probably be said of Montreal.

Since climate is Miami's main attraction, Canadians have long been among those who have answered its call. Anglophone Canadians mix easily with Bostonians and Philadelphians and Jews from Montreal or Toronto are not distinguishable at first glance from those who live in Brooklyn or Long Island, but the Francophones form a community apart. As in Old Orchard, there are motels and clubs in North Miami Beach catering specifically to them. The Petit Québec nightclub in the sprawling Castaways motel does a roaring business offering service and entertainment in French, and it is far from alone. In the 1970s and 1980s the city of Hollywood, midway between North Miami Beach and Fort Lauderdale, became the heart of the Québécois presence in Florida. More French than English is often heard on Hollywood's broad expanses of sandy beach and along its crowded beachfront strip of restaurants and souvenir shops — and not just at establishments with names like Frenchie's or La Gaspésienne. Montreal and Quebec City papers are flown in daily during the winter tourist season, and some of Quebec's less distinguished musical acts and nightclub performers play to appreciative crowds. From an office near downtown Hollywood, well away from the distractions of the beach, Jean Laurac, a veteran of Montreal show business tabloids, puts together *Le Soleil de la Floride*, the latest and — if its hefty volume of advertising is any indication — the most successful of several attempts to establish a lasting French-language paper in Florida. Published monthly, its pages are filled with features on tourist attractions, practical hints for visitors and a steady supply of community gossip. It also enables businesses ranging from Chinese restaurants to air conditioning repairers to peddle their services to the tightly-knit Francophone market.

Nobody seems quite certain how big this market really is, although there have been some extravagant conjectures. Laurac, like many others, divides Québécois in Florida into three categories: the year-round population, which he estimated in 1989 at about 50,000; seasonal visitors who spend three to six months a year in Florida and often own the housing they stay in, about 100,000; and short-term tourists, about 500,000 to 600,000 a year. That gives a total greater than one-tenth of Quebec's overall population, but some estimates have run much higher and Laurac's figures seem as reasonable as any. Naturally a group this size is going to possess very considerable commercial clout. A broad range of retail and service establishments—many but by no means all of them run by Québécois—take pains to deal with their clients in French. Video rentals, bingo games, and Sunday Mass are all available in French; so are legal and dental services, car repairs, plumbing, dry cleaning, and real estate services. Some medical clinics even accept Quebec health insurance cards for full or partial payment. Hollywood and some of the neighbouring communities provide something as much like a home away from home as Québécois are apt to find anywhere south of the Canada–U.S. border.

Canadians, whether English- or French-speaking, not only travel to southern Florida: they bring their money with them. Not surprisingly, one of the main concentrations of Canadian investment has been the Miami area. Some of these investments are small-scale, but others involve more massive amounts of money. Most such investment has gone into tourism and real estate development, but light manufacturing and other domains have also been affected. Because Québécois investment tends to be unusually visible, some Floridians have singled it out for criticism. A former general manager of the Hollywood Chamber of Commerce, Bob Potenziani, decided it was a problem in his city and said so to anyone who would listen, including several reporters. He told the Miami *Herald*:

> These people are poor neighbours and poor citizens.... They form into their own cliques.... Many refuse to speak English.... They won't participate in the community. Some fly the Canadian flag. This attitude has got to stop. It's childish. There is still the United States of America, and we're not going to allow splinter groups to form at the expense of the community. If they want to stay among their own kind and act like this, why don't they stay in Canada in the first place?

Potenziani accused French Canadians of driving up real estate prices to the detriment of the community:

> Tourists have contributed to the economy but not people who've bought real estate. They've only bought what other people have built and inflated the prices. They can't solve their problems at home so they bring them down here.

But he wasn't entirely favourable to French Canadian tourists either:

> You walk along the beach and you think you're in France. I've had customers from other states tell me they won't come back because they don't feel at home here.

Potenziani said that reaction to his comments in the *Herald* was almost uniformly favourable, but most Floridians in positions of influence have long been hospitable toward foreign investment and are willing to tolerate a few Canadian flags to get it. Potenziani's outbursts were considered bad for business, and pressure from the state secretary of commerce led him to quit his job.

Southern Florida's population continued to shoot upward in the 1980s, and Hollywood was far from immune. The Québécois dominated much of the eastern part of town near the beach; families of Cuban descent moved into new subdivisions on the west side of town; and some of Hollywood's longtime English-speaking inhabitants began to feel a bit squeezed. Chris Garrett, executive vice-president of the Chamber of Commerce, was careful to avoid outbursts of the sort that got Potenziani into trouble. Garrett said in a 1989 interview that French Canadians were very much appreciated in Hollywood, but that he found them to be quite self-contained and felt relations could be a bit better. He expressed disappointment that relatively few French-speaking business people had joined the Chamber of Commerce, and contrasted this with the broader Hispanic participation. He also hinted they could be doing more to reverse the slow deterioration of the area around the beach. There can be little doubt that French Canadians in Florida—like other minorities—prefer to stick together: many of them are older people who speak little or no English, and many of these have clustered together in mobile home communities and condominium developments. Québécois who buy this kind of housing may not intend to squeeze out neighbours of other ethnic backgrounds, but that is often the result: one real estate agent with a largely Québécois clientele said that once a project reaches a threshold where forty or forty-five per cent of its occupants are

French Canadians the proportion will quickly shoot up beyond eighty per cent as other residents sell out and move away. But a similar process has long been a familiar characteristic of ethnic or racial population shifts throughout the United States.

A sizable majority of the Québécois who take up seasonal or permanent residence in Florida are approaching or already past retirement age, but a substantial number of younger people have also followed the lure of the sun, hoping to build careers in the south, often in tourism or the building trades, and Florida is not the only place where a warm climate and a booming economy have proved an irresistible lure to emigrants from Quebec. Southern California has also drawn great floods, generally a younger crowd than in Florida, which may be why any attempt at cultural cohesiveness seems to have been left behind. Canadians, both English- and French-speaking, abound in that endless suburban sprawl known as Los Angeles, but it is hard to pinpoint any neighbourhood where they have formed recognizable communities. There does exist an *Association Québec–Californie* which organizes activities such as film showings and Christmas parties, but while groups ranging from Koreans to Salvadorans have established a highly visible presence in Los Angeles the same cannot be said of French Canadians, who have blended in with a degree of unobtrusiveness that would stun Floridians.

Unlike their forebears who migrated to the New England mill towns to escape economic distress at home, many of the recent working-age transplants in Florida have already done well at home and arrive with sufficient capital to buy housing or set up small businesses: even the less ambitious soon discover that although wages may sometimes be lower than in Quebec, so too are living costs. They came south to escape the harsh northern winters and immerse themselves in a glamorous subtropical lifestyle, and who is to say that this is somehow wrong? Countless other North Americans have dreamt this facet of the American Dream and have done just the same.

Something else that differentiates these Québécois from migrants of an earlier era is that, although they may stumble on—and indeed become part of—what amount to small-scale re-creations of the society they left behind, few seem to harbour illusions of being able to perpetuate their distinctive Quebec identity very far into the future. Their children attend classes in English, and even if many parents insist that they speak French at home these same parents also want to see them become good Americans. (The Irish bishops of New England might well have had an easier time with French Canadians like these.) That does not mean that the French language is about to die out in Hollywood or in its other Florida enclaves. The continuing influx of new arrivals and the comings and goings that keep jumbo jets full and highways crowded will provide cultural sustenance for years to come; but should these steady transfusions from Quebec one day start to dry up, as they did in New England, the cultural defences of French Canadians could well crumble even faster in Florida than they did farther north.

For the present, however, French Canadians can still live the American Dream in Florida without having to jettison more than a small part of their cultural past. Michel Tremblay arrived in 1976 from the Lac St. Jean region of central Quebec with his wife and two young children. Four years later, he bought the Entrada Motel in downtown Hollywood. By the late 1980s the motel was drawing a winter clientele that was three-quarters French-speaking, and Tremblay hoped to do the same in the summer. The motel bar still attracted mainly *Américains*, but plans were afoot to instill a French-Canadian *ambience* there as well. Steve Tremblay, the owner's son, now helps manage the motel and talks English just like an American. He never learned to write in French although he can speak the language: his mother insisted on it. Michel Tremblay is happy with his move:

> Here we've got the sun and the beach. We've got everything we want. There's a drug problem here, but that's true in Quebec also. People here sometimes seem lazy to us; we come from a northern tradition, and we work faster. But this is home to me now. I own a property on Lac St. Jean and had thought of spending six months a year there and six months here. But Quebec has only a few warm days a year. It made me feel depressed.

He knows quite a few Quebecers who have gone into business in Florida, and some who discovered the hard way that doing business there isn't as easy as it may seem.

> There are quite a few Québécois who returned home after being taken to the cleaners. You have to have a good lawyer [his daughter was studying law in Miami]. My generation are all keeping their Canadian citizenship, but the second generation are all going to be Americans. My children both speak French, but when we have grandchildren, we'll have to see how things turn out.

Jean-Guy Fournier is someone else who has found his paradise in Florida. Once a police officer in a Montreal suburb, he started a company called Quebec Realty Corporation whose head office is in downtown Hollywood, a few blocks from the Entrada Motel.

I came here planning to stay three weeks, and my visit has stretched out to ten years. I have to say it's for the climate, not for the hospitality. I find the Americans are a bit cold. But here you get into your car in the morning, and the engine starts.

Fournier has witnessed two trends in recent years: more Québécois are visiting Florida during the summer, turning it into a year-round affair; and more of them are buying Florida real estate well before they reach retirement age. As the French-Canadian community expands it creates a snowball effect that makes it easier for others to follow.

The legal niceties of immigration, however, have provided plenty of gossip, much of it repeated in a low whisper. It is an open secret that several thousand Québécois — neither the Miami office of the U.S. Immigration and Naturalization Service nor the Canadian consulate in Atlanta seemed to have a clear idea of the numbers — came to Florida as visitors and remained illegally as workers. (This is in addition to thousands more whose immigrant status was legalized under a sweeping amnesty offered in the late 1980s to anyone who could prove at least five years' residence.) But the immigration service has bigger fish to fry in southern Florida; its agents are kept busy stemming the flow from the Caribbean and Central America. They are far too busy to spend much time hassling Québécois, who have proved by and large to be economically self-sufficient, to make few demands on the region's overburdened social services, and to contribute little to Florida's crime rate. When the immigration service does snare anyone it is usually on a tip from somebody motivated by jealousy, blackmail, or personal animosity. The threat of being deported for staying more than six months a year in the U.S. without legal papers is less worrying to most Canadians than the risk of losing their provincial health insurance coverage for being in Canada *less* than six months a year.

But these cares and woes seem far removed from the rolling surf and the toe-warming sand whose magnetic charm has lured so many people from so far away. Some of those to be seen on a typical day are speaking French, just as countless millions across the broad interior of the continent might be doing today had the eighteenth century turned out differently. History may have deceived them, but these people and others like them will continue to pursue a dream, the same dream that has motivated so many of their compatriots in the past and will continue to influence Quebec life in years to come.

8

Nation and State, Language and Culture

AT THE OPENING of the final decade of the twentieth century the traditional concept of the nation-state was again under attack in Canada as it was elsewhere. The strides toward the unification of markets across international boundaries in North America and elsewhere, and the ambitious course plotted by the once quarrelsome states of Europe toward the free movement of goods, labour, and capital, were leaving national governments with narrower spheres in which to operate. At the same time secessionist pressures in places as disparate as Kirghizia, Catalonia, and Quebec prodded central governments into yielding more power to local bodies. Government authority was also nibbled away by the growing ability of multinational corporations to move capital and other resources from one part of the globe to another. New forms of association and regional sovereignty were becoming necessary.

The traditional nation-state concept was also running into trouble for the simple reason that it only rarely corresponds to reality. Japan and Sweden are states composed almost entirely of a single national group sharing language, customs and common origins, but far more typical are states such as Canada or Nigeria or the Soviet Union where more than one language is widely spoken and where distinct national or ethnic groups dominate in particular geographic zones, with the unavoidable consequence that internal tensions occasionally flare up.

Moves toward regional integration and national disintegration seemed to be taking place concurrently, but these tendencies are less contradictory than they may appear at first glance, especially if you happen to be a member of a national minority: a Scottish nationalist or a Catalonian autonomist, for example, may enjoy the spectacle of European Community headquarters in Brussels siphoning authority away from the traditional centralizers and oppressors in England or Castile. Every nationality is a minority within the European Community, and no longer can an overbearing majority within any one country exert quite the same degree of control. This may be less true in North America because of the overwhelming size and influence of the U.S.A., but the movement toward a continental free trade zone nonetheless made supporters of Quebec independence confident that a sovereign Quebec would be part of a larger trade grouping, and thus would not be cast economically adrift. Whether the forces of economic integration will generate irresistible pressure toward cultural homogeneity is another question.

As this was written Quebec's constitutional direction was far from certain. The collapse of the Meech Lake constitutional accord in June 1990 was a setback for those who wanted Quebec to stay in the Canadian family but with formal recognition as a distinct society and with some increased autonomy. The Meech deal might only have postponed for a few years a more radical political transformation, but its demise was linked to serious resistance to such changes in much of Canada and sent support for Quebec independence temporarily soaring in public opinion polls over the following months. It also produced a flood of provincial and federal commissions of inquiry into constitutional reform.

Canadian historians used to speak endlessly of the country's two founding peoples, ignoring the descendants of the aboriginal peoples who inhabited Canada long before the French and British arrived; but it was a Cree member of the Manitoba legislature, Elijah Harper, who drove the decisive nail into the Meech Lake coffin. Events inside Quebec that same year—most notably the Mohawk sieges at Oka and Kanawake in a bitter dispute over ancestral lands, and the Cree lawsuits aimed at halting new phases of James Bay hydroelectric development—made it clear that any redefinition of Quebec's place in the world would have to take account of the small but prickly aboriginal presence in its midst. There are distinct societies within Quebec also, quite apart from the Anglophone and immigrant minorities.

At many moments since the end of the French colonial era, however, Quebec has been more concerned with defining itself in relation to those outside its borders. The conservative élites that complied readily with the British regime shared the disquiet of many in other British North American colonies at the radical republican experiment to the south, and an influx of people fleeing that experiment helped to accentuate the conservatism of society north of the border. When representatives of several remaining British colonies met in the 1860s to discuss unity and independence, Quebec's political élites may have shared the desire of their partners to build political structures that would distinguish them from the Americans, but they also took great care to get guarantees of language and religious rights that in turn would distinguish them from their English-speaking neighbours in the new Canadian confederation.

Earlier generations of Quebec nationalists, from Henri Bourassa to Maurice Duplessis, often objected to ways the federal government wielded power, but rarely did they argue that Quebec as a distinct national entity must form a separate nation-state. Beginning with a few radicals in the 1960s, however, and growing to encompass much of the political mainstream in the 1970s and an apparent majority by 1990, Quebec's rising independence movement came to regard national affirmation and the creation of a sovereign state as indissociable. At the same time developments both within North America and on the broader international stage have changed the nature of the sovereignty attainable by Quebec, or indeed by any other national entity. Many Quebec *souverainistes* see political independence as the ticket to cultural survival, but in an era of shifting trade and investment patterns no economically alive part of the world can evade the effects of interdependence. A sovereign Quebec secure in control of its destiny, and free trade with the U.S.A. to ensure an opening to the world: independence and interdependence, blending harmoniously—or at least that is what the vision promises.

Ideas of nation and state continue to evolve, very closely linked to language and culture. The continuing dominance of the English language in Montreal's economic life until as recently as the late 1970s, and the tendency of immigrants to identify themselves with the English-speaking minority, rang alarm bells that evoked two very different responses. In Ottawa the Liberals under Pierre Trudeau passed the Official Languages Act in 1969 aimed at giving French equal status with English in federal institutions across Canada (bilingualism already being the norm within federal institutions in Quebec). Trudeau's dream of coast-to-coast bilingualism made some modest inroads but foundered on the hard rock of demographic reality: outside Quebec and contiguous parts of Ontario and New Brunswick the French-speaking population of Canada is very sparse. The response from the Quebec government was rather different. While Trudeau strove valiantly to promote his vision of Canada *tout entier* as a national homeland to be shared by French and English alike, Quebec saw itself as the indisputable heartland of French North America — a view supported by every census ever taken — and judged that the battle for the survival of the French language would have to be fought on Quebec soil. Successive governments, beginning with the Union Nationale under Jean-Jacques Bertrand, continuing with the Liberals under Robert Bourassa and reaching an apogee of sorts with the Parti Québécois under René Lévesque, passed a series of increasingly stringent measures designed to reverse the encroachment of English and promote the paramountcy of French.

For a variety of reasons language has become central to Quebec's cultural identity. The homogenization wrought by North American mass culture has inserted its tentacles deeply into Quebec. The fervent religious faith that once served as a distinguishing factor is all but gone. Quebec's distinctive traditional architecture has yielded to nondescript suburban bungalows and wretched commercial strips. *Fèves au lard* have lost out to cardboard hamburgers from McDonald's. The traditional jigs and reels are now just a vague folkloric memory, but disco dancing thrives.

None of this is meant to suggest that Quebec has thrown in the towel when it comes to cultural creativity. A glance at recent offerings in the performing arts and literature, not to mention such phenomena as the renowned Cirque du Soleil, attests to the contrary. Much of this output is distinctively Québécois without having to hide behind language barriers. But what of the truly mass conveyers of popular culture, television and pop music? U.S. penetration in these areas is a worldwide phenomenon to which neither the English-speaking nor the French-speaking part of Canada is immune. Nevertheless there are some startling differences. Home-grown drama series are often the most popular TV programs in Quebec, and Statistics Canada, which compiles data on television-viewing habits along with so much else, has reported that French-speaking audiences have shown

a general trend...away from foreign drama programs and towards a greater consumption of programs in the light entertainment and information categories. This movement has resulted in an overall decline in the Francophone consumption of foreign content. In 1987, 62 per cent of the viewing by Francophone audiences was of Canadian programs, continuing an upward trend from 52 per cent in 1984.... Canadian programs have made up a progressively smaller proportion of Anglophone viewing time in recent years, declining from just under 30 per cent in 1984 to 26 per cent by 1987.

This suggests that language may indeed provide an effective barrier against any overwhelming penetration by U.S. programming.

In popular music, however, U.S. influence seems all but invincible. If

Quebec's radio airwaves offer some respite from wall-to-wall U.S. offerings, it has much to do with the regulation of the Canadian Radio-television and Telecommunications Commission, a federal body, requiring French stations to limit vocal music in English to thirty-five per cent. To many outsiders such a quota may appear stringent. No regulations set quotas on record sales, however, and some estimates suggest that up to three-quarters of all records sold in Quebec come from the United States. One article in *La Presse* described a youth who, between two classes on Quebec's cultural heritage, runs to the Ed Archambault music emporium across the street from the Université du Québec à Montréal to get the latest Billy Joel album. This youth is likely to remain representative of Quebec for some time to come.

During the long public debate on free trade with the United States, English Canadians were told by supporters of the agreement that European integration was not making Italians any less Italian or Danes any less Danish. In Quebec this argument was not widely used because it seemed self-evident. Québécois, unlike many English-speaking Canadians, seemed confident that closer economic integration with the United States would not seriously threaten their cultural survival. This insouciance about the cultural effects of U.S. penetration did not, however, reflect a deep-rooted cultural confidence. The theme of cultural survival is still a staple of public discourse in Quebec, as it has been for decades if not centuries. At almost every turn Anglophones, immigrants, a faltering birth rate, and the slant of federal policies have been blamed directly or indirectly for putting the French language in jeopardy, but U.S. influence has rarely been faulted. People who spend their vacations in Florida find English commercial signs in Montreal worrisome, and Billy Joel fans favour tougher language regulations to reinforce the position of French.

For centuries Québécois have lived side by side with Americans but have rarely been forced into political propinquity with them. While day-to-day disputes arise with Ontario, the United States is associated in the minds of many Québécois with more positive thoughts. Hordes of vacationers and shoppers, and in earlier generations hordes of emigrants, have been drawn southward by warm weather or economic bounty. As a result, the United States has become too familiar to be regarded as truly foreign. And unlike many English-speaking Canadians who have maintained sentimental ties with Britain or other mother countries overseas, the Québécois feel few links to any overseas homeland. Despite the efforts to renew ties with France that have been made since 1960, Quebec's historical relationship with that country is just too far in the past. The Québécois are quite thoroughly rooted in North America.

This sense of North American identity is sometimes grounded in the concept of Canada, but not always. In 1969 René Lévesque told *Le Magazine Maclean*:

> I've never had any feeling of being Canadian, but I've always had an incredibly strong sense of being North American. The place where I'm most at home outside Quebec is the United States.

A generation later this sentiment appeared to have some currency in public opinion. A Toronto *Globe and Mail* – CBC poll in the spring of 1991 found that twenty-nine per cent of those polled in Quebec said they "agreed" or "strongly agreed" with the statement: "I have more in common with Americans than I do with Canadians living in other provinces." In the rest of Canada only sixteen per cent of the respondents answered similarly.

Phil Edmonston, the bearded former U.S. marine who in 1990 became the first New Democrat ever elected to Parliament from a Quebec riding, said in an interview that he detected a real spirit of kinship toward Americans among the Québécois.

> It's funny, but they seem to embrace the very country which poses the greatest threat of assimilation and takeover. The U.S. tends to be seen in a benevolent light. Americans are not seen as *têtes-carrées*, ["squareheads", a pejorative slang term for English Canadians]. Americans are seen not as English but as an offshoot of the English just as Québécois see themselves not as European French but as an offshoot of the French. Ontario faces a disadvantage because it carries a hundred years of anti-French cultural baggage. Americans aren't seen to have that same cultural baggage.

There has even been some modest support in Quebec for political union with the United States. A *Maclean's* magazine poll in 1989 found that while fourteen per cent of all Canadians favoured joining the U.S.A., the proportion rose to twenty-three per cent in Quebec: this means that among Canadians outside Quebec support for the proposition worked out to about eleven per cent. If Québécois were twice as likely as English Canadians to want to become part of the U.S.A., it may reflect as much as anything else a feeling of not really belonging to Canada, or of not wanting to belong to Canada. A fledgling party calling itself Parti 51 because it wanted Quebec to become the 51st state of the U.S.A. presented several candidates in the 1989 Quebec election, but they won only a handful of votes. Nevertheless some recognition does exist that, however precarious the state of the French language in much of Canada (a study based on 1986 census data concluded that only sixty per cent of Francophones living outside Quebec spoke French at home), rates of assimilation are still far lower than in formerly French-speaking pockets of New England or Louisiana.

Despite their own concerns about cultural survival, the Québécois have often been prone to take a condescending attitude toward the cultural insecurity felt by some English-speaking Canadians, portraying them as second-rate Americans who have failed to forge a distinct identity. Even André Laurendeau, who learned otherwise during his cross-country travels in the mid-1960s as co-chair of the Royal Commission on Bilingualism and Biculturalism, was moved almost to despair during a visit to Windsor while he was reading George Grant's pessimistic *Lament for a Nation*. He wrote in his journal:

> This is really a book not to be read in Windsor, which gives the impression of being a working-class suburb of a large American city.... In Windsor they really do live in the shadow of Detroit and they say they are happy about it, which is a good summary of the Canadian situation and of Grant's book.[67]

Quebec's cultural status has tended to be viewed in more flattering terms. François-Marie Monnet, a former correspondent in Canada for *Le Monde* of Paris, wrote in *Le Défi québécois*:

> In the current "revolution" in lifestyles, which is particularly visible among the young, Quebecers have no reason to envy their neighbours to the south; they are less inclined to imitate the Americans than to compete with them and, sometimes, to be ahead of them, a precedence that comes from belonging to a society that has a human scale and is therefore still fairly easily accessible, while young Americans are often forced to retreat into a marginal group in order to recapture the feeling of belonging to a society where they have an active function. [Authors' translation]

Young Québécois are part of the mainstream of Quebec culture, and the culture they are part of is clearly a mixed one. This is not in itself unusual — most modern cultures are products of a variety of influences — but Quebec, again like many other societies, has its purists who maintain that it should not be so. Cultural purism was the basis of Quebec nationalism for several generations. It has powerful proponents even now, but even purists have to contend with reality, and part of that reality is society's susceptibility to outside influences. In a position paper on cultural policy Dr. Camille Laurin, the Parti Québécois minister of state for cultural development, came up with a concept to explain this susceptibility: the "provincialization" of Quebec culture, which Dr. Laurin argued was the result of Quebec's political status as a province of Canada. He described a provincial culture as a limited culture, one that can deal with only certain aspects of reality. A province is "confined, it invents little. It holds on."[68] According to this argument, the longer Quebec remained a province, the worse things would get.

There was considerable validity to Dr. Laurin's observation that Quebec culture, or at least the distinctive and unique part of that culture, had a more limited scope than it had had two generations earlier, but there were plausible explanations for this phenomenon other than the growing provincialization suggested by Dr. Laurin. This narrowing of scope coincided with industrialization, urbanization, secularization, and the Quiet Revolution—in other words, with a significant *broadening* of spirit in Quebec society as a whole. What happened, and what disturbed Dr. Laurin, was that this process lowered the barriers between Quebec and other societies, and especially between Quebec and other societies in North America. The range of opportunity and experience open to the Québécois was much greater than it had ever been, but the proportion of that opportunity and experience that was specifically Québécois was much smaller. Even though the success of the old Quebec in maintaining a distinctive identity was to be valued, its manner and method of remaining apart were no longer appropriate. A new way had to be found, a way that was suited to a modern society.

Of the elements that traditionally kept Quebec apart the only one that remains in a reasonably healthy condition is the French language. Because it now stands virtually alone, the importance attached to language by Quebec nationalist thinkers has increased. René Lévesque wrote in his 1967 manifesto, *Option Québec*:

> Being ourselves is essentially a matter of keeping and developing a personality that has survived for three and a half centuries.... At the core of this personality is the fact that we speak French. Everything else depends on this one essential element and follows from it or leads us infallibly back to it.

André Bernard, a Université du Québec political scientist who endeavoured to interpret for English Canada what Quebec wants, also concluded that central to what it wants is the French language: "French is, ultimately, what Quebecers fight for."

Quebec is not the only society that has faced the problem of trying to maintain its language and other national characteristics in the face of changing economic relations, a changing demographic situation, and changing values. This could almost be described as the central problem of modern nationalism, the form of nationalism that grew up in the nineteenth century in response to the desire of some of the submerged peoples of Europe to establish their own place in the enlightened industrial world that was then emerging. American sociolinguist Joshua Fishman, who has delved deeply into the relationships among values, language, and nationalism, has identified the goals of these national movements as unity, authenticity, and modernity. If the simultaneous pursuit of modernity and authenticity is something of a balancing act in any culture, it is even more so in a society where not so long ago resistance to modernity constituted the very definition of authenticity. For many older liberals in Quebec, especially those of Pierre Trudeau's generation who came to political maturity in the Duplessis era, modernity was irrevocably associated with *anti*nationalism.

This brings us to a further complication. The Québécois, and French-speaking North Americans generally, are fighting for their national existence not in multilingual Europe but on a continent dominated by a single culture and a single language: to resist the English language is to resist one of the dominant forces on the continent. These complications help to explain why Quebec culture can never rest easy: to survive it must maintain aspects of distinctiveness in a society that has constant access to one of the greatest homogenizing forces of modern times, the American Dream.

In the 1990s however, as in the 1960s, there were forces challenging the homogeneity of the Dream even within the United States itself. The 1980s were a period of cultural and social retrenchment in the U.S.A., perhaps best exemplified by a movement for formal recognition of English as the country's sole official language; but by 1990 resistance to cultural uniformity was again gathering strength. As usual, much of that resistance was concentrated within non–English-speaking cultural communities, especially but not exclusively among Spanish-speaking Americans. A parallel challenge appeared within the academic community, where assumptions of the inherent superiority of Western culture in general and Anglo-Saxon culture in particular came once again into question. These challenges elicited a vigorous reaction from some Americans who perceived them as a threat to the cultural cohesion of their country. Rarely has cultural pluralism in the United States been so strongly espoused—and rarely has it been so strongly opposed. As the United States entered the 1990s it appeared to be in the early stages of an intense cultural struggle whose outcome was far from assured.

These developments occurred too late to have much impact on the status of French as a spoken language in the United States, but their effects will no doubt spill over into Quebec, and indeed may influence Quebec's culture as much as anything that happens within Quebec itself. If the existence of Quebec as a modern, North American, and yet distinctive society can no longer be assured by keeping out the American Dream, it may yet benefit from a redefinition of that Dream. Despite all the contradictions, all the difficulties in explaining both to insiders and to outsiders that it is a feasible enterprise, Quebec must continue to pursue the American Dream, but in its own way.

Notes

1 Latouche, "Quebec and the North American Subsystem."

2 Monnet, *Le Défi québécois*, p. 181.

3 Bouchard, *Les 36 cordes sensibles*, p. 131.

4 Lysiane Gagnon, "Le 'Mon' Oncle des Etats" (Montreal *La Presse*, 13 April 1985).

5 Vallières, *Un Québec impossible*, pp. 31–32.

6 Morison, *European Discovery: Northern Voyages*, p. 252.

7 Ibid., p. 323.

8 Groulx, *Notre grande aventure*, p. 50.

9 Marxist historian Stanley Ryerson uses a quotation from Champlain to make the latter point (*The Founding of Canada*, p. 83).

10 *Evangeline*, Part 1, canto 1.

11 The Canada–Guadeloupe controversy is treated extensively in Clarence W. Alvord, *The Mississippi Valley in British Politics* (2 vols. Cleveland: Arthur H. Clark, 1917); the London pamphlet war on the subject was discussed by William L. Grant in "Canada versus Guadeloupe: An Episode of the Seven Years' War" (*American Historical Review* 17, July 1912, pp. 735–43).

12 In the early history of Canada the term "Canadian" was used specifically to denote French Canadians, a usage we have adopted in the early pages of this book. Until well into the twentieth century, in fact, French Canadians often referred to themselves as *Canadiens* (or its dialect variant *Canayens*) and to their English-speaking compatriots as *les Anglais*. (Some *indépendantistes* now reverse this and use

Canadien to refer exclusively to English-speaking Canada.) The term *Québécois* (originally, a resident of Quebec City) did not begin to supplant "French Canadian" until the 1960s, and it remains ambiguous: it is often used in both French and English to mean "Quebec Francophone", but in French it can of course encompass Quebecers of any stamp.

13 There have been many attempts to understand the reasons for British policy toward the American colonies in the years following 1763; perhaps the most cogent is Charles M. Andrews' *The Colonial Background of the American Revolution* (New Haven: Yale University Press, 1924). Among the more interesting recent treatments of the subject is John Shy's "Thomas Pownall, Henry Ellis, and the Spectrum of Possibilities, 1763–1775," in *Anglo-American Political Relations, 1765–1775*, ed. Alison G. Olson and Richard M. Brown (New Brunswick, N.J.: Rutgers University Press, 1970).

14 *Journals of the Continental Congress*, 1, pp. 82–90 and 105–113.

15 Along with a hundred or so other Canadians Clément Gosselin served in Washington's army, and after the revolution he received a grant of a thousand acres in upper New York State and became a prominent citizen, although he returned periodically to Quebec and his many children were all baptized in his old homeland. (Ernest L. Monty, "La Révolution américaine: les canadiens-français et la révolution," *L'Union*, the official publication of the Union St. Jean Baptiste d'Amérique, March 1976).

Pierre de Sales la Terrière was jailed for three years, then banished to Newfoundland. Medicine had been his profession in France, and when he returned to Quebec in 1783 he set up a practice there, but five years later a new Licensing Act was proclaimed and la Terrière could neither produce his French certificate nor pass the alternative examination (he attributed this to the "unfairness of the Board"). Like immigrant doctors in later years he couldn't practise medicine without the right credentials, so he went to Boston and enrolled in Harvard University's new medical school, becoming its first graduate. He returned to Quebec City where he presented his Harvard degree only to have it rejected, but this time he passed the examination and practised medicine quietly in Quebec until his retirement in 1810. (Léonard F. Bélanger, "A Canadian Physician in the 18th Century," *University of Ottawa Medical Journal* 16, May 1972.)

16 Fleury Mesplet, the French printer from Philadelphia who had printed the Congress's *Letter to... Quebec*, and who came to Montreal with Benjamin Franklin, had no time to publish any revolutionary propaganda before the British re-entered the city, but he settled in Montreal and in 1778 founded the city's first newspaper, *La Gazette du Commerce et Littéraire*. Early issues of the paper spoke less than respectfully of the church, the judges, and the courts, and Mesplet was interned in Quebec City. Three years later he revived the *Gazette* in a toned-down form and it

has survived under a succession of publishers, most recently Toronto-based Southam Inc. Its name is one of the few things about the *Gazette* that has not changed: the newspaper that started out as an organ of the American Revolution has spent the greater part of its long lifetime as one of the stuffiest Tory papers in Canada.

17 Jefferson to Robert P. Livingston, 18 April 1802. Quoted in Lyon, *Louisiana in French Diplomacy*, pp. 152–53.

18 25 October 1803. *Debates and Proceedings in the Congress of the United States, Eighth Congress* (Washington: Gales and Seaton, 1852), pp. 480–81.

19 London *Standard*, 19 September 1862. Karl Marx quoted this in *Theories of Surplus Value* (part 2, chapter 18).

20 *Niles' Weekly Register*, 23 May 1816, p. 230.

21 "Montreal Annexation Manifesto," Montreal *Gazette*, 11 October 1849.

22 Mgr. L.-F.-R. Laflèche, *Quelques considérations sur les rapports de la société civile avec la religion et la famille* (Trois-Rivières, 1866), quoted in Cook, *French-Canadian Nationalism*, pp. 92–106. See also Monière, *Le Développement des idéologies*, pp. 177–182.

23 Quoted in Walton, *The Story of Textiles*. (The verse contains a bitter pun: something given "to boot" was a gratuitous extra thrown in to sweeten a deal.)

24 For the mill girls, see Josephson, *The Golden Threads*, and Nancy Zaroulis, "Daughters of Freemen: The Female Operatives and the Beginnings of the Labor Movement" (Eno, *Cotton Was King*).

25 W. Sutherland, *On the Present Condition of United Canada As Regards to Agriculture, Trade, and Commerce* (1849; quoted in Ouellet, *Histoire économique et sociale*).

26 Hogan, in *Le Journal de Québec*, 12 July 1855 (authors' translation; quoted in Ouellet, *Histoire économique et sociale*, p. 498).

27 Fall River *L'Indépendant*, 19 February 1886.

28 Since the early eighteenth century the Métis have formed an indigenous Francophone population on both sides of the western Canada–U.S.A. border: they are the people who would have made up Louis Riel's prairie republic. The descendants of "country marriages" of French (later French-Canadian) fur traders with Native women, they have had few historical or sentimental ties with other North American Francophone groups. The term *Metis* (without the accent) has lately been extended to cover Anglophones with a similar history, perhaps to replace the Prairie habit of referring to any respectable person of mixed blood as "French" in order to avoid using the invidious term "half-breed". The Metis have increasingly made common cause with Native peoples in the political struggles of the late twentieth century.

29 The British and U.S. commanders, each charged with evicting the other, found themselves in agreement that hostilities would serve no useful purpose; whereupon they settled down to a joint occupancy of the disputed territory until such time as their respective governments could think of a better solution.

30 Yolande Lavoie of Statistics Canada gives an estimate of nine hundred thousand (*L'Emigration des québécois aux Etats-Unis de 1840 à 1930*, Quebec: Editeur officiel du Québec, 1979, p. 45). At the 1980 Conference on Franco-American Studies at Assumption College, Worcester, Massachusetts, she estimated that, had there been no emigration, and had the absence of emigration had no effect on the Quebec birthrate (which she admits is unlikely), there would have been nine million French-speaking Québécois in 1971 instead of the actual four-and-a-half million. On the same occasion Ralph D. Vicero, chair of the Department of Geography, California State University at Northbridge, estimated a net emigration of 340,000 for the period 1850–1900. Assuming that this rate of emigration was valid for the whole period of Lavoie's study would provide an estimate of 530,000 emigrants for her ninety-year period.

31 Other mutual benefit societies have also been active among New England Franco-Americans, notably the Quebec-based Société des Artisans; the Société de l'Assomption, the national society of the Acadians, which was founded in Massachusetts in 1903 but later moved its head office to Moncton, New Brunswick, where it has an imposing presence; and the Franco-American Foresters, who broke away from a predominantly Irish organization, the Catholic Foresters, after a linguistic and cultural dispute in 1905 and were eventually absorbed into the Association Canado-Américaine. For a detailed discussion of these societies see Chevalier, "French National Societies".

32 Mopsy Strange Kennedy and Steven D. Stark, eds., *Let's Go: The Student Guide to the United States and Canada 1972–1973* (New York: E.P. Dutton, 1972, pp. 89, 93, 107).

33 London *Standard*, 3 January 1888, report of speech by Calixa Lavallée to the congress of musicians.

34 Marx to Friedrich Engels, 25 August 1879 (Karl Marx, *On America and the Civil War*, ed. and trans. Saul K. Padover, New York: McGraw-Hill, 1972, p. 45).

35 "Uniform Hours of Labor," in *Twelfth Annual Report* of the Massachusetts Bureau of Labor Statistics.

36 "The Canadian French," in the *Thirteenth Annual Report*.

37 Language maintenance was by no means a universal pattern. The 1940 census listed 1,751,100 Americans of Yiddish and 3,766,820 of Italian mother tongue, but about ninety-seven per cent of these were either immigrants or the sons or daughters of immigrants. By contrast, nineteen per cent of the German speakers, thirty-seven per cent of the French speakers, and thirty-nine per cent of the Spanish speakers were of the third or later generations (Kloss, *American Bilingual Tradition*, table 1-5, p. 14). The energy that other groups poured into language maintenance was reserved by U.S. Jews for the maintenance of their religion, and they continued to enjoy a lively group life, as did the Italians. See also Horace Kallen, *Americanism and Its Makers* (Bureau of Jewish Education, 1944); and Gordon, *Assimilation in American Life*.

38 For Lodge's racism and his contributions to the racist cause see Higham, *Strangers in the Land*, pp. 96, 101–105, 141– 42; for the contradictions in his thought, and especially for the effect on it of having to submit himself periodically to an ethnically diverse electorate, see Saveth, *American Historians*, pp. 51–62.

39 For the Fall River controversy see the accounts in Silvia, "The Spindle City", pp. 379–413; Chevalier, "French National Societies", pp. 98–105; and Rumilly, "Histoire des Franco-Américains", pp. 105–112.

40 Sorrell, "The Sentinelle Affair," p. 82.

41 For a comparable discussion of the more urban setting of Drummondville, see Hughes, *French Canada in Transition*.

42 One of Eaton's rivals in the steel business, George Humphrey of the National Steel–Hanna Mining empire, put together a consortium of five U.S. steel companies—Armco, National, Republic (Cyrus Eaton's company), Wheeling, and Youngstown Sheet and Tube—and formed an alliance with Hollinger Mines, the Canadian company that held the claims in the Labrador Trough. Bethlehem Steel, the second-largest U.S. steel producer, joined the group later on; the giant of the industry, U.S. Steel, was initially sceptical of the whole proposition but later formed its own company to mine ore in the area, Quebec Cartier Mining. See Black, *Duplessis*, pp. 585–87; William T. Hogan, S.J., *Economic History of the Iron and Steel Industry in the United States* (4 vols., Lexington, Mass.: D.C. Heath, 1971), vol. 4, pp. 1482–83; and T.H. Janes and R.B. Elver, *Survey of the Canadian Iron Ore Industry During 1958* (Ottawa: Department of Mines and Technical Surveys, Mineral Resources Division, 1959), p. 59.

43 The "one cent a ton" allegation was not quite fair. According to the 1946 legislation under which the company undertook its operations, Iron Ore was committed, like other mining companies producing in the province, to pay a duty of a percentage of its annual profits, plus an annuity of $100,000: in the early years its production was in the neighbourhood of ten million tons, so it was the annuity that represented approximately one cent a ton. Conrad Black, the admiring biographer of Duplessis who has become president of Hollinger, makes much of this misrepresentation and argues that the company's payments were an adequate return to the province. This claim is at least as questionable as Lapalme's. The post-Duplessis government of Premier Jean Lesage thought differently, and in 1965 more than doubled the duties levied on mining companies.

44 U.S. interest revived shortly after the election of President Dwight Eisenhower. Initially cool to the seaway, Eisenhower was brought around by members of his cabinet, especially by his persuasive secretary of the treasury, the steel magnate George Humphrey (see above, n. 42). The Eisenhower administration worked actively for the project, and steel money financed a pro-Seaway lobby in Congress.

45 "Epilogue" in Trudeau, *The Asbestos Strike*.

46 For a sympathetic view of the strike see Trudeau, *The Asbestos Strike*. For a view sympathetic to the companies and Duplessis, see Black, *Duplessis*, pp. 514–526 & 537–38.

47 Dion-Lévesque's translation of Whitman's "I Dream'd in a Dream" in *Walt Whitman*, p. 184.

48 *Destruction and Reconstruction* (New York: D. Appleton & Co., 1879), pp. 44–45.

49 The years since Kerouac's death have been somewhat kinder to his reputation than the years of his life. Although the Beat Generation, like most media phenomena, was short-lived, the work of its more substantial artists has been lasting, and Kerouac's in particular has shown strange and stubborn persistence. The inventory of Kerouaciana, in addition to his own books, has included a number of biographies, a biographical drama, a bibliography, an edition of *On the Road* containing an anthology of critical essays, a "chicken-essay" by Victor-Lévy Beaulieu, and several issues of *Moody Street Irregulars*, a "Jack Kerouac newsletter" published in New York, as well as a number of documentary films.

50 Jarvis, *Visions of Kerouac*, p. 19.

51 Monière, *Le Développement des idéologies*, pp. 326–27 (Authors' translation).

52 Fullerton, *The Dangerous Delusion*, p. 56. The chief obstacle to such a loan was the nervousness of the United States about the contribution to its balance-of-payments deficit of large U.S. investments in foreign securities. The Hydro-Quebec issue was believed to have been one of the catalysts for President Kennedy's imposition of an interest equalization tax to curb such borrowings.

53 "La Baie James: Un cas d'espèce" (1975), unpublished report prepared for the Science Council of Canada by Eric Goudreau, Pierre Dansereau, Louis-Edmond Hamelin, and Guy Rocher (Authors' translation).

54 James Bay was first talked about with a cost of $2 billion, and in his announcement speech Premier Bourassa mentioned a figure of "$5 or $6 billion"; but the first serious figure, released to the natural resources committee of the Quebec National Assembly in 1974, was $11.9 billion. Two years later, before the same committee, this was revised upward to $16.2 billion, and there were many, including some Hydro-Quebec engineers, who did not believe it would be completed for less than $20 billion. The project actually came in at $15.1 billion, after having been slightly scaled down.

55 Hydro-Quebec received roughly 0.9 cents per kilowatt-hour for the electricity it sent to New York, as compared to a 1978 average of 2.3 cents it charged its commercial customers, 2.1 cents to its residential customers, and 1.3 cents to its industrial customers (*Audience de l'Hydro-Québec devant l'Office national de l'energie*, 1976; Hydro-Quebec, *Annual Report*, 1978). There were two categories, "summer power" and "interruptible power" (because its availability was not guaranteed).

Summer power exports are logical: heavily air-conditioned New York uses more electricity in the summer than in the winter, and heavily heated Quebec does the reverse. For years Hydro-Quebec aggressively promoted electric heating, which not only reduced Quebec's dependence on oil but also required the additional generating capacity that created Hydro's ever-increasing summer surpluses. According to 1979 Hydro-Quebec estimates, every year 40,000 new electrically heated homes were built and 20,000 existing dwellings were converted to electric heat: this represented an increase of 400 megawatts a year for domestic heating alone—400 megawatts that were not needed in the summer. (*La Presse*, 4 August 1979, "Le Chauffage des maisons québécoises à l'aube de l'ère postpétrolière: L'Hydro prête à prendre la relève".)

Interruptible power was sold to New York under a separate agreement, year round. It was pure surplus, power Hydro-Quebec could generate but could not sell at home. Since it was peak-period power it could be comparatively expensive: Hydro's price was based on eighty per cent of what it would probably cost the U.S. utilities to produce the power themselves—perhaps triple the summer surplus price. Surplus power might be available for sale as interruptible because of above-average precipitation in the watersheds of Hydro's dams, or because new hydro plants generally produce more than their rated capacity when they first come into service; but in any case it was Hydro-Quebec's practice to build new plants before they were needed in Quebec if there were customers for the power elsewhere.

56 See for example K.M. Chrysler and Carl J. Migdail, "Crisis Across the Borders," *U.S. News and World Report*, 13 December 1976; Herbert E. Meyer, "Business Has the Jitters in Quebec," *Fortune*, October 1977; "Secession vs. Survival: A Proud Province Raises the Fear That a Nation Could Come Apart," *Time*, 23 February 1978; Bill Gladstone, "A Tale of Two Cities: Is There a Future for Jews in Montreal?" *National Jewish Monthly*, February 1978; Sylvan Meyer, "The Silent Exodus: A 'Sixth Sense' Is Uprooting Thousands of Quebec's Jews," *Miami Magazine*, March 1978; Joy Allen and Robert Samsot, "Canada in Crisis," Long Island *Newsday*, 12–15 March 1978; Andrew Malcolm, "Montreal Mausoleum," New York *Times*, 2 September 1979.

57 Lisée, *Dans l'oeil de l'aigle*, p. 211.

58 Ibid., p. 479.

59 Metropolitan Life, also a heavy investor in Quebec securities, once defined its investment criteria as safety, yield, and the public interest, in that order. In 1979 Metropolitan singlehandedly forced up the interest rate on a New York City bond issue, costing the corporation's home city half a million dollars a year: it is hardly likely that any greater weight would be given to the public interest in a French-speaking province on the other side of the Adirondacks. With billions of dollars invested, insurance companies hold immense power over the future of Quebec.

(Geoffrey Stokes, "Met Life's Quiet Sellout of New York," *Village Voice*, 1 Jan. 1979.)

60 Johnson quotations from Doris Kearns, *Lyndon Johnson and the American Dream* ([1976] New York: New American Library, Signet, 1977) pp. 68–71, 175, 279.

61 Erna Newman Paris, "The Cajun Connection," *Weekend*, 25 June 1977.

62 Some time later, the Democratic National Committee in Washington received a letter from one of the authors requesting a French copy of the Democratic Charter. The director of the research library replied that "the Democratic Charter does not expressly provide for issuance of a charter to be printed in French." He did, however, send along an English copy of the Charter, which contained the following passage: "There shall be authentic texts of this Charter published in all of the official languages of these United States, which include French and Spanish, as well as English." When this contradiction was brought to Landry's attention he sent a scathing letter to the Democratic National Committee. His efforts eventually bore fruit: he was pleased to report several years afterward that the Democratic Charter had been translated not only into French and Spanish but into Hawaiian as well.

63 Quoted in Fraser, *Quebec Inc.*, p. 46.

64 Fraser, *Quebec Inc.*, p. 161.

65 The term *Brayon* is commonly used on the Canadian side for people from this region of mixed Quebec and Acadian heritage.

66 In the nineteenth century Miami was a carefree and isolated bayside village with closer ties to the neighbouring Bahamas than to the rest of the United States, but after Henry M. Flagler pushed his Florida East Coast Railroad through in 1896 it grew quickly. By the 1920s the tourist boom had become a land-buying frenzy until a devastating hurricane in 1926 ended the boom and gave Miami a head start on the Depression. Miami's spectacular postwar growth has been somewhat more orderly than the boom of the 1920s, but it has had much the same spirit.

67 Laurendeau, *Journal*, p. 322 (authors' translation).

68 Camille Laurin, *La Politique québécoise de la langue française* (Quebec: Éditeur officiel du Québec, 1977).

Selected Bibliography

Adamic, Louis. "Tragic Towns of New England." *Harper's Monthly Magazine* May 1931.

Albert, Abbé Thomas. *Histoire du Madawaska.* Quebec: Imprimerie franciscaine missionaire, 1920.

Ammon, Harry. *The Genet Mission.* New York: W.W. Norton, 1973.

Angers, Trent. *The Truth About the Cajuns.* Lafayette: Acadian House, 1989.

Asbury, Robert. *The French Quarter: An Informal History of the New Orleans Underworld.* [1936] New York: Capricorn Books, 1968.

Baird, Charles W. *History of the Huguenot Emigration to America.* 2 vols. New York: Dodd and Mead, 1885.

Beard, Charles A., and Mary R. Beard. *The American Spirit: A Study of the Idea of Civilization in the United States.* New York: Macmillan, 1946.

Beaulieu, Victor-Lévy. *Jack Kerouac: A Chicken-Essay.* Trans. Sheila Fischman. Toronto: Coach House Quebec Translations, 1975.

Black, Conrad. *Duplessis.* Toronto: McClelland and Stewart, 1977.

Bonier, Marie-Louise. *Débuts des la colonie Franco-Américaine de Woonsocket, Rhode Island.* Framingham: Lakeview Press, 1920.

Borduas, Paul-Émile, et al. *Refus global.* Montreal: Mithra-mythe éditeur, 1948.

Bouchard, Jacques. *Les 36 cordes sensibles des québécois.* Montreal: Editions héritage, 1978.

Bourassa, Henri. *L'Affaire de Providence et la crise religieuse en Nouvelle-Angleterre.* Pamphlet. Montreal: 1929.

Bourassa, Robert. *Power from the North.* Englewood Cliffs, N.J.: Prentice-Hall, 1985.

Brebner, John B. *The Neutral Yankees of Nova Scotia: A Marginal Colony During the Revolutionary Years.* New York: Columbia University Press, 1937.

Burt, Alfred Le Roy. *The Old Province of Quebec.* [1933] Toronto: McClelland and Stewart, Carleton Library, 1968.

Cable, George W. *The Creoles of Louisiana.* New York: Charles Scribner's Sons, 1885.

Casanova, Jacques-Donat, and Armour Landry. *America's French Heritage.* Paris and Quebec: La documentation française and the Quebec Official Publisher, 1976.

Chassé, Paul P., ed. *Anthologie de la poésie franco-américaine de la Nouvelle-Angleterre.* Providence: Rhode Island Bicentennial Commission, 1976.

Chevalier, Sr. Florence Marie, S.S.A. "The Role of French National Societies in the Sociocultural Evolution of New England from 1860 to the Present." Ann Arbor: University Microfilms, 1973.

Clay, Floyd Martin. *Coozan Dudley LeBlanc: From Huey Long to Hadacol.* Gretna, La.: Pelican Publishing, 1973.

Cook, Ramsay, ed. *French-Canadian Nationalism: An Anthology.* Toronto: Macmillan, 1969.

Dales, John H. *Hydroelectricity and Industrial Development: Quebec 1898–1940.* Cambridge, Mass.: Harvard University Press, 1940.

Desbarats, Peter. *Réné: A Canadian in Search of a Country.* Toronto: McClelland and Stewart, 1976.

Dion-Lévesque, Rosaire. *Silhouettes franco-américaines.* Manchester, N.H.: Publications de l'association Canado-Américaine, 1957.

Donaldson, Scott, ed. *"On the Road" by Jack Kerouac: Text and criticism.* New York: Penguin, 1979.

Eno, Arthur L., ed. *Cotton Was King: A History of Lowell, Massachusetts.* Somersworth, N.H.: New Hampshire Publishing Co., 1976.

Everest, Allan S. *Moses Hazen and the Canadian Refugees in the American Revolution.* Syracuse, N.Y.: Syracuse University Press, 1976.

Feldman, Elliot J., ed. *The Quebec Referendum: What Happened and What Next, A Dialogue the Day After with Claude Forget and Daniel Latouche.* Cambridge, Mass.: Harvard University, University Consortium for Research on North America, 1980.

Fishman, Joshua A. *Language and Nationalism: Two Integrative Essays.* Rowley, Mass.: Newbury House, 1972.

Fishman, Joshua A., et al. *Language Loyalty in the United States: The Mainte-nance and Perpetuation of Non-English Mother Tongues by American Ethnic and Religious Groups.* The Hague: Mouton, 1966.

Fraser, Matthew. *Quebec Inc.* Toronto: Key Porter, 1987.

Fullerton, Douglas H. *The Dangerous Delusion: Quebec's Independence Obsession, As Seen by the Former Adviser to Réné Lévesque and Jean Lesage.* Toronto: McClelland and Stewart, 1978.

Gatineau, Félix. *L'Histoire des Franco-Américains de Southbridge, Mass.* Framing-ham, Ma.: Lakeview Press, 1919.

Gordon, Milton M. *Assimilation in American Life: The Role of Race, Religion, and National Origins.* New York: Oxford University Press, 1964.

Groulx, Lionel. *Notre grande aventure: L'Empire français en Amérique du nord (1535–1760).* [1958] Montreal: Fides, 1976.

Guide français de Fall River, Mass., contenant l'histoire de la colonie et l'almanach des adresses avec illustrations. Fall River: L.J. Gagnon et cie., 1909.

Guthrie, John A. *The Newsprint Paper Industry: An Economic Analysis.* Cam-bridge, Mass.: Harvard University Press, 1941.

Haley, Alex. *Roots: The Saga of an American Family.* Garden City, N.Y.: Doubleday, 1976.

Hamelin, Jean, and Yves Roby. *Histoire économique du Quebec 1851–1896.* Montreal: Fides, 1971.

Hansen, Marcus Lee. *The Immigrant in American History.* [1940] New York: Harper & Row, 1964.

Higham, John. *Strangers in the Land: Patterns of American Nativism 1860–1925.* [1955] New York: Atheneum, 1967.

Hogue, Clarence, André Bolduc, and Daniel Larouche. *Québec: Un siècle d'électricité.* Montreal: Libre expression, 1979.

Hughes, Everett C. *French Canada in Transition.* [1943] Chicago: University of Chicago Press, Phoenix Books, 1963.

Jarvis, Charles E. *Visions of Kerouac: The Life of Jack Kerouac.* Lowell, Mass.: Ithaca Press, 1973.

Jones, Howard Mumford. *O Strange New World: American Culture: The Forma-tive Years.* New York: Viking, 1964.

Josephson, Hannah. *The Golden Threads: New England's Mill Girls and Magnates.* [1949] New York: Russell & Russell, 1967.

Kerouac, Jack. *Doctor Sax: Faust Part Three.* New York: Grove Press, 1959.

———. *Lonesome Traveler.* [1960] New York: Ballantyne Books, 1973.

———. *Vanity of Duloz: An Adventurous Education 1935–46.* [1968] New York: G.P. Putnam's Sons, Capricorn Books, 1978.

Kloss, Heinz. *The American Bilingual Tradition.* Rowley, Mass.: Newbury House, 1977.

Lanctôt, Gustave. *Canada and the American Revolution 1774–1783.* Trans. Margaret M. Cameron. Toronto: Clarke, Irwin, 1967.

Lapierre, Eugène. *Calixa Lavallée: Musicien national du Canada.* Montreal: Fides, Publications de la société historique de Montréal, 1966.

Latouche, Daniel. "Quebec and the North American Subsystem: One Possible Scenario." *International Organization* 28, 4 (Autumn 1974): 938.

— — —. "La Vraie nature de la révolution tranquille." *Revue canadienne de science politique* 7, 3 (September 1974).

Laurendeau, André. *Journal tenu pendant la Commission royale d'enquête sur le bilinguisme et le biculturalisme.* Montreal: VLB éditeur / Le Septentrion, 1990. In English as *The Diary of André Laurendeau.* Trans. Patricia Smart and Dorothy Howard. Toronto: James Lorimer and Co., 1991.

Lauvrière, Émile. *La Tragédie d'un peuple: Histoire du peuple acadien de ses origines à nos jours.* 2 vols. Paris: Librairie Henry Goulet, 1924.

LeBlanc, Dudley. *The Acadian Miracle.* Lafayette: Evangeline Publishing, 1967.

Lisée, Jean-François. *Dans l'oeil de l'aigle.* Montreal: Éditions du boréal, 1990. In English as *In the Eye of the Eagle.* Trans. Arthur Holden, Kathe Rothe, and Claire Rothman. Toronto: HarperCollins, 1990.

Lyon, E. Wilson. *Louisiana in French Diplomacy 1759–1804.* Norman: University of Oklahoma Press, 1934.

Maillet, Antonine. *La Sagouine: Pièce pour une femme seule.* [1968] rev. ed. Montreal: Editions Léméac, 1974. In English as *La Sagouine.* Trans. Luis de Céspedes. Toronto: Simon and Pierre, 1979.

Massachusetts Bureau of Statistics of Labor. *Twelfth Annual Report.* Boston: 1881.

— — —. *Thirteenth Annual Report.* Boston: 1882.

Melvin, Charlotte Lenentine. *Madawaska: A Chapter in Maine-New Brunswick Relations.* Madawaska, Maine: Madawaska Historical Society, 1975.

Metalious, Grace. *Peyton Place.* New York: Julian Messner, 1956.

— — —. *No Adam in Eden.* New York: Trident Press, 1963.

Miner, Horace. *St. Denis: A French-Canadian Parish.* [1939] Chicago: University of Chicago Press, Phoenix Books, 1963.

Monière, Denis. *Le Développement des idéologies au Québec des origines à nos jours.* Montreal: Editions Québec-Amérique, 1977.

Monnet, François-Marie. *Le Défi québécois.* Montreal: Quinze, 1977.

Morison, Samuel Eliot. *The Oxford History of the American People.* New York: Oxford University Press, 1965.

———. *The European Discovery of America: The Northern Voyages A.D. 500–1600.* New York: Oxford University Press, 1971.

New England-Atlantic Provinces-Quebec Center. *The French in New England, Acadia, and Quebec.* Orono: University of Maine at Orono, 1973.

Old Orchard Beach Historical Society. *Old Orchard Beach Then and Now.* Old Orchard Beach, 1978.

Ouellet, Fernand. *Histoire économique et sociale de Québec 1760-1859.* Montreal: Fides, 1966. In English as *Economic and Social History of Quebec, 1760-1850.* Toronto: Macmillan, 1980.

Quintal, Claire, ed. *The Little Canadas of New England.* Worcester, Mass.: Assumption College French Institute, 1983.

Reed, Revon. *Lâche pas la patate: Portrait des acadiens de la Louisiane.* Montreal: Parti pris, 1976.

Roby, Yves. *Les québécois et les investissements américains (1918–1929).* Quebec: Les Presses de l'université Laval, 1976.

Roy, Jean-Louis. *Maîtres chez nous: Dix années d'Action Française.* Montreal: Editions Léméac, 1968.

Rumilly, Robert. *Histoire des Franco-Américains.* Montreal: Robert Rumilly, 1958.

Ryan, William F., S.J. *The Clergy and Economic Growth in Quebec (1896–1914).* Quebec: Les Presses de l'université Laval, 1966.

Ryerson, Stanley. *The Founding of Canada: Beginnings to 1815.* Toronto: Progress Books, 1960.

Sauriol, Paul. *The Nationalization of Electric Power.* Trans. Kina Buchanan. Montreal: Harvest House, 1962.

Saveth, Edward N. *American Historians and European Immigrants 1875–1925.* New York: Columbia University Press, 1948.

Silvia, Philip T. "The Spindle City: Labor, Politics, and Religion in Fall River, Massachusetts, 1870–1905." Ann Arbor: University Microfilms, 1974.

Sorrell, Richard Sherman. "The Sentinelle Affair (1924–1929) and Militant 'Survivance': The Franco-American Experience in Woonsocket, Rhode Island." Ann Arbor: University Microfilms, 1976.

Sosin, Jack M. *Whitehall and the Wilderness: The Middle West in British Colonial Policy, 1760–1775.* Lincoln: University of Nebraska Press, 1961.

Thériault, Sr. Mary-Carmel. *La Littérature française de Nouvelle-Angleterre.* Montreal: Fides, Les Publications de l'université Laval, 1946.

Tocqueville, Alexis de. *Democracy in America.* [1835] New York: New American Library, 1956.

Tremblay, Rodrigue. *Indépendence et marché commun Québec–E.U. (manifeste économique).* Montreal: Editions du jour, 1970.

Trofimenkoff, Susan Mann. *Action Française: French Canadian Nationalism in the Twenties.* Toronto: University of Toronto Press, 1975.

Trudeau, Pierre Elliott. *The Asbestos Strike.* Trans. James Boake. Toronto: James Lewis & Samuel, 1974.

Trudel, Marcel. *Chiniquy.* Trois-Rivières: Editions du bien public, 1955.

Vallières, Pierre. *Nègres blancs d'Amérique.* Montreal: Parti pris, 1968.

— — —. *Un Québec impossible.* Montreal: Editions Québec/Amérique, 1977.

Vicero, Ralph Dominic. "Immigration of French Canadians to New England, 1840–1900: A Geographical Analysis." Ann Arbor: University Microfilms, 1969.

Wallace, Donald H. *Market Control in the Aluminum Industry.* Cambridge, Mass.: Harvard University Press, 1937.

Wallot, Jean-Pierre. *Intrigues françaises et américaines au Canada 1800–1802.* Montreal: Editions Léméac, 1965.

Walt Whitman: ses meillenres pages traduites de l'anglais par Rosaire Dion-Lévesque. Quebec: Les Presses de l'université Laval, 1965.

Walton, Perry. *The Story of Textiles: A Bird's-Eye View of the History of the Beginning and the Growth of the Industry by Which Mankind is Clothed.* Boston: John S. Lawrence, 1912.

Williams, T. Harry. *Huey Long.* [1969] New York: Bantam Books, 1970.

Zangwill, Israel. *The Melting-Pot.* [1909] Rev. ed. New York: Macmillan, 1923.

Acknowledgements

I FIRST BEGAN looking into the connection between Quebec and the United States in 1976. There were three separate starting points: the obvious pro-Americanism of the then newly elected Parti Québécois government, electricity exports and their relation to Quebec's financial ties with Wall Street, and the fragile revival of Franco-American identification in New England spurred by *Roots* and the U.S. bilingual education program. I was curious about what lay behind these phenomena and how they intertwined. I completed a manuscript on this subject in late 1979; for a variety of reasons it was not published at the time, although it did serve as my thesis for a Master of Arts in Liberal Arts degree at Clark University in Worcester, Massachusetts.

It was a source of great satisfaction to me when, a decade or so later, Eric Hamovitch expressed interest in revising and updating the manuscript for publication, and Between The Lines expressed interest in publishing it. Eric's changes and additions not only preserved but enhanced the points I had hoped to make. Leo Serroul's mastery of computers helped cross the hurdle presented by the technological revolution that had occurred since I started work on the project, and Ann Phelps's rigorous yet sensitive editing brought the manuscript to its present form.

It is impossible to thank individually all the people who helped us by sharing information, insights, and ideas in formal interviews and informal conversations: in Quebec, Ottawa and Toronto; in Quebec and Canadian government offices in the United States; in U.S. academic, business and political circles; in Florida, Louisiana, California and throughout the Franco-American archipelago. This book is extraordinarily dependent on such input, and we are very grateful to all of those who provided it.

Robert Chodos
New Hamburg, Ontario
October 1991

Index

Printed in Canada